THE MONEY-LAUNDERERS

Keith —
good hunting

GW00702291

For a complete list of Management Books 2000 titles
visit our web-site on http://www.mb2000.com

THE MONEY-LAUNDERERS

Bob Blunden

2000

First edition published in 2001 by Management Books 2000 Ltd

This second edition first published in 2009 by Management Books 2000 Ltd
Forge House, Limes Road
Kemble, Cirencester
Gloucestershire, GL7 6AD, UK
Tel: 0044 (0) 1285 771441
Fax: 0044 (0) 1285 771055
Email: info@mb2000.com
Web: www.mb2000.com

British Library Cataloguing in Publication Data is available

ISBN 9781852525897

Preface

This is the second edition of a book which was first published a few months prior to the terrible events of September 11th 2001. I did comment at that time that I was worried that writing a book may make me seriously famous (a favourite saying of an old friend and prolific author). Well the publication certainly led to invitations to speak at various conferences, and post September 11th being interviewed on various television stations and in the media to discuss terrorist funding, but as for being seriously famous I think infamous would be a closer assessment.

Money laundering has become even more of a topical subject since that time but the actual meaning of the term has been hijacked by various governments to show how active they are in their anti-money laundering measures. It is now used to define any proceeds of crime that the criminal has deposited in a bank account or used to purchase assets. However, in its correct usage, 'money laundering' is the process of hiding illegal funds through a variety of processes until the money at the end of the laundering cannot be identified as proceeds of crime. This fact makes a mockery of the current vogue of charging criminals for 'money laundering' when all they may have done is put the proceeds of their crime into a building society account in their own name without attempting to hide the money.

This new edition includes some of the earlier articles and identifies many of the new laws, government and anti money laundering risk assessments, money laundering and blacklisted financial centres.

I hope that you enjoy this book as much as one individual who had a signed copy of the first edition in his office which was found by the Serious Fraud Office during a raid in respect of an alleged £3 million 'boiler room' fraud. My note said 'keep it clean' – whether he did or not only the investigation and forthcoming trial will prove.

Thank you to all who purchased the first edition and to new readers I hope that you enjoy the book.

Bob Blunden
March 2009

Contents

Introduction

I would like to tell you a story

Charlie West is a serious criminal and is also a respected businessman with a thriving antiques business in Yorkshire. Alan Jenkins is also a serious criminal and manages one of the North of England's leading casinos. Both manage an extensive drugs trafficking empire and both look like successful businessmen, dressing in conservative clothes with none of the ostentatious gold jewellery beloved of the nouveaux riches or the Arthur Daleys of this world.

It is mid-Sunday afternoon, that time of day in London's East End when the lunchtime pub-goers have returned home to the Sunday roast, some verbals from the wife and an afternoon's sleep in front of the television. The stall holders in the various street markets are packing up and street traffic is, for a change, relatively light and no longer represents the daily vision of one large car park moving in one-yard jumps. A black Audi proceeds down the City Road towards Old Street. Charlie checks his watch, glances in the rear view mirror – the road behind is empty. 'Great,' he says, and turns into the one-way system at the top of Shoreditch. In the boot of the car are two cases containing two million pounds in cash.

Alan or 'Kosher' to his close friends, stretches his arms and rummages for a cigarette. 'So, we're almost there, Charlie?'

'Yep, we should have it all sorted within the hour – then we'll go up West – OK?'

The Spitalfields area of London has, in the profound wisdom of the local authority, been renamed Banglatown in recognition of the large Bangladeshi community. Curry emporiums, leather warehouses and Asian food stores stand cheek by jowl with a few remaining Jewish businesses, evidence of a previous influx of refugees from distant shores.

Small offices overlook the narrow streets where just over a hundred years ago Jack the Ripper stalked his unfortunate prey. In more recent years, 'the Firm' held sway until the twins' incarceration and their subsequent death.

Charlie drives up Brick Lane and parks near the old Ind Coope brewery in Hanbury Street. Without digressing from this edge-of-the-seat story – the spot where Charlie parks is exactly outside where number 29 Hanbury Street stood until demolished for the brewery construction. This was the scene of the Ripper's murder of Annie Chapman, whose body was found dismembered in the back yard. Anyway, back to my story ...

Charlie makes a quick call on his mobile phone, not being particularly concerned about the call being traced as the phone was one of the pay-as-you-go models, purchased for cash from Woolworths in Leeds, thus making the user completely anonymous. He ends the call, nods to Kosher and they get out of the car, remove the cases and quickly enter a door located between two Indian restaurants.

At the top of the narrow staircase, they open the door, enter a small room and are greeted by two Asian men who quickly check the contents of the cases. They are then ushered into the inner office where Rashmid Gautama quickly rises from his chair and greets Charlie with a firm handshake. 'It's good to see you again, Charlie.' He passes the torn half of a cinema ticket to Charlie who carefully places it in his wallet.

'OK, the usual 5% to you Rashmid?'

Rashmid nods and, after a farewell handshake, Charlie and Kosher give the car keys to Rashmid, leave the flat and walk west towards Liverpool Street station and a taxi to take them towards the bars and clubs of Soho, prior to their return north by train. The car had been rented, using false documents, from a national car hire group and is returned to a local franchise operator early the following day, the keys being deposited in a customer courtesy box as no staff are on duty to check the car in.

Rashmid quickly splits the money into numerous packages which are then taken by hand to various Asian businessmen operating Asian cash & carry and wholesale warehouses in the area, the cash soon being lost in a web of loans, cash income and creative accounting that even the best forensic accountant in the world would find difficult to unravel. Some of the cash will end up in legitimate bank accounts in High Street banks, being treated as business income.

Forty-eight hours later, in the Gold Souk in Dubai, a tall Australian walks into one of the many gold vendors and passes the torn half of the cinema ticket to a Pakistani sitting in a plush leather chair behind a large display counter. The vendor opens a drawer pulling out half of a cinema ticket and fits the two halves together – a perfect fit. He signals to an assistant who takes the ticket to a small office a few streets away. Later that day, gold is packaged and sent to the office where it is then sold to another vendor. The torn half of a playing card is then given to a courier who takes it in his wallet on a flight to Amsterdam.

The courier, mixing with the tourists in Amsterdam's red light district, bumps into a street vendor, passing the playing card to him. Later that night, the other half of the card is matched and within a few hours, drugs have been loaded onto a coaster heading for Humberside the following day, with a cargo of timber. The drugs are dropped off while the vessel is slowly heading up the River Ouse towards Goole, a crew member throwing the packages into some bushes on the riverbank. Two men, in a van parked in the small village of Blacktoft, watch the packages being thrown and quickly retrieve the drugs, loading them under several boxes of wet fish, purchased earlier at Kingston Upon Hull fish market. They then head for the M62, Leeds and Manchester. The drugs are for sale on the street only seven days after

Charlie's visit to Rashmid.

Various 'dealers' collect the cash from the addicts and twice a week the funds are taken to a Casino in Leeds. Charlie likes a flutter and usually comes out on top with substantial cash winnings. The funds not 'won' by Charlie became part of the Casino's legitimate income. The Casino's profits are paid by dividends to shareholders every year. The main shareholder is a trust company set up several years previously in an offshore jurisdiction and administered by a local attorney. The dividends are invested in property, blue chip shares, bearer bonds and pension funds.

In the meantime, Charlie's antique business is doing quite well, and the manager of his bank is only too happy to check out Charlie's business plan with supporting accounts to extend a business loan for the new shop in Harrogate. Of course, antique dealers like dealing in cash, so each week, buyers acting for Charlie visit the various antique markets and centres buying some good pieces for cash, money that several hours previously had been taken from drug addicts in Manchester and Liverpool. Although some of the antiques are retained, the majority are sold back to the trade or to collectors through the auction rooms. Cheques from auction houses could be seen by the bank as legitimate funds, which, although declared in the annual accounts, are well worth the expense of tax and commissions.

Once a month, Charlie and Kosher go on a buying expedition to London where they invariably meet either Rashmid or his family and, once a month, drugs are smuggled into the United Kingdom to meet the demands of the Leeds/Manchester drugs market. Other drugs such as cocaine and cigarettes (a good, new lower-risk market due to the differential between UK and European prices) are sourced from other criminal organisations.

This 'story' (sorry – I'm no Ian Fleming, and the characters are fictitious) briefly outlines some of the methods by which the criminal will both launder his funds and hide them from the scrutiny of the authorities. In this particular case, the Asian Hawallah system was used by the suppliers and other, more conventional money laundering schemes through the casino and antiques trade were used by Alan and Charlie. I would comment that the Asian/Chinese underground banking systems used by the Triads and Asian organised crime, are probably the most difficult in the world to unravel and investigate satisfactorily.

You may think that this story is a bit dated as, yet again, the drugs trade is used to illustrate money laundering. Unfortunately, the majority of dirty money still originates from that business. In this particular example, the drugs purchased were heroin, which you will read later is controlled by the Asian gangs – thus the Hawallah secret banking system is more likely to be used. Of course, money obtained from other crimes will be laundered in different ways and this book details some of the methods used by the criminals to hide their funds, whatever the crime. More about them later – but what is money laundering?

Money laundering

Money laundering is the process of hiding the proceeds of crime by depositing the financial benefits into a layered sequence of accounts that an investigator will find difficult to unravel to identify the true source of the money. Under the various proceeds of crime laws throughout the world any criminal who is arrested and charged with a crime that has resulted in financial benefit is usually charged with money laundering as the proceeds have usually entered the financial system. However the major crime organisations **integrate their illegal funds into the cash collected by legitimate sources.** Terrorists, organised crime organisations (mafia) or drug dealers are usually set up as what appear to be legitimate tax-paying businesses, submitting accounts that conceal the proceeds of their criminal activities. These are the real money launderers and investigations attempting to establish an audit trail of the movement of funds through various 'shell' companies and jurisdictions can be very difficult, sometimes almost impossible, to complete successfully.

For example, the criminal who has sold £100,000 worth of drugs will need to bank the money rather than stash it in a box under his bed. It is obvious that he will not wish it to be placed in a bank account with his own name. So he opens an account in a false name or organisation.

Yes, since September 11th you will have found it difficult to open a bank account without a cart load of identification documents. Equally the cases of identity theft have increased dramatically over the past few years. As I write this book I see that a little old lady has just been sentenced to 5 years imprisonment for benefit fraud using hundreds of false names to obtain over £1million in cash. Apparently this fraud took place in a hidden room behind her bedroom wardrobe – it certainly puts a new angle on what is hidden in the wardrobe.

So back to our drugs dealer. By setting up a legitimate business, especially a cash rich business such as a casino, cash & carry warehouse or antiques salesroom, he can launder his money

Yes it is that simple.

Recipe of ingredients

Cash or valuables that are proceeds of criminal activity (criminal activity can be drug production and selling, smuggling, theft, blackmail, murder, terrorism, tax evasion and any crime, that if committed, results in financial gain)

Equipment required

- **Financial institutions:** (banks, investment advisors, lawyers, accountants, insurance companies or any facility that can process the profits of the criminal enterprise).
- **Company formation agents:** to provide off-the-shelf companies to use as a dressing to conceal the true taste, origin and colour of the money.
- **Employees:** who are prepared to process the dirty money contrary to law and legislation.
- **Computer:** to process electronic fund transfers through the anonymity of the internet.
- **Regulatory Body:** that is either corrupt, ineffective, or lacking in statutory powers.

Instructions

Find the most beneficial financial institution, and deposit the funds using either a shell company, an alias, or a legitimate front individual or organisation. Let funds settle, then transfer through a sieve of individuals, organisations, etc., mixing with legitimate business revenue. Invest final fund realisation into legitimate business or to fund further criminal enterprise. The better the mix the better the results.

Yes, this 'cooking' recipe is contrary to the usual concept of money laundering which is seen as a washing cycle to clean dirty money. But before you get into this book (and wash your hands afterwards), I believe that it is important to consider the main ingredients and equipment (the washing machine) needed in the money laundering process, as closing down and proper control of any of these main 'equipment' factors can ensure that the launderer goes elsewhere. Also I see that the FSA in London can mean two things, the Financial Services Authority or the Food Safety Agency, so 'recipes' are, perhaps quite relevant.

The proliferation of company formation agents is still a loophole that requires both review and legislation. Whereas I am all for free enterprise, the ease with which the dishonest can set up companies with fictitious directors, shareholders and so on in many jurisdictions is a major problem and headache when looking for the true, beneficial owners of an organisation.

1

How It Works

I have updated this book so that it remains (hopefully) an easy read and helps you to gain an understanding of the background, the danger signs, the legislation and consequences of the processing of dirty money. I have added a number of chapters to describe the issues relating to specific sectors (real estate, trusts, accountants and dealers in precious metals and stones). In order to make each of these chapters complete for the purposes of the reader in that particular sector, there is inevitably a slight element of duplication regarding the general principles.

In the aftermath of September 11th 2001, the problems of money laundering have multiplied, with the additional scenario of funding of acts of terror throughout the world. The unholy alliances between the South American drug cartels, the Mafia, Russian organised crime and the Asian gangs, meaning that joint ventures in the sale of drugs, arms (including nuclear weapons) money laundering and murder are just the tip of a very big iceberg. The criminals have obviously taken lessons from the multinationals in their style of management, organisation and anti-competitive alliances thus achieving a highly organised, sophisticated and ruthlessly run operation. It is worth recalling that famous quote in The Godfather – 'It's not personal – it's just business.'

This multi-billion-pound business allows the organised crime 'executive managers' to bribe and recruit accountants, lawyers, bankers and employees within those organisations that can process the proceeds of their criminal activity. Awareness of this potential problem is essential as part of any organisation's compliance standards. It's no good having good controls and procedures if you have the proverbial rotten apple in the barrel. Later in the book, I have detailed the need to look beyond the obvious.

The ever increasing use of the internet means that e-money can be transferred anywhere in the world the touch of a button with the source unidentifiable. In addition, there is the old style criminal who still needs to convert the proceeds of crime to clean money. Recent press reports show that tobacco smuggling into the UK is now bigger business than drugs, with higher profits and less risk. Obviously, all of these 'profits' need to be banked and invested away from the gaze of the authorities.

In an ideal crime, the proceeds of that crime are hidden so that recovery by the loser is impossible and all evidence is hidden.

Even in the incident of murder, the perfect crime is where the killer hides the body or bodies from discovery. The body becomes a missing person if reported as such, or just disappears unannounced and unreported. The activities of Fred West in Gloucester where bodies were hidden in walls and under floors in his house were a prime example of hiding the evidence to conceal the crime. The concealment of cash is no different – the criminal wishes to hide the evidence – and in today's high speed financial market, it is easier to hide cash than a body.

I do not envy you the problem, but hope that the following chapters will alert you to what is happening and how a few simple controls and checks may keep the dirty money away from your business.

On top of this problem many of the world's established financial institutions are currently in meltdown, mainly caused by the avarice in the financial sector. I wonder how many disgruntled employees facing redundancy are paying no more than lip service to money laundering controls and one must question what 'know your client ' checks were made prior to granting large mortgages (sometimes 150%) in a market which has imploded dramatically. However it is very important to differentiate between money laundering and terrorist funding:

- **Money laundering** is the cleaning of *dirty money* (money obtained through crime).
- **Terrorist funding** is the use of money, *usually clean,* for the funding of terrorism thus making the *money dirty.*

What is money laundering?

Money laundering is the procedure to conceal the origins of criminal proceeds so that they appear to have originated from legitimate sources. The individuals who complete this process are:

- concealing true ownership and origin of criminal proceeds
- maintaining control of these funds
- changing the form of their ill gotten gains
- obscuring the movement of the funds.

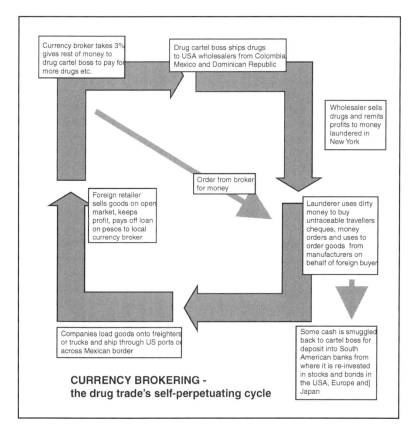

Currency broker takes 3% gives rest of money to drug cartel boss to pay for more drugs etc.

Drug cartel boss ships drugs to USA wholesalers from Colombia, Mexico and Dominican Republic

Wholesaler sells drugs and remits profits to money laundered in New York

Order from broker for money

Foreign retailer sells goods on open market, keeps profit, pays off loan on pesos to local currency broker

Launderer uses dirty money to buy untraceable travellers cheques, money orders and uses to order goods from manufacturers on behalf of foreign buyer

Companies load goods onto freighters or trucks and ship through US ports or across Mexican border

Some cash is smuggled back to cartel boss for deposit into South American banks from where it is re-invested in stocks and bonds in the USA, Europe and] Japan

**CURRENCY BROKERING -
the drug trade's self-perpetuating cycle**

Before the enactment of money laundering laws around the world, this concealment was easy as the various financial centres were only too happy to accept deposits of funds. One only has to look at the amount of money stolen by the Nazis and deposited in Switzerland to get the general idea. Whatever the changes in laws, the detrimental effect on a country's social fabric where money laundering occurs, has meant that the world map of where one can 'hide' funds is constantly changing.

The three stages of money laundering are universally recognised (in line with a washing machine cycle) as:

1. **Placement** (immersion)
2. **Layering** (heavy soaping)
3. **Integration** (spin drying)

1. Placement

This is the physical disposal of the criminal proceeds. The majority of such proceeds are cash which the criminal wishes to place in the financial system. In the case of drug revenue, this placement is needed to finance the business, whether that be to pay bribes, contract 'enforcers' or purchase transportation such as aircraft, boats, vehicles and so on.

Placement can include:

- depositing cash at a bank (often intermingled with clean funds to obscure any audit trail), and converting this cash to a readily recoverable debt
- physically moving cash between jurisdictions
- making loans in cash to businesses that appear to be legitimate or are connected to legitimate businesses
- purchasing high value goods for either personal use or as gifts
- purchasing the services of high value individuals
- purchasing negotiable assets in one off transactions
- placing cash in the client account of a professional intermediary.

A large proportion of the cash receipts from the US drugs market is used to buy merchandise from cash and carry warehouses which is then exported back to South America for resale by various 'retailers'. Jeffrey Robinson in his book, *The Merger,* and recent press reports comment about the increase in Argentinean tourists to Paraguay, looking for duty free goods, and identify Ciudad del Este in that country as a centre for this type of trade, where visitors can buy anything at very reasonable prices.

This placement is also known as the immersion phase of the money laundering wash cycle. Originally, the money launderer would split the funds into small amounts below the $10,000 reportable sum and use 'couriers' to deposit these smaller amounts in various banks where counter-cheques or currency was obtained, then paid into dummy companies. This is called 'smurfing'.

Why smurfing? Well, you know those strange little blue men running around everywhere in Holland. The Dutch got so fed up with their takeover of the national culture, which, in my opinion was due to eating funny cakes in Amsterdam cafés, that they deported them to that melting pot of cultures, the good old USA. Here they gained employment running round banks depositing cash. If you believe that, I now know why you are reading this book!

One area that is excellent for placement is the antiques trade. Every day, a large number of people travel around the country visiting antique shops and auctions buying antiques for cash. So, say you have £100,000 to launder – it's simple. Check out the illustration overleaf.

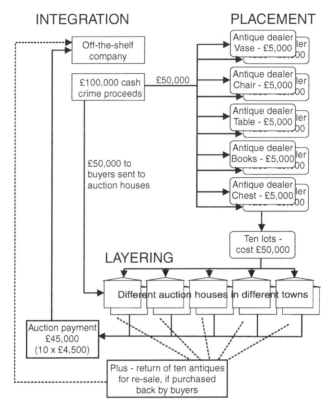

Step One   Get a formation agent to set up a company so you have a name and a registered office address – cost £100.

Step Two   Drive around the country using the new company name to purchase antiques for cash. Let's say you have 10 pieces costing £5,000 each (total cost £50,000).

Step Three   Split the stock between ten auction houses, ideally in ten different towns.

Step Four   Either let the pieces be sold to the highest bidder or use a 'friend' to buy the pieces back (using the £50,000 balance of your dirty money).

Step Five   The auction house receives £5,500 in cash for each piece (£5,000 hammer price plus 10% buyers commission). They send you a banker's draft for £4,500 (hammer price less seller's commission).

These are clean funds which you can bank as part of your new legitimate business, and you can sell the pieces again. These sales have cost you £10,000 which any criminal will accept as a reasonable expense of cleaning the money.

Auction houses, like expensive car dealers, are required to report suspicious transactions. The key word is 'suspicious'. As mentioned, hundreds of people buy antiques for cash at auctions and from antique dealers every day. Hardly any of these transactions are reported. Any business where cash is the normal method of payment such as fast-food outlets, video rental stores, casinos, bookmakers and so on are excellent venues for the placement of dirty money.

Another system is to tour the horse or greyhound racing tracks and purchase for cash winning tickets (obviously paying the punter a bonus) then claim the winnings backed up with a receipt. This is one of the latest schemes used by the criminal to launder drug money. Francis 'the Belgian' Vanverberghe, the mastermind behind the famous French Connection case, where drugs were shipped into New York from Marseilles concealed in a car, was recently murdered in Paris and evidence found on his body confirmed that he was operating such a scheme. This is yet another method for you to clean your dirty money.

2. Layering

This stage is where the money is separated from its criminal source by the creation of layers of transactions designed to disguise the audit trail and to give an appearance of legitimacy. Usually this is achieved by a wide variety of methods according to the opportunity given to, and the ingenuity of the criminals and their advisors. The layering stage is often called the heavy soaping stage.

Layering may include:

- rapid switches of funds between banks and/or jurisdictions
- use of cash deposits as collateral security in support of legitimate transactions
- transferring cash through a network of legitimate and 'shell' companies across several jurisdictions (see Bank of New York case in Chapter 3)
- resale of goods/assets.

The Brinks-Mat gold bullion robbery and the subsequent laundering of the cash proceeds is an excellent example of layering. I shall detail the sequel of events in respect of that case in Chapter 3.

3. Integration

The final part of the wash cycle is the integration of the criminal funds as being legitimate, having been successfully immersed and layered. This stage is sometimes called the Spin Dry cycle. The proceeds are integrated back into the economy in such a way as they appear to be legitimate. The antiques example shows the three stages with the integration of the banker's drafts received from the auctioneers.

Examples of activities at the integration stage include:

- **False or inflated invoices** – paying inflated or deflated invoices for exports/imports provides an effective way to integrate the proceeds of crime in and out of an economy (this is a favourite ploy of the Russian crime syndicates). For example, exports to Japan from Russia have been deliberately under-invoiced by Russian businesses. Fish exports to Japan in 1994 were, according to Russian records, some 7,000 tonnes valued at $90.4 million whereas the Japanese claim imports to the value of 56,000 tonnes or $ 622 million. During the same period, crab exports were similarly under-invoiced by some $537 million. Something fishy was obviously going on.

- **Real estate** – criminals use a shell company to purchase property then sell the company with its assets for a 'legal' profit (used by the Brinks-Mat robbers to launder some of the proceeds of the sale of the stolen gold bullion).

- **Front companies** – the corporate secrecy laws in some countries permit the formation and operation of companies that do not reveal their true owners, only names of nominee directors. These companies, operated by criminals, lend themselves their dirty money in an apparently legitimate transaction and pay themselves 'interest' on the 'loan'. The interest can be treated as a business expense for tax purposes with a reduction in tax liability.

- **Foreign bank complicity** – hinders detection because it conceals activity relating to money transfers. With the assistance of corrupt bank officials, dirty money is used as security against legitimate loans. Bank secrecy laws make the chances of detecting such loans minimal. (Liechtenstein's financial businesses are under investigation for this type of activity.)

Some banks in Russia have made loans to dummy companies who subsequently invest the money in offshore companies controlled by the same bank. The dummy company defaults in repayment of the loan and the offshore company channels the money through more banks so as to obscure the origin. The promissory notes of the defaulting company are assigned to a third company who allow the lending bank to write off the original loan. This type of scam is also prevalent in Africa and I remember during an investigation into money laundering by an Indian Hawallah dealer, discovering 'loans' amounting to millions of pounds to various 'companies' for construction of bottling plants and so on. Every 'loan' was subsequently written off.

Effect on financial centres

At the end of the last century, the proceeds of crime had grown tremendously. Whereas earlier in the 20th century, headline news was provided by the incidence of large crimes such as the Great Train Robbery, the French sewer bank robbery, the Knightsbridge safe deposit box heist and more recently, the failed Millennium Dome jewel heist ('I was only here for de Beers'), the growth of organised crime, especially in the drug trade, provided the organised crime syndicates with income beyond their wildest dreams.

This organised crime business, although the subject of various books and government reports, has to a degree been seen as part of the society that we live in. Only when a criminal is convicted are the public aware of the extent of the crime and possible money laundering.

Some sources put the dirty money income as $1 trillion dollars worldwide and that some 300 billion US dollars are currently circling the globe. The drug trade obviously has serious effects on a country's social fabric, with increases in crime to support drug habits, increase in AIDS and other health matters associated with drug usage and all that this means to the health and crime enforcement budgets of a nation.

When a financial centre is seen to be an easy conduit for dirty money, two things happen.

- The criminals, whether they be robbers, fraudsters, drug barons or despots, will be attracted like flies to a jampot, and this will result in ...
- The World Powers, i.e. the USA and EC plus international bodies such as the United Nations, World Bank and so on, will attempt to close these financial centres down.

Obviously, a financial centre likes to pride itself on integrity, customer/client confidence and as an attractive place to invest funds. In other words – a centre of financial excellence. Therefore any incident of 'crime' involving a financial business within a financial centre, especially where the involved business is seen to have acted in a naive manner, brings unwanted publicity to the centre of excellence. Closure of a business or financial centre is going to cause unemployment and a drain on the local economy. The Barings Bank debacle not only embarrassed the

City of London but caused the bank to collapse with subsequent unemployment and economic issues.

The need to ensure that the financial centres do not become the proverbial jam pots or, in money-laundering terminology, 'sinks', has resulted in a range of regulations and legislation. The lack of adherence to the law and regulations by some financial businesses has made the UK an ideal place to hide or launder money.

Sources of dirty money including areas of high risk

The main source of dirty money is from the world-wide drug trade originating in Central America and the Far East. This is followed by the influx of criminal profits from the old Soviet bloc, embezzlement by various despots in Africa and the old Soviet bloc, the illegal diamond trade, exchange control violations and the proceeds of any crime.

The problem is how can you be expected to identify that the cash deposit, wire transfer or whatever is the proceeds of crime?

It would be great if the new client entering your business speaks Spanish or Russian, wears dark glasses, lots of gold jewellery, smokes a large cigar and makes you an offer that you cannot refuse. Easy – he is obviously a crook and you can send him on his way. Unfortunately it's not that simple. The drug barons have had years of practice in the art of money laundering and have set up systems so complex one needs to be an Einstein to unravel the web of transactions to identify the true source and beneficiary of the funds. So the source is invariably hidden and you are not going to see a transaction from a Colombian or Russian Bank.

Money laundering is about 'sleight of hand'. One author likened it to a magic trick for wealth creation and is the closest anyone has come to alchemy.

Al Capone and Bugsy Moran used coin-operated laundromats to disguise revenue from gambling, prostitution, racketeering and violation of the Prohibition laws and many claim that this is where the term 'money laundering' originated. This is wrong – the term perfectly describes the cycle of transactions that the dirty money passes through so that it comes out clean at the other end.

> *'It's not our business to inquire into our clients' morals.'*
> Hong Kong banker

So the sources of dirty money are worldwide, as crime is a multinational business – only the rapidly disappearing ice caps are relatively clean. Since the publication of the first edition of this book in 2001, the Financial Action Task Force ('FATF') has evaluated anti-money laundering controls all over the world. Whereas there used to be a number of unregulated financial centres that, because of their lack of anti money laundering measures, were being used to launder dirty money (these countries were called 'sinks' and were listed as non-cooperative), the list is now currently empty.

However, in spite of this, money laundering is continuing, and increasing. Recently while on holiday in Latvia I took a sum of sterling into a bank to exchange for the local currency. The cashier did not ask for a passport and did not know who I was. I had a similar experience in a side-street bureau de change. Recently two young Chinese students were murdered in Newcastle. Apparently they were operating an online betting scam and despite declared income of less than £20,000, over £200,000 was passed through their bank account in less than a year. This fact only became apparent when the police investigated the murder. I wonder what money laundering procedures their bank had?

The situation in Latvia and other jurisdictions demonstrates to me that the FATF only look at the general picture of the jurisdiction's banking systems and not the detail. So as far as I and the professional fraud investigator are concerned the 'sinks' still exist.

Various offshore jurisdictions have been and are still licensing International Business Corporations (IBCs) which for an average $1,000 start up fee give anyone the right to incorporate a company in any language. IBCs are permitted to use any suffix that any company anywhere in the rest of the world can use such as Ltd, Inc, GmbH, SA, NV, whether they have business in those countries or not. It is impossible from the company's name to decipher what it does, or where it does it. It allows the company to pretend that it does something that it doesn't, and is somewhere where it isn't.

No minimum share capital is required and an IBC is exempt from local tax and stamp duties. There is no requirement to file annual accounts or hold general meetings. In addition, to maximise security of assets, they are permitted to transfer, domicile, re-acquire and re-issue shares for cash in any currency, or for any form of consideration. The shares can be bearer or nominative and to really complete the web, they can list other companies as directors so that it is impossible to find out who actually owns the company.

The latest offer is the facility to purchase banking licences. For under £20,000 one can have your very own financial institution. The sales brochures claim that it 'Provides access to the international credit market, as well as the international mutual funds market and securities market. It allows the bank to conduct FOREX transactions and, with minimal expense, solve the problems of liquidity.'

Formation Agents in London and on the web offer IBC formation and banks for sale with branch offices in Moscow and St Petersburg.

Crime syndicates also use any jurisdiction where money laundering controls are either weak or non-existent. Cyprus was allegedly used to launder $1 billion per month and the Russians had formed some 8,000 shell companies in that jurisdiction. Since then the banking authorities in Cyprus have revoked a large number of licences and the request of Turkey and North Cyprus to join the European Union has galvanized a clean-up operation of dubious banks and shell companies.

The Russians have also met Colombian drug cartels and Italian Mafia in the Caribbean where there are some 450 banks (many with no offices) registered in the Cayman Islands, and some three dozen banks have been registered in Antigua in the last few years, including at least four Russian owned and one Ukrainian bank (usually no more than an office with a computer).

The European Union Bank, chartered in Antigua, offered internet banking with all of the money laundering facilities that type of operation could offer. However, the bank recently collapsed and investors' money disappeared. Another BCCI?

Since then the Stanford International Bank in Antigua has been involved in an alleged $9.2 billion investment fraud with potential laundering of the ill-gotten proceeds and everyone is queuing up outside the bank looking for their money. Someone has even had the audacity to claim that it was just not cricket. This appears to be yet another classic money laundering case as one of the banks servicing the organisation blew the whistle on the lack of transparency in relation to the numerous large wire transfers made (I can see a complete book about this scam).

Then the aptly named Mr Madoff did the proverbial runner with $50 billion of clients' money; he has since admitted fraud and money laundering and will spend the rest of his life behind bars.

Israel implemented anti-money laundering legislation and a strong Financial Intelligence Unit in 2002 after a decade of no money laundering controls and laws.

Companies in Russia only have to produce documents showing that they are importing something and they can transfer funds out of the country. These documents are usually false. Great Britain is a popular destination and the money has been washed in the City of London, sheltered in the Channel Islands and spent on property.

Although much has changed in the past seven years and the FATF blacklist is empty, with many jurisdictions having cleaned up their financial centres, nevertheless many countries in the world are still vulnerable to the laundering of dirty money through their, often secretive, financial institutions.

In Southern Africa it is estimated that at least $20 billion is laundered each year, the money deriving from corruption, fraud, diamond smuggling, etc., and in many of the countries such as Tanzania the banking and anti-money laundering controls are practically non-existent. Recently airline staff flying from South Africa to Europe have been arrested for the smuggling of considerable quantities of cocaine.

Corruption of course is rife throughout the dark continent and external aid frequently ends up in the pockets of crooked politicians. Even *Playboy* magazine recently published an article detailing how Guinea Bissau is now the main hub of the cocaine trade from Central/South America to Europe.

President Mugabe of Zimbabwe is currently hiding money in Hong Kong and Thailand. Where are those jurisdictions' anti-money laundering controls and procedures?

In South America, except for a couple of jurisdictions, lawyers do not have to abide by any legislation in respect of money laundering laws.

Indications and tell-tale signs

The main vulnerabilities of money laundering are the following identified points:

- cross-border flows of cash
- entry of cash into the financial system
- transfers within and from the financial system
- acquisition of investments and other assets
- incorporation of companies and formation of trusts.

According to the Bureau for International Narcotics and Law Enforcement Affairs, US Department of State, Washington DC, the following criteria are used by drug money managers for the laundering of their drugs sales revenue:

- failure to criminalise money laundering from all serious crimes or limiting the offence to narrow predicates such as prior conviction of a drug trafficking offence
- rigid bank secrecy rules that cannot be penetrated for authorised law enforcement investigations or that prohibit or inhibit large value and/or suspicious or unusual transaction reporting by both banks and non-bank financial institutions
- lack of adequate 'know your client' requirements to conduct financial transactions or allowed use of anonymous, nominee, numbered or trustee accounts
- no requirement to disclose the beneficial owner of an account or the true beneficiary of a transaction
- lack of effective monitoring of cross-border currency movements
- no reporting requirements for large cash transactions
- no requirement to maintain financial records over a specific period of time
- no mandatory requirement to report suspicious transactions or a pattern of inconsistent reporting under a voluntary system; lack of uniform guidelines

from which to identify suspicious transactions

- use of bearer payable monetary instruments
- well established non-bank financial systems, especially where regulation, supervision, and monitoring are lax
- patterns of evasion of exchange controls by nominally legitimate businesses
- ease of incorporation, especially where ownership can be held through nominees or bearer shares, or where off-the-shelf corporations can be acquired
- no central reporting unit for receiving, analysing and disseminating to the competent authorities large value, suspicious or unusual transaction financial information that might identify possible money laundering activity
- limited or weak bank regulatory controls, or failure to adopt or adhere to the Basle Principles for International Banking Supervision, especially in jurisdictions where the monetary or bank supervisory authority is understaffed, underskilled or uncommitted
- well established offshore financial centres or tax haven banking systems, especially jurisdictions where such banks and accounts can be readily established with minimal background investigations
- extensive foreign banking operations, especially where there is insignificant wire transfer activity or multiple branches of foreign banks, or limited audit authority over foreign-owned banks or institutions
- limited asset seizure or confiscation capability
- limited narcotics and money laundering enforcement and investigative capabilities
- jurisdictions where there are Free Trade Zones where there is little government presence or other supervisory authority
- patterns of official corruption or a laissez-faire attitude toward the business and banking communities
- jurisdictions where the US dollar is readily accepted, especially jurisdictions where banks and other financial institutions allow dollar deposits
- well established access to international bullion trading centres in New York, Istanbul, Zurich, Dubai and Mumbai
- jurisdictions where there is a significant trade in or export of gems, particularly diamonds
- jurisdictions with large parallel or black market economies
- limited or no ability to share financial information with foreign law enforcement.

So how does your organisation measure up? Would it be possible to launder money through your company?

Vigilance

Although the regulatory bodies do not wish you to become detectives, there is a need and requirement to maintain vigilance so as to deter criminals from using your business for the purpose of money laundering. The task of detecting crime remains with the various law enforcement agencies, and your task is to maintain a duty of vigilance to avoid assisting the process of money laundering and to react appropriately should such an attempt be made. However, the regulatory bodies are making you self-policing and I think you can be likened to 'special constables'.

Most regulatory bodies see that vigilance encompasses the following control elements:

- verification
- recognition of suspicious customer transactions
- reporting of suspicion
- keeping of records
- training.

The regulatory bodies also recommend that a financial service business can perform their duty of vigilance by having systems that enable them to:

- determine (or receive confirmation of) the true identity of customers requesting their services
- recognise and report suspicious transactions to the appropriate regulatory body
- keep records for a prescribed length of time
- train key staff
- liaise closely with the appropriate regulatory body on matters concerning vigilance policy and systems
- ensure that internal audit and compliance staff regularly monitor the implementation and operation of vigilance systems
- ensure that all staff (new, temporary and existing) are subject of pro-active vetting

...and that you should not enter into a business relationship or complete a significant one-off transaction unless the above mentioned systems have been fully implemented.

Obviously the scale of these systems will depend on the size of the business but whatever the size the systems have to meet the standards set by the regulatory body.

The legislation usually calls for the appointment of a Reporting Officer and/or a Prevention Officer. Obviously the size of your business may necessitate combining the responsibilities.

Whatever the size of your business, the duty of vigilance begins with the start of the business relationship or a significant one-off transaction and continues until either comes to an end. However the keeping of records continues as a responsibility.

It is very important to note that **all key staff are at risk of being or becoming involved in criminal activity if they are negligent in their duty of vigilance. They should be aware that they face criminal prosecution if they commit any of the offences which we shall detail in Chapter 14.**

When employees move on to new employment within the financial services business, they may find a customer from their previous employment who had been the subject of suspicion and they have a duty to report such matters to their new employer.

We have discussed the effect on financial centres earlier, but the lack of duty of vigilance has a number of serious consequences. These can be summarised as:

- commercial failure by losing one's good market name, position and the incurring of non-productive costs and expenses
- the possibility of the regulatory body raising concerns in respect of the business being a fit and proper financial operation
- the risk of criminal prosecution and heavy financial and/or custodial penalties
- the risk to the employee of losing one's reputation, and criminal prosecution.

When the duty of vigilance is examined in relation to the legislation, it is important to note that two of the relevant offences are concerned with assistance given to the criminal. There are two aspects to such assistance:

1. the provision of opportunity to obtain, disguise, convert, transfer, conceal, retain or invest criminal proceeds; and
2. the knowledge or suspicion on reasonable grounds (actual or, in some cases, imputed if the person should have had a suspicion) of the person assisting that they are dealing with the proceeds of criminal conduct.

Involvement is avoidable on proof that knowledge or suspicion was reported to the regulatory body in accordance with the vigilance policy of your business. While prompt reporting removes the criminality from assistance, it is important to note that:

- any reporting which prejudices an investigation by either tip off or leak may constitute an offence
- any failure to report knowledge or suspicion may also constitute an offence.

2

Know your client(s)

This is without doubt the most important defence against the money launderer. A few years ago, I carried out a review of non-resident Indian clients for an American Bank based in London. The bank were concerned that some of their clients may have been involved in the Bombay Stock Exchange Fraud where millions of dollars were lost and disappeared. I found that the checks completed by the bank on these clients were so minimal that they may as well not have bothered. Many had given residential addresses which I found to be rented accommodation where the clients had resided for a few days.

One client had a corner shop in a small town in Sierra Leone (probably the poorest country in the world) yet he had deposited nearly $3 million. No accounts had been provided to support the deposits and there was a reasonable opinion that the money came from illegal diamond smuggling (which is rife in Sierra Leone). There were many similar examples where examination of the client assets showed there were doubts about the origin of the funds. If the bank had completed properly designated background checks, many of the clients would not have been accepted and the risk of censure by the Bank of England eliminated.

A recent check I completed for a stockbroker on a potential client revealed that his residential address was an office rented to a company whose registered office was a semi-detached house in South London. His massive investment company registered in Jersey had a share capital of £2 with no published accounts and his other Jersey company had been struck off two years previously.

When asked about eight years that were missing from his CV, which he claimed had been spent rebuilding a $18 million chateau in the South of France, he admitted that he had been arrested by the French police and held in custody for 10 months for suspected money laundering. If he was as rich as he claimed, why did he spend all of that time in custody?

Similarly, a proposed new Chief Executive for a new to-be-launched PLC was found to have withheld the fact that his previous company (he was chief executive) was involved with the Mafia in the USA and had been prosecuted for corruption and fined $26 million. A number of people had been murdered, or had committed suicide.

The legislation makes it clear that verification of customer(s) is very important and guidelines have been issued. For example, when verifying individuals, it is advised that the following checks should be considered:

- full name(s) used
- date and place of birth
- nationality
- current permanent address including post code
- telephone and fax number
- occupation and name of employer
- specimen signature
- documents including passport, national identity card, Armed Forces identity card and driving licence if it bears a photograph.

Most of these checks can be completed using credit databases, but it is important that such checks are not completed on face value. A recent investigation by a well known fraud investigator in London showed that he could obtain good credit references for Adolf Hitler, Lord Lucan and Napoleon Bonaparte.

One has to ask the question whether the permanent home address as shown on an electoral roll is actually owned by the applicant or is the property rented. If owned, are the deeds in the applicant's or another name? In the UK, electoral rolls, land registry documents and such like can provide this important verification, but in other countries and jurisdictions such data is not so readily available.

We all know that a check of an employer or company may reveal an offshore organisation with nominee directors and we recommend that consideration should be given to:

- using a professional research agency should you not have the facilities to complete meaningful checks and/or
- apply a weighting system to the verification of the information supplied and set pass criteria.

Be suspicious of those customers who are reluctant to provide normal information or provide minimal, false or misleading information. Also the customer who provides information which is expensive for you to verify. You know the one – he has £2 million to invest and shows a Mongolian passport with an address 'Tent 6 – Umshal Ful U, Outer Mongolia'. These are obviously the ones that you need to report as suspicious.

However, proceed with caution. It may be worthwhile to check out the difficult information as the client may be genuine. One needs to make a commercial decision on whether it is worth spending money to verify the identity as the client may prove to be an excellent, genuine customer. It is matter of sifting out the genuine from the false.

It is also important that you are not driven by the promise of money where what looks like a good deal that will increase the bonus is pushed through the system without the appropriate caution being taken.

The legislation, as I shall detail later, now affects most businesses from banks, accountants, lawyers, insurers and estate agents to car dealers, casinos, money transfer services and so on.

All new account clients should be treated with caution and as verification subjects. This particularly applies to 'friends' introduced by current customers/clients – the old school tie is dead and offers little in mitigation if you are caught providing facilities to launder dirty money.

The importance of checking documents cannot be over-emphasised. With today's computer technology, forgeries are simple and the old control measures of signature verification are, to put it bluntly, useless. If in doubt, the services of a forensic expert can prove to be invaluable. Recently I contacted a company who were advertising various financial services such as offshore accounts, credit cards, work permits and other doubtful services such as anarchist handbooks. The proprietor advised that the Isle of Man was the best place to hide money as that is where he had hidden OJ Simpson's assets. This was probably no more than the proverbial bullshit, but what interested me was the offer of passports. He claimed that for £4,000 he could get me an African passport, and for £7,000 an Irish one. He advised that the more money I was prepared to spend, the better the jurisdiction of the passport. Obviously, the money launderer with all of his cash can afford to buy whatever he wishes. In other words, treat the production of a passport with caution. In fact the Portuguese Government has stated that many of their overseas consulates have been burgled with a large number of passports being stolen. As you will shortly read, Mr Kenneth Noye, one of the Brinks-Mat gold and money launderers, used false passports to conceal his identity.

Currently it is estimated that there are at least 20 million false identities in the United Kingdom, created by organised gangs who apply for new national insurance numbers and then create fictitious individuals who can then use the new numbers to claim benefits and proof of identity for other frauds. The UK Government admitted that there were at one time 81 million NI numbers for a population of 60 million. Of course one has to consider that the Government do not really know how many people are living here. Recent news stories claimed that 139,000 Poles have returned home because of the failing UK economy, yet figures show that only 22,000 came here?

This type of fraud is on the increase; identity theft has risen in the UK from 24,000 cases in 2001 up to 77,000 last year. In the USA identity theft is costing the country $50 billion in fraud and has affected 8.2 million people with a growth of identity theft of children to such an extent that one child in every classroom in the US has had their identity stolen.

This highlights the need to pay more than lip service to customer/client verification as it means that to pay more than lip-service to customer/client verification as it means that one in three NI numbers in circulation is false!

The following details what the regulatory bodies see as appropriate vigilance depending on what type of financial business you are operating. Obviously these recommendations are based on experience and should help prevent the money launderer using your business to launder their dirty money. I have analysed various guidelines and have divided the recommended vigilance deemed appropriate between the various types of financial businesses. So I apologise for the following boring bit, but it is essential reading for anyone with a responsibility for prevention of money laundering.

The loss of personal data by the Government and some financial institutions obviously increases the risk of false identity records. Then the recent theft of blank passports highlights the inadequate security in many government agencies. The Government has now admitted that it cannot guarantee the security of personal data, and the real nail in the coffin is the latest loss of personal tax data from the Governments' Gateway site. The fraudsters, terrorists, etc., must be having a good laugh.

Banks & financial businesses

Banks should be vigilant when opening new accounts, doing business with non-account customers, accepting safe custody or safe deposit box business, deposit taking, lending and doing business involving marketing and self-promotion.

So what is suspicious?

Account opening

As we mentioned a couple of pages back, take care with those customers who are reluctant to provide normal information or provides minimal, false or misleading information – the type who tells you that he works for an official agency and has been sworn to secrecy and if he tells you anything he may have to kill you.

Non-account

All non-account clients should be treated with caution and as verification subjects. This particularly applies to 'friends' introduced by current customers/clients. It's no good thinking that all of your client's friends and associates are as honest and trustworthy as them.

Safe deposit boxes and safe custody facilities

Unless the customer is established and has been verified, extreme care should be taken in the acceptance of boxes, parcels and sealed envelopes. Full verification procedures should be taken especially in respect of non-account customers. Our previous comments re non-account customers are relevant.

Deposit taking

As explained, the criminal needs to get his dirty money into the banking system to initiate the cleaning cycle. The depositing of funds, usually cash, is often the only avenue open to him or her. So what deposits are suspicious? What do you look for? Unless you have a satisfactory explanation and can verify the source of the funds as being legitimate, substantial cash deposits, singly or in accumulations, should be regarded as suspicious. This is particularly relevant when the following factors apply.

- The business in which the customer is engaged would normally be conducted in cheques, banker's drafts, letters of credit, bills of exchange or other instruments, but not cash – especially such high amounts. In simple terms, large cash deposits from an international freight company would probably be suspicious.
- The cash deposit appears to be credited to the account for immediate conversion to a bankers order, money transfer or any other negotiable or readily marketable money instrument indicating rapid movements in and out of the account.
- Deposits are received by other banks and one becomes aware of the regular consolidation of such funds from those accounts prior to a request for onward wire transfer or transmission elsewhere. Only constant examination of the client's accounts would identify this trend.
- The customer or its representatives avoids direct contact with the bank.
- The use of nominee accounts, trustee accounts or client accounts appear to be unnecessary or inconsistent with the customer/beneficiary's normal business.
- Numerous accounts are used when fewer would suffice for no apparent commercial reason (usually to disguise the scale of the deposits).
- Numerous individuals (especially people whose names do not appear on the account mandate) are used by the customer to make deposits.
- Frequent small deposits are made which, when taken together, are substantial.
- There is frequent switching of funds between accounts in different names and in different jurisdictions.

- Payments out of the account are made the same day and in the same amount as deposited that day.
- A substantial cash withdrawal is made from a previously dormant or inactive account.
- A substantial cash withdrawal is made from an account which has just received a large credit from overseas.
- Use is made of a third party (professional firm or trust company) to deposit cash or negotiable instruments, especially if these are immediately transferred between client or trust accounts.
- Use is made of bearer securities outside a recognised dealing system in settlement of an account or otherwise.

Lending

Very frequently, loans, mortgages and the issuing of credit and charge cards are used by money launderers at the layering or integration stages. Secured borrowing is an effective method of layering and integration because the legitimate financial business (the lender) has a genuine claim to the security of the loan between the criminal and those seeking to confiscate such assets.

Obviously if a law enforcement agency or prosecution service is granted, by a court, the seizure of a convicted criminal's assets (HM Customs & Excise usually seize any assets used in the completion of a crime – the American DEA have frequent auctions of aeroplanes, boats, exotic cars, etc.) and a financial business has a secure charge on that criminal's asset, expensive litigation may follow to ensure that the charge is honoured.

Marketing & self promotion

Should a customer not provide a satisfactory explanation, either

- declining to provide information which would make them eligible for credit or other banking services, or
- making insufficient use of normal banking facilities such as higher interest rates for large credit balances,

they may be regarded as suspicious.

Electronic transfers

In an effort to ensure that the SWIFT system is not used by money launderers, the Financial Task Force (FATF) have asked SWIFT to request that all users of the system when sending SWIFT MT100 messages (customer transfers) identify both remitting customer and recipient. Any customer who is reluctant to provide those details or provides details of a recipient who is located in an unregulated or loosely regulated jurisdiction and where criminal activity such as drug trafficking or terrorism is high, should be viewed as suspicious.

Investment business

This type of business is not usually cash based and payments are made by cheque or transfer from another financial services business. The problem is that those payments can be from an unregulated bank by means of cheque, draft or wire transfer and there must be some responsibility to ensure that one knows who one is dealing with. Some experts will argue that such payments means that the Placement Stage has already been achieved and such transactions are in the Layering part of the wash cycle. Just because it has reached this stage, if all goes wrong and the wheel falls off, the fact that the crooks have laundered dirty money through your business is publicity that you will not want.

Obviously the payment of cash for investment products should be investigated fully as part of know-your-client.

As mentioned, the investment business is at risk at the layering stage as the liquidity of investment products is attractive to launderers as it allows them to quickly and easily move the criminal proceeds from one product to another, mixing them with lawful proceeds thus facilitating integration.

The risk of integration is also high as:

- opportunities to liquidate investment portfolios containing legal and illegal funds while concealing the latter are relatively easy
- the variety of available investments is extensive
- transfer between investment products is easy

Those investments at particular risk are:

- collective investment funds and other pooled funds (especially when unregulated)
- high risk/high reward products due to the fact that the launderer's cost of funds is by definition low and the potentially high rewards accelerate the integration and money laundering process.

Borrowing against security of investments

As mentioned previously, secured borrowing is an effective method of layering and integration because the legitimate financial business (the lender) has a genuine claim to the security of the loan made to the criminal and from those seeking to confiscate such assets.

Verification

Investment businesses will note the particular relevance in their case of exceptions to the need for verification, i.e.

Customers dealing direct

Where a customer deals with the investment business direct, the customer is the applicant for business to the investment business and accordingly determines who the verification subject(s) is(are). In exempt cases, as mentioned above, a record should be maintained indicating how the transaction arose and recording details of the paying financial services business branch sort code and account number or other financial services product reference number from which the cheque or payment is drawn.

Intermediaries and underlying customers

Where an agent/intermediary introduces a principal/customer to the investment business and the investment is made in the principal/customer's name, the principal/customer is the verification subject.

Nominees

Where an agent/intermediary acts for a customer (whether for a named client or through a client account) but deals in his own name, then the agent/intermediary is a verification subject (unless the applicant for business is an EC regulated financial services business) and the customer is also a verification subject.

If the applicant for business is an EC regulated or locally regulated financial services business, the fund manager may rely on an introduction from the applicant for business (or other written assurance that it will have verified any principal/customer for whom it acts as agent/intermediary). Such introductions should follow the verification procedures as detailed in know-your-customer procedures.

Delay in verification

Where verification has not been completed in a reasonable time, then the business relationship or significant one-off transaction in question should not proceed any further.

Where an investor exercises cancellation rights, or cooling off rights, the repayment of money arising in these circumstances (subject to any shortfall deduction where applicable) does not constitute 'proceeding further with business'. As such cancellations can offer a route to launder money, investment businesses should be alert to any abnormal exercise of cancellation/cooling off rights by any investor, or in respect of business introduced through any single authorised intermediary. In the event that such an abnormal exercise of rights becomes apparent, the matter should be treated as suspicious and reported through the usual channels. In any case, repayment should not be made to a third party.

Redemption prior to completion of verification

If the transaction is a significant one-off transaction or is carried out within a business relationship, verification of the customer should be completed before the customer receives the proceeds of the redemption. Investment businesses can be considered to have taken reasonable measures of verification where payment is made:

- to the legal owner of the investment by means of cheque, where possible crossed 'account payee', or
- to a bank account held (solely or jointly) in the name of the legal owner of the investment by any electronic means of transferring funds.

Switch transactions

There is no requirement for verification where it is a switch where all of the proceeds are directly reinvested in another investment which itself can, on subsequent resale, only result in either:

- a further reinvestment on behalf of the same customer
- a payment being made directly to him of which a record is kept.

Savings vehicles and regular investment programmes

Except in the case of a small one-off transaction, and subject to mandatory checks, where a customer has

- agreed to make regular subscriptions or payments to an investment business, or
- arranged for the collection of such subscriptions or payments,

the investment business should undertake verification of the customer or satisfy themselves that such verification is exempt under the regulations.

Where the customer sets up a regular savings scheme where money invested by him is used to acquire investments to be registered in the name or held to the order of a third party, the person funding the cash transaction should be treated as the verification subject. When the investment is realised, the person who is then the legal owner (if not the person who funded it) should also to be treated as a verification subject.

Reinvestment of Income

A number of retail savings and investment vehicles offer customers the facility to have income reinvested. The use of such a facility is not seen as an entry into a business relationship and such reinvestments do not require verification of client.

Suspicious transactions

Unless one has a satisfactory explanation, the following transactions should be regarded as suspicious:

- introduction by an agent/intermediary in an unregulated or loosely regulated jurisdiction or a sensitive jurisdiction
- any delay or want in the provision of information thus hindering completion of verification
- any transaction involving an undisclosed party
- early termination especially at a loss caused by front end or rear end charges or early termination penalties
- transfer or assignment of the benefit of a product to an unrelated third party or assignment as collateral
- payment into the product by an unrelated third party
- use of bearer securities outside a recognised clearing system where a scheme accepts securities in lieu of payment.

Fiduciary services

Many attorneys and financial businesses carry out fiduciary services in the setting up of trusts for clients. Unfortunately, with their inherent confidentiality, trust funds are a perfect place to launder dirty money.

It is considered good practice to ensure that key staff complete engagement documentation (client agreement, etc.) duly signed at the time of entry.

As with other financial service businesses, it is important that verification of new clients include:

- the verification of the settlor and/or the principal beneficiaries whenever a settlement is made or when accepting trusteeship from a previous trustee or where there are changes to principal beneficiaries or the settlor
- the verification of the identity of the underlying beneficial owners of any company that you have been requested to form
- documentation and information in respect of the new client for use by the

administrator who has the daily management of the new client's affairs should include a note of any required further input on verification from any agent/intermediary of the new client, together with a deadline for the supply of such data.

Suspicious transactions

In addition to the due diligence undertaken prior to and at the commencement of providing fiduciary services, there is an obligation to monitor the activities of the entities to which it provides services and in the absence of satisfactory explanation the following should be regarded as suspicious:

- any request for or the discovery of an unnecessarily complicated trust or corporate structure involving several different jurisdictions
- payments or settlements to or from an administered entity which are either of a size or source which had not been expected
- an administered entity entering into transactions which are either unrelated to the anticipated or have little or no obvious purpose
- use of bearer securities or cash outside a recognised clearing system in settlement of an account or otherwise
- the establishment of an administered entity with no obvious purpose
- sales invoice values that exceed the known or expected value of the goods/services
- sales or purchases at inflated or undervalued prices
- a large number of bank accounts or other financial products all receiving small payments which in total amount to a significant sum
- large payments of third party cheques endorsed in favour of the customer
- the use of nominees other than in the normal course of fiduciary business
- excessive use of wide-ranging powers of attorney
- unwillingness to disclose source of funds
- the use of PO boxes for no apparent advantage or necessity
- failure or tardiness to complete verification
- administered entities that constantly make substantial losses
- unnecessarily complex group structure
- unexplained subsidiaries
- high turnover of shareholders, directors, trustees or underlying beneficial owners
- the use of numerous different currencies for no apparent purpose
- arrangements established with the apparent objective of fiscal evasion.

Insurance

Offshore insurance business, whether life assurance, pensions or other risk management business, presents a number of opportunities to the criminal for money laundering at all of its stages. What can be easier than paying cash for the purchase of a single premium product followed by early cancellation and reinvestment?

Examples of insurance products at risk from money launderers are:

- requests from clients to purchase insurance products where the source of funds to purchase the product is unclear or inconsistent with the customer's financial standing
- an urgent or sudden request for the purchase of a substantial policy with a lump sum payment by an existing client whose other policies, etc. are completely out of character with the new purchase
- any request for an insurance product that has no discernible purpose and a reluctance from the client(s) to divulge the reason for the investment
- to purchase an insurance product using a cheque drawn on a third party account
- client(s) who are not interested in the performance of the investment, but are more concerned about early cancellation and surrender value.

Verification requirements

Surrender prior to completion of verification

Whether the transaction is a significant one-off transaction or is carried out within a business relationship, verification of the client is required before they receive the surrender proceeds.

A life insurer is considered to have taken reasonable verification measures where payment is made either:

- to the policy holder by cheque crossed account payee, or
- to the bank account held in the name of the policyholder by electronic transfer.

Switch transactions

If the significant one-off transaction is switched to another policy of insurance where all of the proceeds are directly paid to the new policy and on surrender will result in:

- a further premium payment on behalf of the same client or
- a payment made directly to the client of which a record is kept verification is not required.

Employer sponsored pension or savings schemes
In all transactions undertaken on behalf of an employer sponsored pension or savings scheme the insurer is required to undertake verification of

- the principal employer, and
- the trustees of the scheme (if any),

and may need to verify the members if they as individuals seek personal investment advice unless the employer/trustees have been verified and the principal employer confirms the identity and address of the investor in writing.

Suspicious transactions

- applications from potential clients from overseas for business where a comparable service can be provided closer to home
- application for business outside the insurer's normal pattern of business
- any introduction from an agent/intermediary in either an unregulated or loosely regulated jurisdiction or where criminal activity is prevalent
- any delay in the provision of information needed for verification purposes or the lack of the full details required
- any proposal involving an undisclosed third party
- early termination of product especially at a loss caused by front end loading, or where cash was tendered and/or the refund cheque is to a third party
- 'churning' at the client's request
- transfer of the product's benefit to an unrelated third party
- use of bearer securities outside the recognised clearing system in settlement of an account
- insurance premiums higher than market levels
- large, unusual or unverifiable insurance claims
- unverified reinsurance premiums
- large introductory commissions
- insurance policies for unusual/unlikely exposures

Terrorists

'Know your client' procedures are obviously extremely important in respect of possible terrorist money laundering. This book now includes a review of indicators and operating methods for various types of terrorist financing. A short time ago I completed an assignment where I had to check an offshore bank's client database to see whether any clients were listed on various government blacklists. Out of some 21,000+ names I found two that were deemed to be suspected or linked to terrorist organisations. All businesses handling large sums of money on behalf of customers or clients should carry out such an audit.

Summary

The various regulatory authorities throughout the world have given general guidance on verification. The main points made are as follows.

- A financial services business undertaking verification should establish that every verification subject relevant to the application for business actually exists.
- All of the joint applicants for business should be verified.
- Where there are a large number of verification subjects, it may be sufficient to carry out full verification on a limited group such as senior members of a family, principal shareholders, main directors, etc.
- Primarily, the verification should be in respect of the parties operating the financial services product. Where there are underlying principals, the true nature of the relationship between the principals and signatories should be established and verification completed on these principals especially where the signatories act on the instructions of the principals. These principals will include beneficial owners, settlors, controlling shareholders, directors, major beneficiaries, etc. The level of verification will depend on the exact nature of the relationship.

3

The Classic Cases

The Lansky legacy

It's better in the Bahamas

US Bureau of Narcotics File

Name: Meyer Lansky

Aliases: Meyer Suchowlansky, Bugs Meyer, Morris Lieberman

Description: born 7-04-02 Grodno, Poland,Jewish, 5'5", 145 lbs, brown
             eyes, grey brown hair, Naturalised Brooklyn, NY, 9-27-1928

Localities frequented:
    Resides 612 Hibiscus Driver, Hallandale, Fla.
    Frequents Gold Coast Lounge, Hollywood, Florida, Miami, NY and Las
    Vegas

Family background:
    Divorced from Ann Citron, children from first marriage, Bernard, Sandra,
    Paul. Second wife, Thelma Schwartz. Mother Fenke (deceased) brother
    Jack.

Criminal associates:
    Lucky Luciano, Guiseppe Doto, Francisco Saveria, Anthony Accardo,
    Santo Trafficante, Jack Lansky.

Criminal history:
    FBI/791783, NYCPD ? B70258 records date from 1918 and includes
    arrests for petty larceny, felonious assault, bootlegging, gambling,
    narcotics.

Business:
    Has interests in Havana Riviera, Capri Hotel, and Sans Souci Gambling

---

Casino, all in Havana, Cuba and Flamingo Hotel, Las Vegas.

Modus Operandi:
One of the top non-Italian associates in the Mafia controls gambling in partnership with leading Mafiosi. Finances large scale narcotic smuggling and other illicit ventures.

'You can buy an airstrip, or an island. You can buy citizenship. You can buy protection. You can buy justice. And should your drug cargo get seized by the Police, you can even buy it back.'

Carl Hiaasen and Jim McGee
'A Nation for Sale', *Miami Herald*, 23 September 1984

Meyer Lansky was one of the first criminals to use his brain rather than muscle. Born in Poland and raised in New York, a 9th grade drop-out, he became the highest ranking non-Italian in what was called The Syndicate, and was known as the mob's accountant. Today he is remembered as the patron saint of money launderers.

When Al Capone was sent to prison for tax evasion, Lansky had a theory:

'Any money that the Inland Revenue Service does not know about is not taxable.'

He then embarked on a search of ways to hide money and he quickly discovered the benefits of numbered Swiss bank accounts. Later he became instrumental in financing The Flamingo as a casino/hotel complex in a small Nevada town that was to grow into the gambling capital of the world, Las Vegas. What better way to launder the proceeds of crime.

He then convinced the mob to take their 'income' offshore, first to Havana with the blessing of President Batista, and then with the arrival of Castro, who threw the Americans out, to the Bahamas. Money from the United States was laundered through the Casino in Nassau where it became Casino profit deposited into local banks and then transferred back to various accounts in the USA.

Lansky secured the Bahamas as the mob's offshore financial centre by funding Lynden Pindling, a self styled 'Black Moses of the people', in his political aspirations. Pindling became Prime Minister and a corrupt regime ensued. Only recently the Bahamas Government addressed the problem of money laundering with new legislation being enacted to clean up the island's image and to become accepted by FATF as being a cooperative financial jurisdiction. Their legislation calls for the reporting of 'unusual' transactions as opposed to 'suspicious'.

In the 1970s, the Bahamas began to woo Colombian and other drug traffickers and the islands were used as airfields and harbours for drugs in transit to nearby

Florida and the Carolinas.

A Royal Commission formed in the 1980s to investigate the drug trade in the Bahamas found corruption in the courts, police and government. Pindling and other ministers were found to have deposited millions of pounds in excess of their salaries into various bank accounts.

Local banking laws with strict secrecy regulations, which make local banking officials from manager to teller criminally liable if they reveal details about their clients and their transactions, made it impossible for foreign law enforcement agents to investigate suspect transactions.

Money arrived originally stuffed in beer cartons (Meyer) and later in suitcases, bin liners and so on. Bank tellers were paid a commission to count the money, this being usually 2%. After safely depositing the cash, it was wire transferred to a foreign bank. North Americans preferred Canadian or US banks, whereas Colombians preferred Panamanian banks. To conceal the money trail even more, Bahamian shell companies with nominee directors were set up and funds were paid into bank accounts in the shell company name from where it was wire transferred to another shell company in Panama.

To show the growth of the Bahamas drug trade, one only has to look at The Royal Bank of Canada's Bimini branch who, in 1977, transferred only $0.5 million to the Nassau branch, yet by 1984 that figure had increased to over $24 million. These transactions were all in respect of cash deposits. The bank, when asked, could not identify the funds coming from any ordinary business transaction. Bimini has a local population of 2,000, and 500 allegedly work in the drug trade.

The Bahamas banking system was dominated by Canadian banks. Of the six most important banks, four were Canadian and the other two were British and American. When American and Canadian authorities became frustrated with the Canadian banks' lax attitude to money laundering, they were stonewalled by the banks who claimed that the Bahamas banks operated under Bahamas law, not Canadian. However the US investigators eventually won a landmark court decision and the Bank of Nova Scotia was fined $1.8 million.

Subsequently, the other banks set up anti-money laundering procedures, but there was no noticeable decline in dollar deposits. Bimini has been shut down as a drug centre and the Royal Navy and American agencies have reduced the volume of actual drug traffic through the islands. Stopping the traffic does not of course stop the money laundering. However, as mentioned, new legislation currently being enacted has improved the anti-money laundering controls and regulations in this jurisdiction. Notwithstanding, Lansky certainly left a legacy of awesome proportions.

At the same time, corrupt politicians have made and hidden fortunes in the US and in other jurisdictions during the period of prohibition, rationing and to date.

The Nazis

Then the biggest criminal gang of all, the Nazis, decided not only to rob their own country but everyone else as well. Just prior to the Second World War the German gold Reserves were very small and certainly insufficient to wage a war.

With the invasion of most of Europe and subsequently Russia, the Nazis amassed a fortune in gold, artwork, precious stones and currency, much of which ended up in personal bank accounts and safe deposit vaults (including mines and being buried).

Safehaven operations

Prior to the Germans looting various countries' gold and money reserves, many of the countries concerned took steps to secure their reserves by moving the funds out of the country. Poland moved theirs to Romania but the funds were subsequently seized by the Nazis when they invaded that country, too. The French shipped their reserves to the United States; the Belgians entrusted the French who shipped those reserves to Dakar. When Dakar became part of Vichy France the Nazis received the Belgian reserves. Most of Holland's reserves were shipped to London.

Although neutral, the US Government froze all assets held in the USA on behalf of any country overrun by the Nazis (Denmark, Norway and all European countries except England). In addition they issued a blacklist (very similar to today's anti-money laundering blacklists) of prohibited individuals and companies. Similarly, the transfer of property in occupied countries was deemed to be illegal.

It was then declared (Declaration of Gold Purchases 22 February 1944) that the US (Britain and USSR made similar declarations) would not recognize the transfer of gold from the Axis or buy gold from any country that had not broken relations with the Axis.

Operation Safehaven was launched to recover assets looted by the Nazis. Unfortunately rivalry between the US Treasury and State Department hindered the success of the operation. Part of the operation was the investigation into the use of foreign neutral countries to facilitate the Nazi operations. Switzerland was used as a financial centre for the laundering of gold and cash, Sweden for operations of the Siemens steel, ball-bearing production and heavy industry, and Spain/Portugal for oil/mineral supplies.

The oil supply question proved an embarrassment in that the oil from South America was being shipped by Standard Oil (Esso), an American company, and whereas petrol rationing was making life difficult on the eastern seaboard of the US, Spain had no such rationing and a lot of the oil was shipped on to Nazi Germany, who refuelled their military machinery, no doubt including U-boats that were sinking tankers taking oil to Russia, England and the USA.. When requested to think about stopping these supplies, Esso threatened to interrupt supplies to the USA. The supplies to Spain continued.

At this stage of the war the Office of Strategic Services ('OSS') became more involved. Unfortunately in Switzerland the OSS head was Allen Dulles, later to become head of the CIA – the airport for the capital of the USA was named after his family: Dulles International. I wonder whether this was due to the flight of Nazi capital to South America? Dulles had earlier been exposed, during a joint British/American operation, as having allegedly spied on Americans and was suspected of being sympathetic to the Nazi cause. Historians claim that he was deliberately sent to Switzerland to see if he would take the opportunity to help Nazis while there. Apparently aware of being under surveillance it is claimed that he used his Vatican connections to help Nazi 'clients', using Vatican couriers to help launder the assets received from Germany. (*The Vatican having agreed to help Dulles so as to recover their own assets in Germany and to further their anti-communist philosophy.*)

Gregory Rozman, a Slovenian Bishop was trying to transfer huge quantities of Nazi gold and western currency secreted in Swiss banks during the war. Rozman had been sent to Switzerland with the aid of Dulles' friends within the intelligence service. Although attempts were made to stop these transfers the funds soon ended up in the hands of Nazis now residing in Argentina. Dulles had allegedly fixed the transfer.

In 1945, the US Treasury accused Dulles of laundering the funds from the Nazi Bank of Hungary to Switzerland with the aid of a German agent Hans Bernd Gisevious (an OSS agent working in the Reichsbank). The US State Department took over the investigation and it was dropped.

During his tenure in Switzerland, Dulles' career was marked by several money laundering cases. The Nazis tipped Dulles off that the Swiss codes had been broken and Dulles switched his operation to the banks of Belgium, Luxembourg and Leichtenstein, laundering the funds through Japan using Vatican couriers.

After the war these banks refused to allow allied investigators to look at their books. It is suspected that the Germans were able to launch the Battle of the Bulge as a complete surprise as Dulles is alleged to have advised the Nazis that that the Japanese code had been broken at a vital time. Shortly after this warning the SS told the German High Command to use tighter code security and to stop using the radio. The Germans stopped using Ultra, using couriers instead, and their subsequent attack through the Ardennes was a complete surprise.

Dulles and his colleagues are claimed to have used a great deal of influence to ensure that US investments in Nazi Germany were not seized for repartitions. In Switzerland the SS had purchased a large amount of stock in American corporations and laundered their money through the Chase and Corn Exchange banks. The W R Grace Corporation (no not the bearded batsman) hired Pan Am clipper flying boats to transport Nazi gems, currency, stock and bonds to South America. These operations were the product of money laundering for the Nazis. A number of US Army officers admit that not all of the Nazi gold was handed over to them; one officer claimed to have been in a large vault filled with gold, gems and currency that never appeared in any US files.

As Dulles was still so closely associated with the German industrialists (see Appendix 1 for further details of Dulles's German connections) it is claimed that he was unwilling to give the attention to Safehaven that Washington expected. An agent sent to Berne unearthed:

- Gold and bonds looted from Europe and deposited in certain Swiss Banks
- Funds from Deutsche Verkehrs-Kreditbank of Karlsruhe to Basle.
- Stocks and bonds held in Zurich for the Nazi Party
- Numerous Nazi accounts in Swiss francs in various banks
- Nazi cash and property held in Liechtenstein
- A Reichsbank account for 2 million francs in Switzerland
- 45 million Reichsmarks held in secret Swiss bank accounts

Dulles was also a friend of the American Director of the Bank for International Settlements as well as the previously mentioned top Nazi banking officials.

After the investigation into his money laundering he resigned and returned to America where he met Thomas McKittrick, the former head of the Bank for international Settlements. The Nazis had moved considerable funds from Switzerland to Argentina and Dulles soon went to work for a large number of Argentinian clients. It is claimed that the boom in the Argentinian economy was due to the influx of Nazi money.

Oh yes, and remember our old friend, the architect of money laundering, Meyer Lansky. He, it is alleged, visited Switzerland and managed to obtain some of the Nazi assets himself.

Dulles's alleged involvement in money laundering and drug trafficking continued (see 'CIA black operations', page 72).

Of course, while all this was going on many of the Nazis plundered Germany's now substantial Gold reserves and looted art treasures. This robbery is listed as the greatest gold robbery ever, making Brinks-Mat look like a child's game. Much of this gold, etc., was no doubt laundered. A short synopsis of this robbery is set out in Appendix 2.

Tricky Dicky

It was in 1973 that the term money laundering first appeared in print and it was reported as such during the Watergate scandal. In 1972, Richard Nixon took the first steps to secure his tenure of the White House and created a committee – The

Committee to Re-elect the President – 'CRP' bizarrely pronounced 'creep' although in retrospect, I can think of better pronunciation.

Nixon's formal law partner, Attorney General John Mitchell, was named to run CRP, but the real drive began a year earlier when Mitchell, and Secretary Maurice Stans, began building a war chest. Major donors were the American Dairy Industry (Nixon had raised milk subsidies) and Howard Hughes who is reported to have handed $100,000 to Nixon's closest friend, Florida banker, Charles 'Bebe' Rebozo. Disgraced financier Robert Vesco, who at the time was under investigation by the Justice Department, arranged a cash donation of $200,000.

Mitchell and Stans approached American Airlines for $100,000 and the chairman, George Spater, was faced with the predicament of how to divert corporate funds that were otherwise accountable. He contacted a Lebanese company called Amarco and asked them to submit a false invoice for commission on sales of aircraft parts to Middle East Airlines. The $100,000 was paid and Amarco deposited the funds into their Swiss bank account from where it was wire transferred to their account in New York. Their New York agent withdrew the money in cash and paid it to Spater who passed it on to Mitchell and Stans.

Braniff Airlines, who needed to raise and hide a $40,000 donation, similarly arranged for a false invoice to be submitted to their Panama office for goods and services. They then supplied the office with a batch of unaccountable blank tickets which were sold to passengers who paid cash for their airline tickets. This money was funnelled through a Dallas construction company before showing up in Braniff's books to cover the shortfall.

Ashland Oil arranged a similar scheme, the money coming from their Gabob subsidiary and washed through Switzerland from where it was withdrawn in cash and carried back to the USA in an executive briefcase. Gulf Oil laundered their donation through their subsidiary in the Bahamas.

As congress were about to pass legislation about the reporting of donations and prohibiting anonymous ones, Mitchell and Stans decided to raise as much as possible before the deadline. Using an old Mexican connection that would guarantee such donations could not be traced, they targeted private citizens as well as other corporations.

Among the donations, were four cashiers' cheques totalling $89,000, all made out by different American banks, and payable to a Mexico City lawyer, Manuel Ogarrio Daguerre. The four cheques were mailed to Miami where they were paid into a bank account of a real estate salesman, Bernard L Barker. He was instructed that, if questioned about the funds, to say that it was his share of a land deal with an anonymous Chilean businessman. If then asked why he withdrew the $89,000 in cash, he was to answer that the deal fell through and he had to repay the commission.

Then it all went wrong. Our intrepid pair decided to use some of the fund to finance a burglary at Watergate. Even after the quick arrest of the five burglars, our duo did not think that anyone would be able to discover and trace funds paid to CRP. However, after the Washington Post scoop, every journalist in the USA wanted to get in on the act.

The New York Times discovered the Mexican connection and investigators got into Barker's bank account and found a fifth cheque payable to a Nixon Fund raiser in the Mid West. When interviewed, he admitted that he had paid it to Stans. Further investigations revealed that CRP had washed $750,000 through Mexico and that Stans had a huge cash slush fund in his office at CRP.

The irony of this case was that, in 1973, money laundering was not illegal anywhere in the world.

The treasure of La Mina

La Mina is Spanish for The Mine and Colombia's drug cartels dubbed one of their money laundering organisations with that name.

In 1991, Vahe and Nazareth Andonian, together with Raoul Vivas, were sentenced to 505 years imprisonment without parole. They had laundered drug monies for the Colombian Medellin cartel and the proceeds of heroin sales from Turkish drug traffickers.

The Andonians were in the jewellery business in Los Angeles and when La Mina was discovered, it had been operating for some 15 years. Due to pressure from the law enforcement agencies in Florida, the Colombians had relocated to Los Angeles. By the late 1980s, LA banks were producing a $3.8 billion cash surplus – a 2,200% increase in four years.

Basically the banks were awash with cash deposits and, as they had more cash than needed for normal daily business, the surplus was paid into the Federal Reserve Bank. Whereas in the rest of the USA, the Federal Reserve Bank was reporting a deficit of some $16.5 billion, Southern California was in surplus.

Vivas was approached by the Colombian drug cartels with an offer that he could not refuse. On the table was the offer of a 5% handling fee to launder $500 million a year. He immediately formed two front companies in Montevideo, Letra SA to deal in gold, and Cambio Italia SA to operate as a currency exchange business. An office was opened in the Los Angeles jewellery centre at 610 South Broadway in the heart of the city's diamond trading district.

The plan was simple – all of the drug money collected around the USA would be sent to a front company in New York's jewellery district from where it would be taken by courier to the Los Angeles office. Vivas used this money to purchase gold in all of its various forms where the dealer was prepared to accept cash payment at a purchase price over the odds. The gold materials would be melted down and mixed with silver so that it represented South American gold.

Dummy gold was then exported to the USA by Letra with appropriate documentation, the dummy gold was destroyed on receipt and replaced with the newly smelted 'South American' gold. This gold was sold in New York and the now laundered, clean, money from the sales wired to Cambio Italiana who paid Letra SA who in turn paid the money to the Colombians.

Due to the large amounts of cash being handled by Vivas, the system was in danger of collapse so he brought the Andonian brothers, who operated a number of jewellery businesses, and a Syrian, Wanis Koyomejian, who operated a gold dealing company Ropex, into the scheme.

As the business expanded even further, Vivas brought in friends in Miami, Houston and New York.

Meanwhile the Medellin cartel's financial representative Eduardo Martinez Romero was introduced to a New York mafia-connected drug trafficker, Jimmy Brown, and during their first meeting he bragged about the Vivas' 'La Mina' operation. Brown suggested a separate laundering operation through Atlanta and some $12 million was laundered through that city.

However, $1 million of drugs money was seized by the authorities in Atlanta and at a meeting between Romero, Brown, and an associate Alex Carrera, in Panama, Romero insisted that the $1 million be paid back by Brown. At a second meeting in Aruba between the same parties, plus the man in charge of the Atlanta operation, Romero, after too many drinks, boasted again about La Mina, claiming that it had washed $28 million in the last 45 days with a wash cycle of 48 hours. It was agreed that the Atlanta operation would take a commission cut to 6% to repay the lost $1 million and match the 48 hour wash cycle. Romero continued to brag over the next few months, being unaware that Brown's real name was John Featherly, and Carrera's real name was Cesar Diaz (both being undercover Drug Enforcement Agency agents) and that the Atlanta operation was being run by the Agency as a sting.

In San Francisco, a bank officer at Wells Fargo Banking Corporation, noted that the Andonian brothers had, in just under three months, deposited $25 million in cash into an account at one of the branches. He telephoned the Internal Revenue Service.

At Los Angeles Airport, a shipping clerk was checking a cargo of scrap gold from a jeweller in New York being sent to a gold dealer called Ropex in Los Angeles. One of the boxes was ripped open and he noted that it contained, not gold, but cash. He reported it to his management who contacted Ropex. Ropex claimed that there had been a mix up and that they knew all about it. The cash was from the jeweller hoping to find better short term interest rates in Los Angeles. The shipping company sent the cargo to Ropex, but being unhappy with Ropex's explanation, notified the FBI.

A surveillance operation code named 'Polar Cap' was initiated with hidden video cameras throughout the Los Angeles jewellery district and in New York. Phone taps were placed on various telephones, people were followed and garbage was collected. The garbage included various documents such as invoices with contacts in Canada, Mexico, and the United Kingdom, plus cancelled cheques identifying bank accounts as well as lists of friendly gold dealers. The operation became the biggest in the history of US law enforcement.

A task force from the FBI, Drug Enforcement Agency, Internal Revenue Service, Customs and Bureau of Alcohol, Tobacco and Firearms, plus the US Immigration and Naturalisation Service arrested everyone. Evidence of 1035 bank accounts in 179 banks throughout the Americas and Europe was found. 127 indictments were served and Vivas and Romero were extradited to the USA. Some $1.2 billion had been laundered. The US authorities not only seized assets and froze bank accounts, but fined foreign banks with US branches for their wilful participation in La Mina.

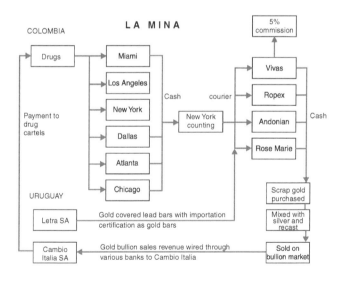

The investigation spread to Switzerland where the first female Justice Minister, Elizabeth Kopp, resigned in the wake of her husband's involvement in money laundering where it was found that his company Shakarchi Trading was involved with drugs money seized in Los Angeles, it being en route to his company from the Andonian brothers. He also had meetings in Zurich with representatives from Ropex.

Elements of this case and the recent expose of Liechtenstein's dubious activities highlight the use of technology to identify money launderers' activities. In the United Kingdom, GCHQ at Cheltenham and the US Secret Service communication centre in Yorkshire, monitor communications, whether telephone, satellite, internet or whatever, between locations where national security may be threatened. Obviously the activities of organised crime are subject to surveillance. Recently the national press revealed that e-mails are to be subject of surveillance.

In effect, this means that, should your business become involved in money laundering, it is likely that communications from your business will be monitored. With the ever-increasing use of CCTV systems in town centres for security purposes, evidence of a target money launderer entering your premises is readily available.

The seizure of garbage in this case and the discovery of evidence is worthy of comment. During an investigation into money laundering in London, garbage dumped on the pavement outside a private bank in Mayfair was examined by me, and although it did not identify any evidence of money laundering, highly confidential personal bank account data was discovered. I had the account details and bank balances of most of Hollywood's movie star population. This data could of course be used by the criminal fraternity.

As one can see from the flowchart on page 55, the money laundering in this case was quite a simple scheme that collapsed due to errors being made by the main players involved. The drugs cash was placed in the system by using it to purchase gold and silver for cash, the gold/silver was then resmelted and layered into the genuine gold market by using it to replace 'false' gold imports, and the resulting clean funds from the sale of that 'South American' gold were integrated back to the drug cartels.

Brinks-Mat

I have included this case as it contains all of the elements of classic money laundering with some similarities to La Mina.

On 26 November 1983, several criminals broke into the Brinks-Mat warehouse near London's Heathrow airport. After terrorising the guards they entered the underground vaults and stole 6,400 gold bars with a market value of £ 26,369,778.

Within a month, the police had four of the men in custody and a year later three of the four were sentenced to 25 years imprisonment. Unfortunately, the police had still not recovered one ounce of the stolen gold.

One of the three convicted men, Mickey McAvoy had friends including the owner of a mini-cab firm, Brian Perry, and John Lloyd who lived with Jeannie Savage (her husband was serving 22 years for armed robbery). Perry and Lloyd contacted Kenneth Noye to help them dispose of the gold. Unlike Perry or Lloyd, Noye had a criminal record and at the time of the robbery was the subject of an investigation by HM Customs & Excise officers looking into gold smuggling and a tax fraud scheme. Using his obvious experience, Noye contacted a John Palmer who had a gold bullion dealership in Bristol called Scadlynn Limited. Also involved in Scadlynn was Garth Chappell who had previously been convicted of conspiracy to defraud.

Noye decided that the gold could be laundered through Scadlynn but it was essential that the serial numbers on each bar were removed. Palmer, who owned his own smelter agreed to melt the gold down and then recast it prior to shipping to Scadlynn. The plan was then to melt the gold again, but mix it with copper and silver coins so that it looked like scrap bullion. This would then be taken to the government Assay Office in Sheffield where each bar would be weighed, taxed and legitimised. Scadlynn would be then free to sell it to licensed bullion dealers who as middlemen would melt the impurities out and market it to the British jewellery trade.

Noye knew from experience that he had to protect himself and flew to Jersey in 1984 where he took £50,000 in £50 notes to Charterhouse Japhet Bank, Bath St, St Helier. Officials at the bank agreed to purchase 11 one-kilo gold bars. At this stage Noye made his first mistake – he kept asking the officials for their assurance that the certificates issued with each bar did not show the bars' serial number. Despite their assurances, he kept asking the question, claiming that if the certificates did show the serial numbers, the deal was off. Finally he accepted their assurances and left the £50,000 as the deposit and returned to London.

The balance of £50,000 was sent to the bank and 8 days later, Noye flew back to Jersey and collected the gold bars and certificates.

He deposited the gold bars in a safe deposit box at the New Street branch of the TSB and flew home with the certificates. It was no accident that he purchased 11 bars and that they matched the stolen gold in size and content. 11 bars weigh 11 kilos or just over 24 pounds and can be carried easily in a briefcase with a nice round value of £100,000. The mistake he had made was that his concerns about the certificates had aroused the suspicions of the bank officials who informed the local police. During his second visit, he was followed and before he landed back in England, the police in the UK had been alerted.

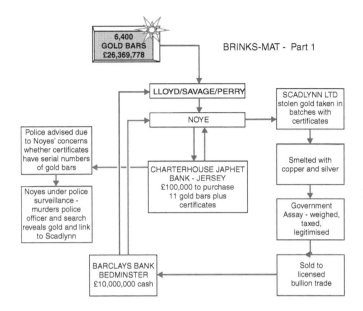

BRINKS-MAT - Part 1

Placement – the gold was now in the system

He could now take 11 bars at a time to Scadlynn and, if stopped, had the certificates as an insurance policy. The arrangement was that Scadlynn would charge the going scrap rate plus VAT. Scadlynn was allowed to keep the undeclared VAT as their profit.

The money would be deposited in the local Barclays Bank at Bedminster in Bristol, where it was withdrawn in cash and paid to Noye, Perry and Lloyd. In five months some £10 million was sent to the three men, usually in black plastic bags in the boot of a car or lorry.

Using a false passport in the name Sydney Harris, Noye deposited his share of the cash into an account with the Bank of Ireland at Croydon. A standing arrangement meant that it was immediately wire transferred to the bank's Dublin office. McAvoy's girlfriend Kathy Meacock and Jeannie Savage used the same Croydon branch on alternative days to make deposits also wired to Dublin.

Meanwhile, Perry had brought in Gordon Parry and a solicitor, Michael Relton. Parry, with Relton's help, deposited £793,500 in cash from Scadlynn into the Bank of Ireland's Balham branch where it was instantly wired to the bank's Douglas, Isle of Man branch. Parry's wife's cousin also helped and deposited a further £500,000 at Balham where it was wired to the Isle of Man.

To confuse anyone attempting to follow the money trail, Parry brought some of the money in the Isle of Man back to the Balham branch into a second account from where it was withdrawn in dribs and drabs to be sent offshore to another bank. During all of this time, the stolen gold was still being sent to Scadlynn for processing.

In August 1984, using a solicitor's introduction from Relton, Parry opened an account at the Hong Kong & Shanghai Bank in Zurich, where he deposited £840,435 in cash. A week later, an unidentified man walked into the bank's Bishopsgate headquarters in London with a sports bag containing £500,000 in cash. He instructed the bank to send it to Zurich.

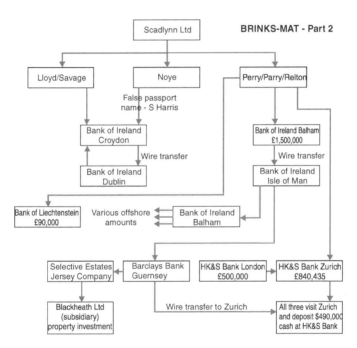

Layering – the cash proceeds were now being circulated to confuse and hide

A few weeks later, Perry, Parry, Relton, a jeweller named Elcombe with his wife, all met in Zurich and opened accounts at the same branch of the HK & S bank. Another £490,000 cash was deposited. Perry and Parry nipped across the border into Liechtenstein where they both opened an account at the Bank of Liechtenstein with £45,000 cash.

Parry then purchased an off-the-shelf company in Jersey called Selective

Estates. An account for the company was opened at Barclays Bank in Guernsey and money from the Isle of Man was transferred into that account. Selective Estates wired those funds from Guernsey to a second HK & S account in Zurich.

In September, Elcombe deposited £65,000 in cash into his Zurich account and the same day Parry walked into the Bank of Liechtenstein with a suitcase containing £500,000 in cash. A few weeks later, Elcombe paid £1,075,000 cash into his Zurich account. So much money was going through Barclays at Bedminster that extra staff were transferred in to cope with the cash.

Noye's Jersey mistake now took a serious turn as the Police, who had been keeping an eye on him after being alerted by the Jersey police, had spotted him meeting with a wanted criminal, Brian Reader. C11, the Metropolitan Police specialist intelligence gathering team, were called in and in January 1985, they placed Noye's house under surveillance. Noye discovered one of the officers in his garden

and the officer was murdered. Noye and Reader were arrested and charged with murder. Ten months later, a jury acquitted them both, but there was enough evidence found at Noye's house to link them with the Brinks-Mat robbery, a small cache of gold bars being found.

Within three days, Palmer and Chappell at Scadlynn had been arrested and that company's affairs were being investigated. On the day the officer was murdered, Elcombe and his wife had left London in Parry's Mercedes with £710,000 in cash stowed in the boot. Two weeks previously, they had made a cash deposit of £453,000 in cash to their account in Zurich.

On the way to Zurich, they were stopped at Aachen by border guards. When asked if they had any money, they declared £45,000, which was their life savings, which they were taking to Switzerland. The guard decided to search the car and found the £710,000 cash under the carpet in the boot. The Elcombes now changed their story and claimed to be antique dealers working out of Belgium. They were detained for questioning. The money was taken out of the car and counted in the border guards' hut where, for some reason, he made a note of serial numbers on a random basis. The German Interpol office was advised and they contacted the British Interpol office. As nothing was recorded about Elcombe, nor whether large amounts of currency had been stolen or the car reported stolen, the Elcombes were released with the cash. However, an officer at Scotland Yard saw the telex messages and that the car was registered to Parry. The name rang a bell and then he realised Parry was linked to the Brinks-Mat investigation, A phone call to the Brinks-Mat situation room confirmed his suspicions and when the team there heard the name Elcombe they begged Interpol to stop them – but it was too late, they had long gone.

On arrival in Zurich, Elcombe deposited £100,000 in his account and opened a new account (720.3) in which he deposited £608,000. A few days later, someone deposited £493,970 in Parry's Liechtenstein account and a week after the murder, Elcombe transferred £1.6 million from his initial account at HK&S Zurich to the new 720.3 account. Parry then closed his Liechtenstein account and transferred the funds to the 720.3 account.

Relton, the solicitor, went to Liechtenstein in April and opened a 'Red Cross account'. These are used by attorneys and tax specialists as foundation accounts, the funds being controlled by an organisation often in the name of a charity under the administration of an attorney. In effect, this type of account usually has written into its charter that a charity is the named beneficiary, the beneficiary is not necessarily the beneficial owner of the account. No one is supposed to know who that is, not even the bank's directors. The true identity is protected by a double layer of bank secrecy and attorney-client privilege. Robert Maxwell used such accounts in Liechtenstein and duly claimed that neither he or his family controlled the funds he deposited there or would benefit from them.

Relton opened this account in the name Moet Foundation, spelt by the bank Moyet. (Moet was Relton's favourite champagne). Relton and Parry deposited £3,167,409.25 into this account. Parry at this stage also made a vital mistake when he paid for a farm purchase with a draft drawn on the 720.3 account in the amount £152,126. He had not checked whether there were funds in the account to cover the draft and in the haste to transfer funds to the new Moyet account, they had not checked to see whether the draft had cleared. Because the bank knew where the funds had gone, they simply transferred the funds back from Moyet to cover the draft. This enabled the Police to identify the Moyet account and its links to the robbers.

Some 15 months had elapsed since the robbery and there was probably only £5 million of gold left. Relton and Parry decided to invest for the future and embarked on a series of property investments. Using the Jersey registered company Selective Estates as an umbrella, they set up a subsidiary called Blackheath Limited. To finance a property purchase in Cheltenham, they wove a complex web of transactions:

1. Relton transferred $300,000 from HK&S Bank Zurich to South East Bank Sarasota, Florida where he had an account.
2. From there, he sent $200,000 to his personal account at Midland Bank, London.
3. He then sent £104,000 to The British Bank of the Middle East (a London subsidiary of HK&S).
4. They wired £103,700 to the solicitors acting for the sellers of the Cheltenham property.
5. Relton then borrowed £250,000 from the British Bank of the Middle East

using his account at HK&S Zurich as security.

The pair used the same money moving scheme again, this time including Jersey, Guernsey and the Isle of Man in the washing cycle. Some £2.1 million was laundered this way and the pair descended on London's Docklands, purchasing several wharfs for £5.4 million and using what looked like legitimate loans to conceal the true origin of the money.

Integration had been achieved

With Noyes' arrest and discovery of the gold at his house, the police investigation into the missing gold and proceeds of the subsequent sale by the criminals led to the arrest of various gang members. All except the Elcombes became guests of Her Majesty and, remember Mr McAvoy? You know, the one who stole the gold in the first place. All he ended up with was a lengthy prison sentence and when released, I suspect he will be looking for a few people who lost him his ill-gotten fortune. In fact, teams of detectives recently descended on a site in Kent associated with McAvoy and proceeded to search for gold allegedly buried there.

With hindsight, it is easy to see where proper anti-money laundering controls may have hindered the criminals. Only one financial institution contacted the authorities and that was not because Noye turned up with £50,000 in cash, but because he kept asking about the serial numbers on the certificates that came with the gold he purchased.

Noye, since his release from prison, continued his life of crime, using false passports to escape to Spain after the M25 road rage murder and allegedly buying a Spanish villa for cash, plus other real estate. One wonders how effective Spanish money laundering laws are?

If anyone is interested, the 11 bars, worth at that time £100,000, remain in a Boots carrier bag within the safe deposit box at TSB in St Helier. The box number and password to obtain the gold is...................... Actually, there was quite a peculiar twist to this story. When Noye was recently convicted of murder at The Old Bailey, the press made enquiries in Jersey to confirm the whereabouts of this gold. It seems to have disappeared.

Recently, the press reported that Marbella on the good old Costa del Crime has become a paradise for money launderers and drug dealers. No wonder Noye decamped to Spain to be with his old associates. Palmer, the Scadlynn smelter, has recently been involved in an alleged massive time share scam in the Canaries, and the trial at the Old Bailey has ended as a mistrial. Until the details of that case become public, one can but speculate as to where the money came from to build all of these apartments in the Canaries.

Lucio Urtubia – the Spanish Robin Hood

A 76-year-old anarchist, bricklayer, bank robber and master forger has funded 'liberation' movements in Europe, Latin America and the United States. Originally fleeing Franco's oppressive Fascist regime, he met up with other anarchists and they robbed banks to fund various revolutionary movements that were active in Paris and Europe in the 50s and 60s.

He decided that it would help those wishing to travel throughout the world to get away from Franco's regime if they could obtain a ready supply of false passports. He then subsequently masterminded the forgery of National City Bank traveller's cheques. These forgeries were so good that not only did they cost the bank tens of millions of dollars, the bank had to suspend the printing and issue of genuine cheques. The fraudulent cheques were used to fund in Uruguay the guerrilla group Tupamaros and in the United States, the Black Panthers.

Lucio was caught in 1980 with a suitcase full of forged cheques but as, after his arrest and imprisonment, the cheques continued to be received at the bank, a decision was made to do a deal. On receipt of the printing plates Lucio would be released from prison. He agreed to this and his days of bank robbing and forging were over.

As previously mentioned, identity theft and forgeries are still increasing in today's world. Only last month the British press reported that 2% of all £1 coins in circulation are forgeries. In fact the same thing happened in South Africa resulting in the particular coin being withdrawn from circulation.

The laughing policeman

One of the richest policeman that you will usually see is the one in the glass case at the end of the pier. You know the one, little children are constantly feeding him money through a slot to make him laugh.

On a more serious note, Anthony Williams, ex-Deputy Director of Finance, New Scotland Yard, made much more. Using his position of trust, he stole some £8 million from his employers over an 8 year period and was finally caught when someone became suspicious of the source of his wealth.

In 1984, Williams was entrusted with the purchase of an aircraft to be used for secret surveillance operations. It was decided to form a private company as cover so Turnbull Associates was formed, with a West London accommodation address. The company purchased a Cessna 404 and based it at Fairoaks airfield. Williams was entrusted with signing cheques in the name D G Turnbull to finance the operation.

On Day One, he stole £3,400 to clear his bank overdraft. Waiting two weeks to see whether the theft was noted, he started to increase the amounts stolen, purchasing a mansion in the country, a flat in London, a villa in Spain, and various properties in and around the village of Tomintoul, Scotland, plus a few cars and expensive holidays.

Although the Yard had implemented audits and simple security measures to detect such anomalies, Williams had been requested to keep the aircraft operation secret and it was he that recommended the setting up of Turnbull Associates with sole control being in his hands. When a superior disagreed and sent a written memo outlining his objections, Williams doctored the memo so that it supported his own ideas.

Once a month, Williams drew up a requisition for funds for the Turnbull account which was primarily fuel and rent, but Williams added a few bogus items for himself. Once he received the money, he wrote cheques to himself and, as time elapsed without discovery, stopped forging invoices and just demanded more money. When threatened with an audit he used the 'need to know' doctrine to stop the auditors and even requested that they make a sworn oath of secrecy (which was not forthcoming) and the threat of audit disappeared.

He then purchased a title and became Lord Williams, formed a company, Tomintoul Enterprises Limited to develop the village and build a hotel.

He then (as with most criminals) made his mistake, requesting a development grant from Moray, Grathspey and Baldenoch Enterprise Board to construct the hotel. Mr Ruane of the Board was prepared to grant £150,000 to refurbish the hotel but requested that Tomintoul Enterprises reveal the source of their funds. Mr Ruane could not understand how someone with a salary of £42,000 could invest millions of pounds into the venture.

When William's bank did not answer requests for details of his funds, the matter was reported to the National Criminal Intelligence Service. Williams was arrested shortly after.

I helped launder £6 billion for the mob

Peter Berlin and his wife Lucy Edwards, a London-based Bank of New York official, Benex International Company Inc ('Benex'), Becs International LLC ('Becs'), and Lowland Inc ('Lowland') appeared at Manhattan Federal Court on 16 February 2000 where all pleaded guilty to various charges including conspiracy to commit money laundering, operating an unlawful banking and money transmitting business, plus aiding and abetting Russian banks in conducting unlawful, unlicensed banking activities in the United States.

They admitted that between late 1995 and September 1999 they participated with others in establishing an illegal banking network that transmitted more than $7 billion through accounts held in the Bank of New York. Specifically they admitted that they:

- conducted unlicensed and unregulated banking operations
- established an unauthorised branch of a foreign bank
- operated an illegal money transmitting business
- laundered money through international fund transfers intending to promote criminal activity including a scheme to defraud the Russian Government of customs duties and tax revenues
- made corrupt payments to a bank employee
- received corrupt payments as a bank officer
- laundered these corrupt payments abroad
- evaded the payment of individual income taxes to the US
- fraudulently obtained visas for Russian nationals to enter the USA

In addition Berlin and Edwards also pleaded guilty to assisting two banks, Depozitarno Kliringovy Bank ('DKB') and Commercial Bank Flamingo ('Flamingo') in establishing branches and agencies in the USA which then conducted illegal, unauthorised banking activities. Benex, Becs and Lowland also admitted conducting an illegal money transmitting service.

The story all started in late 1995 when Berlin and Edwards entered an agreement with various, to date unnamed, individuals, including those that controlled DKB, to open an account in Bank of New York to gain access to banking software – Micro/cash-register – which would enable wire transfers to be made in the new account by themselves. In early 1996, Berlin opened a corporate account in the name BENEX, who were authorised by the Bank of New York to use the software, which was installed in a computer in the offices of General Forex, Forest Hills, Queens, New York.

General Forex was managed on behalf of DKB and the company later changed its name to Torfinex. Using several Russian correspondents' accounts held at Bank of New York, DKB transferred funds into the Benex account on a daily basis. DKB then issued instructions, from its Moscow base, to Torfinex employees in Queens to transfer funds out of the BENEX account using the software to a large number of third party accounts throughout the world. British Intelligence allege that some of these funds were paid to drug barons, contract killers and to YBM Magex. YBM Magex was an American company set up by a Russian (Bogatim) for the manufacture of magnets. A Russian criminal Mogilevitch met Bogatim's brother (a criminal who owned a Polish bank) and a shell company called Pratecs, which incorporated YBM, was floated on the Alberta Stock Exchange. This consortium was used to launder money by the inflation of stock valuations.

In July 1996, a second account was opened called BECS, again the Bank of New York provided software and the same cash movements ensued.

In the Autumn of 1998, Berlin and Edwards were allegedly told that the Flamingo Bank in Russia was being taken over by the Russians behind the original scheme and a new account was opened by Berlin called Lowland. The computer software was issued and set up in an office rented by the Russians in Jersey City, New Jersey. In April 1999, funds were directed into the Lowland account and then wire transferred out to various third parties all over the world.

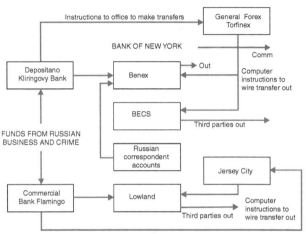

Berlin and Edwards moved to London where she became senior official in charge of the bank's East European operations. She even presented a paper on money laundering at a European Banking Conference. To keep control of the three accounts, they recruited another bank employee, Sventla Kudryavtsev, to manage the accounts and act as a contact with the Torfinex staff. This employee was paid $500 a month by the two for this 'service' and details of all wire transfers through the three accounts were sent to London so that Berlin and Edwards could calculate their commissions.

The Republic Bank in the USA filed a suspicious activity report in August 1998 and the FBI commenced an investigation that involved a number of law enforcement agencies including NCIS in London.

It is important to note that no commercial activity took place by these three companies and the accounts were used to facilitate:

- the transfer of funds out of Russia in violation of currency control limitations and to promote schemes to defraud the Russian Government of duties and taxes
- other criminal activities including the payment of $300,000 in ransom to the kidnappers of a Russian businessman in Russia

The investigation has initially revealed that some $7 billion went through the three accounts at Bank of New York. This equated to hundreds of wire transfers a day in respect of BENEX and BECS accounts, and dozens a day in respect of the LOWLAND account. From February 1996 until August 1999, there were some 160,000 wire transfers. Benex has also been linked with one of the major Russian mafia 'dons' Mogilevitch.

Berlin and Edwards received some $1.8 million in commissions which they hid by laundering in foreign bank accounts. To date they have forfeited $1 million in proceeds which include the contents of two Swiss bank accounts, a securities brokerage account and their London residence. The three companies have agreed to forfeiture of some $6 million held in the accounts at Bank of New York.

The investigation continues with the Swiss authorities now requesting to question the Russian Prime Minister, Mikhail Kasyanov, about a $4.8 billion International Monetary Fund loan which, it is alleged, he laundered through foreign bank accounts after the August 1998 financial crash in Russia. It is alleged that he was involved in a series of complex transfers by which the loan never reached Russia but was absorbed into commercial accounts in the West.

The investigation by the Swiss and FBI has linked the 'missing' funds to the Bank of New York case and unproven allegations of inside knowledge prior to the financial crash has resulted in his nickname of 'Misha Two Per Cent'. Most of the loan has ended up in American accounts belonging to 18 commercial Russian Banks of which many have ceased trading. Investigators have established that on August 14, 1998, some $4.8 billion was transferred from the New York Federal Reserve to accounts at the Republic Bank of New York (the bank that blew the whistle on the Bank of New York). This bank was controlled by Edmund Safra, the billionaire Lebanese banker. He was killed in a fire at his Monte Carlo residence last year and although the death has been blamed on his male nurse, many suspect that his death was due to his cooperation with the FBI and Swiss authorities.

It is important to note that three days after the $4.8 billion was transferred to Safra's bank, the Russian Central Bank defaulted on most of its short term debt and the financial crash ensued. During the following chaos, it is alleged that Safra was instructed by the Russian Central Bank and Russian Ministry of Finance to move the funds quickly into other foreign accounts through a complex series of international transfers. Safra subsequently explained to the FBI the mechanisms that Russians had been using to launder money through American Banks.

As mentioned, there are some important questions to be asked. Certainly American banking regulations were broken, but from the proceeds of crime aspect, one has to consider what crime has been committed. Obviously the use of accounts to launder revenue from drugs, terrorism, prostitution, blackmail and so on are important, but some laws such as currency controls are only relevant locally. Should a Russian businessman find a loophole that enables him to get hard currency out of Russia to a safer financial environment, are those funds dirty money? The Russians have a $2,000 daily limit that they can transfer out and some businesses have admitted that for payment of a small commission they have been allowed to use the BENEX facility to facilitate moving larger sums. Many call this movement of funds Capital Flight. So, going back to the debate of whether such funds are the proceeds of crime, the risk remains that the criminals will also use such a system as BENEX to move their funds, thus creating a mix of capital flight and criminal funds and it all becomes dirty money.

Subsequent FBI investigations have uncovered nine bank accounts through which some $10 billion was laundered for the Russian mafia who allegedly have connections with the Yeltsin family.

The US are more pro-active than most jurisdictions and they currently claim that Russian crime gangs have infiltrated many Western banks and securities firms to help launder their funds. So keep a watch for the sudden change in lifestyle of employees working in at-risk positions.

Some experts have, in the wake of this case, claimed that British money laundering laws are weak and useless as the USA has mandatory reporting of large transactions, whereas the UK puts that responsibility on the financial institution. Insider Trading was made illegal in the USA 50 years before it became an offence in the UK and their stance is certainly more bullish. Britain invented the term 'offshore' and it is rather interesting that the first known reference to such a facility in the sense of an unregulated financial centre referred not to sun soaked islands somewhere, but the City of London.

The Russians

Since the publication of the first edition of this book in 2001, Russia's organised criminal gangs and those from the old USSR have spread their activities throughout the world. The Balkans are now part of the new 'Silk Route' with heroin from the Afghan opium fields, cash, people, endangered species, etc., all passing through the area en route to the Western European marketplace. For example, 80% of illegal shipments sent to Western Europe pass through Bulgaria.

The Russian mafia use the Hungarian currency exchange market for money laundering, Tiraspol is the centre for the manufacture and unregulated sales of arms to customers all over the world and when the Russian Army pulled out of Transinistria, 74 highly sophisticated SAMs went missing, each one capable of bringing down a jumbo jet.

Some 100,000 Russian Jews emigrated to Israel, the criminal element setting up sex trafficking with women being trafficked into Israel, Dubai and China.

In addition, to facilitate their criminal endeavours Russians are producing 'pirate' copies of Windows with virus programmes pre-loaded for subsequent use to steal funds from US and European targets.

The Triads

The Triads are probably the largest criminal organisation in the world, their activities ranging from electronics, gambling, and vice to the massive illegal trade in migrant labour, with some 500,000 people being smuggled abroad from Fuzchow during the period 1985–1995, of which 1/5 arrived in the USA. Whereas the Colombians control the cocaine market, the Triads are the main criminal syndicates behind the heroin market with 60% of the world's supply coming from the Golden Triangle in Burma, Thailand and Laos. This supply is controlled mainly by the Teochiu Triad who have apparently been in the drugs business since 1875 –what one could claim to be a well-established business. The Teochiu are the world's largest ethnic grouping of Chinese expatriates with their own global underground banking system whose money launderers are claimed to be the most skilled in the world with an excellent business management structure. The Teochiu own politicians and lawyers throughout South East Asia with links to the Tiawanese Government, American Mafia, Italian and Russian crime syndicates.

The Triads predate the Roman Empire and were originally known either as a 'hui' (an association) or a 'chaio' (a sect). Various other names were used such as:

hsieh-chaio – (vicious sects)
wei-chaio – (false god sects)
chaio-fei – (bandit sects)
yin-chaio – (obscene sects)
yao-chaio – (perverse sects)

Whereas the Triads now deal with heroin, the origination of their drug trafficking was in the import and sale of opium.

In 1994, the World Bank assessed that more money changed hands for drugs than for food, and on that basis, one can assume that Triad income exceeds the gross domestic product of many nations. One of the Teochiu heroin bosses allegedly has HK$980 million deposited in a Chinese bank in Hong Kong. The authorities cannot seize it as such action may cause a run on the bank and many small depositors would face financial ruin. The profits are reinvested in other illegal operations with the bulk being laundered into legitimate businesses.

Another business operation that provides income of some $4 billion dollars a year is the smuggling of illegal immigrants from China. China has some 300 million people (conservative estimate) who are either unemployed or living on the breadline. Many seek employment overseas and pay the Triad gangs the going rate for transportation by sea or air to Europe or North America. The recent case in the United Kingdom where a large number of Chinese were found dead in a lorry container was undoubtedly part of this business in human misery. It is estimated that there are some 500,000 illegal Chinese immigrants in transit around the world at any given time.

They also operate Cyber Protection Rackets where, by using Denial of Service (DOS) attacks on financial businesses, hold the business to ransom. The Cyber criminals use either High Intensity Radio Frequency (HIRF) guns, Electromagnetic Pulse Cannons (EMP), or Logic Bombs. The first two types of attack weapons were used in the Gulf war to disable Iraqi communication systems and avionics computers and work by firing bursts of electronic power to disrupt computer circuitry and destroy hard disks. Logic bombs are encrypted algorithms hidden in computer systems by sleepers, usually temporary office staff. Activated by a telephone call on a predetermined date, they lock out the computer by encrypting data on the hard disk thus denying access. In other words the computer has been hijacked and the company denied access to its business. An appropriate ransom is demanded on receipt of which a code is given to reverse the encryption.

In London in 1993, two stockbrokers and a merchant bank were blackmailed out of £32.5 million to enable them to regain control of their computers.

Since then, there have been some 60 reported cases with ransoms totalling over £800 million being paid. Of course, many victims do not report the 'incidents' as such bad publicity about their computer security systems is not very welcome.

But perhaps one of the biggest sources of income for the Triad gangs, allied to the use of illegal immigrants, is the revenue obtained from kickbacks in the Far East construction industry. One author estimated that 12% of the construction costs of a Hong Kong skyscraper is written off against kick backs. If one considers that the cost of skyscraper construction is averaging some HK$4 billion, and the Triads take 12% of that on each project, the 'receipts' from each skyscraper are enormous. Extend that revenue across the major cities of the Far East and the amount of criminal revenue is beyond comprehension.

The Triads have linked with Russian organised crime groups and are now recognised as part of the most dangerous organised crime organisations in the world and with some 60 million Chinese living outside of China (this expatriate population being the largest in the World with the exception of the descendants of the African slave trade) the Triads operations are, without doubt, worldwide.

CIA black operations

After the fall of Vietnam and the withdrawal of the French, the CIA discovered that the French had set up an arrangement between the drug producers in the Golden Triangle (Laos, Cambodia, Thailand), the Mafia and themselves to sanction the export of drugs into Europe and America. This drug trafficking became known as *The French Connection*. This top secret CIA operation was known as Operation X.

The CIA, on the withdrawal of the French, sent a top CIA operative (Major General Edward Lonsdale) to Saigon, the CIA being controlled by our friend Dulles. Lonsdale took over the operation, the plan being to use the money to support covert operations. Even after the end of the Vietnam war the CIA continued to remain as principal beneficiary of the drug trade from the Golden Triangle. In 1989 three American Special Forces officers travelled to the remote region Shanland in Northern Burma. A local warlord Khun Sa controlled the Golden Triangle Opium business with an army of 10,000. During a meeting with the Americans he claimed that his total annual opium production for 1989 (900 tonnes) was purchased by the American Government. In 1992 the annual production had risen to 3,000 tonnes. The Americans were amazed at these revelations and arranged a return visit to meet Khun Sa. At this meeting they videoed the meeting and Khun Sa claimed that the American official that he dealt with was a Richard Armitage, the US assistant Secretary of Defence. He also claimed that Armitage used a traffic manager who he named as being Santos Trafficante (the boss of Florida's Mafia).

On the other side of the world, the CIA had set up Operation Watch Tower dedicated to import cocaine from Colombia via Panama into the United States. Colonel Manuel Noriega was on the CIA's payroll and seen as an 'asset'.

Later Celerino Castillo, a former top level Drug Enforcement Agency operative, testified to the US Senate Permanent Select Committee on Intelligence that the CIA were very much involved in the drug trade. The CIA needed funds to pay the Nicaraguan-based Contras to topple the left wing Government of El Salvador (Congress had refused to support the Contras). Colonel Oliver North of the National Security Council was delegated by the CIA to source funds, and an international team of CIA operatives were employed by North, dubbed 'The Enterprise'.

Although, when investigated later, most of North's papers and diaries had been shredded, his notebook was found intact, and one entry states: '14 million to finance came from drugs.' This refers to $14 million earmarked for financing weapons for the Contras.

The money obtained through this drug trade was laundered through banks in Panama and Switzerland. (One of the banks used was the Bank of Crooks and Criminals – BCCI)

The CIA's reason for being involved was originally that the money was needed to fight the perils of communism. However, even after the global collapse of communism and the end of the cold war, the drugs trade has continued to grow and develop. A former CIA Black operative, Ted Shackley, (named as being involved in the Golden Triangle drugs operation), wrote a book *The Third Option* in which he argues that 'low intensity' conflict will continue throughout the world for the foreseeable future, and that the military-industrial complex has a survival blueprint that includes narcotics are part of the equation.

Forgeries

Since the first edition of this book was published the incidence of forgeries and cloned credit cards has increased dramatically. I hate including current statistics as by the time a book goes to print the figures are usually out of date. You may have read about the current high percentage of forged £1 coins in the system, yet more dirty money in the banking system.

One system of forging was of particular interest, bringing a new meaning to money laundering. Apparently dollar washing is good business, but be warned do not try it out wherever you live as the FBI will pursue you throughout the world if you are discovered.

The US dollar notes are printed on paper with a very high (almost 100%) cotton content and each denomination note is exactly the same size. So get a good washing machine, wash the $1 notes clean and then use the now blank notes to reprint with a higher value, say $100. With modern technology 1,000 x one dollar notes easily becomes $100,000. If successful, the forger has to find ways to get round any money laundering prevention systems and get the cash into the banking system or via a cash based business such as a casino.

4

Transaction Examples

The following examples are some of the methods used to hinder identification of the true source of dirty money.

Exchange bureaux

Drafts obtained from foreign exchange bureaux have frequently been used to open accounts in UK banks. Cash smuggled from the USA into Mexico was placed in exchange bureaux (cambio houses) and drafts purchased. The drafts ranged in value between $5,000 and $500,000. After the UK bank account was opened, the funds were then transferred by wire to another jurisdiction.

It is important to ask the question of how did the UK bank accept the drafts and open the account, especially with money laundering legislation? If the bank did not complete proper vetting, the answer is obvious. Of course, if an existing client opened the account with what appeared to be legitimate documentation, the only indication that there may be something wrong would be the origination of the draft.

Bogus property companies

As mentioned in our detail of the Brinks-Mat robbery, bogus property companies can be used to launder money. Recent investigation into drug traffickers importing cannabis from West Africa revealed that some of the proceeds were laundered through a bogus company set up in the United Kingdom. A solicitor set up a client account and deposited £500,000 received from the criminals. This was then transferred to his company's bank account. Acting on instructions from the criminals he used the funds to purchase property on their behalf.

Similarly a client of ours was recently approached by an individual wishing to make substantial investments and attempting to back up his status with the fact that he had a Jersey registered property company with massive property investments in the UK. Needless to say, investigation of the Jersey company did not identify any such investments or business.

Money laundering using cash transactions

There are a variety of 'schemes' that the money launderer will use by converting cash at the placement stage of the laundering process. The following is not a complete list but provides some good examples.

- unusually large cash deposits made by an individual or company whose normal business would be conducted by means of cheques or other instruments
- substantial increases in cash deposits without an apparent cause especially if almost immediately transferred to a destination not associated with the customer
- cash deposited in small amounts by numerous deposits that total a substantial amount (in other words 'smurfing')
- company accounts that show a preponderance of cash transactions where business is normally completed by means of cheques, letters of credit, etc.
- customers who constantly deposit cash to cover requests for bankers drafts, money transfers, etc. (the question is – where does the cash come from?)
- customers who change large quantities of low denomination notes for those of a higher denomination as this can indicate the collection of illegal funds from drug dealers where cash is the normal method of trade
- frequent exchange of cash for foreign currencies
- bank branches that have more cash transactions than normal (see our comments re the Lansky Legacy in the Bahamas)
- customers whose deposits include forged currency or instruments (I can recall investigating the activities of a private bank which was known to contravene exchange control laws appertaining to its home base country in Africa (I was investigating alleged money laundering) and forged US currency was discovered in the Bank's safe. Despite being advised that the currency was forged, the owners of the bank failed to report the transaction to the regulatory body.)
- customers transferring large amounts of money to and from overseas locations with instructions for payment in cash
- large cash deposits made using night safe facilities thus avoiding direct contact with bank staff.

Money laundering using bank accounts

The following styles are frequently used.

- customers who wish to maintain a number of trustee or client accounts which do not appear consistent with the type of business, including transactions which involve nominees

- customers who have numerous bank accounts and deposit cash into each account that in accumulative total are substantial (a form of smurfing)
- any individual or company whose account shows no personal or business banking activity yet is used to receive and disburse large sums of money that have no obvious purpose or relationship to the account holder and/or their business – the recently reported case where it is alleged that a confidant of Russian President Putin into a dormant business account at an Isle of Man bank is a good example of this type of transaction
- reluctance to provide normal information when opening an account, providing minimal or fictitious information, or providing information that is difficult and expensive to substantiate
- customers who have accounts with several financial institutions in the same locality and where regular consolidation of funds occurs prior to requests for onward transmission of the funds (another form of smurfing)
- regular payments out of an account that match deposits made the previous day (used by the money launderer to extend the 'audit trail', the transaction usually going, via several other bank accounts elsewhere, to an account in a jurisdiction where bank secrecy laws make investigation difficult)
- depositing large third party cheques endorsed in favour of the customer
- large cash withdrawals from a dormant/inactive account or from an account that receive an unexpected large credit from overseas
- customers who together or simultaneously use separate tellers to conduct large cash or foreign exchange transactions (another form of smurfing)
- greater use of safe deposit facilities and the use of sealed packets deposited and withdrawn (how often do you check the frequency of safe deposit visits to a particular strongbox?)
- company representatives avoiding contact with the bank
- substantial increases in deposits of cash or negotiable instruments by a professional firm or company, using clients' accounts or in-house company or trust accounts, especially if the deposits are promptly transferred between other client, company and trust accounts
- customers who decline to provide information that in normal circumstances would make the customer eligible for credit or other valuable banking services
- insufficient use of normal banking facilities (avoidance of high interest rates for large balances)
- large number of individuals making deposits into the same account without an adequate explanation (more smurfing).

No doubt there are other methods that the money launderer will use to take advantage of slack or poor controls and awareness.

Money laundering using investment related transactions

Some of the money laundering methods used are:

- purchasing of securities to be held by the financial services business in safe custody where this appears to be inappropriate given the customers apparent standing
- back to back deposit/loan transactions with subsidiaries or affiliates of financial services businesses in sensitive jurisdictions such as Liechtenstein
- request by customers for investment management services (either foreign currency or securities) where the source of funds is unclear and not consistent with the customer's apparent standing
- large or unusual settlements of securities in cash form
- buying or selling of a security with no discernible purpose or in circumstances which appear unusual.

Money laundering by offshore international activity

The following examples should be considered as suspicious transactions:

- a customer that has been introduced by an overseas branch, affiliate or other bank based in countries where production of drugs or drug trafficking may be prevalent
- use of Letters of Credit and other methods of trade finance to move funds between countries where such trade is outside the customer's normal trading pattern or business
- customers who make regular and large payments, including wire transfers, that cannot be verified as bona fide transactions to, or regularly receive regular and large payments from, unregulated jurisdictions, especially those with known links to drug trade and terrorism
- accumulation of large balances that are inconsistent with the normal business turnover, that are subsequently transferred overseas
- unexplained electronic fund transfers by customers on an in and out basis or without passing through a financial services product
- frequent requests for traveller's cheques, foreign currency drafts or other negotiable instruments to be issued outside the normal pattern of trade
- frequent deposits of travellers' cheques or foreign currency drafts originating from overseas.

Money laundering involving financial services employees and agents

This area is often overlooked but is important to monitor as an in-house control. The following examples are typical indications:

- a change in employees' characteristics such as lavish lifestyle, and avoiding taking holidays
- changes in an employee's or agent's performance (the salesman selling products for cash has a remarkable or unexpected increase in performance)
- any deal with an agent where the identity of the ultimate beneficiary or counterpart is undisclosed contrary to normal procedures for the type of business
- money laundering by secured and unsecured lending
- customers who repay problem loans unexpectedly
- requests to borrow against assets held by the financial services business or a third party where the origins of the assets are not known or the assets are inconsistent with the customer's status
- request by a customer for a financial service business to provide or arrange finance where the source of the customers financial contribution to a deal is unclear, particularly where property is involved.

Money laundering by sales and dealing staff

1. New business

Although it may be possible that long-standing clients are laundering money through an investment business, it is far more likely that a new customer will use one or more financial services products for a short period only and they may use false names and fictitious companies. Investment may be direct with a financial services business or indirect through an intermediary who 'does not ask too many awkward questions', especially (but not only) in jurisdictions where money laundering is not legislated against or where the rules are not rigorously enforced.

We recommend that the following situations will require you to make additional enquiries:

- a person or client where verification of identity proves unusually difficult and who is reluctant to provide details
- a corporate/trust client where there are difficulties and delays in obtaining copies of the accounts or other documents of incorporation
- a client with no apparent reason for using the firm's services such as clients

with distant addresses that could find the same service nearer home and those that require services outside the firm's normal trading pattern who could be easily serviced elsewhere
- an investor introduced by an overseas bank, affiliate or other investor both of which are based in unregulated countries or countries known to be involved in the drugs, arms or terrorist trade
- any transaction in which the counterpart to the transaction is unknown.

2. Intermediaries

There are many legitimate reasons for a client's use of an intermediary. However the use of intermediaries introduces further parties into the transaction thus increasing opacity and, depending on the designation of the product, preserving anonymity. Similarly, there are a number of legitimate reasons for dealing via intermediaries on a 'numbered account' basis, but this is also a useful method which may be used by the money launderer to delay, obscure or avoid detection.

Any apparently unnecessary use of an intermediary in the transaction should be investigated.

3. Dealing patterns and abnormal transactions

As mentioned earlier, the aim of the money launderer is to introduce as many layers as possible and this means that the money will pass through a number of sources, different persons and entities. Long standing and apparently legitimate client holdings may be used to launder money innocently, as a favour, or due to the exercise of undue pressure. Examples of unusual dealing patterns and abnormal transactions are:

Dealing Patterns
- a large number of security transactions across a number of jurisdictions
- transactions not in keeping with the investor's normal activity, the financial markets in which the investor is active and the business which the investor operates
- buying or selling of a security with no discernible purpose or in circumstances which appear unusual, e.g. 'churning' at the client's request
- low grade securities purchased in an overseas jurisdiction, sold locally and high grade securities purchased with the proceeds
- bearer securities held outside a recognised custodial system.

Abnormal Transactions
- a number of transactions by the same counterpart in small amounts of the same security, each purchased for cash and then sold in one transaction,

the proceeds being credited to a product different from the original (e.g. a different account)

- any transaction in which the nature, size or frequency appears unusual, e.g. early termination of packaged products at a loss due to front end loading; early cancellation especially where cash has been tendered and/or the refund cheque is to a third party
- transfer of investments to unrelated third parties
- transactions not in keeping with normal practice in the market to which they relate, e.g. with reference to market size and frequency, or at off-market prices
- other transactions linked to the transaction in question which could be designed to disguise money and to divert it into other forms or other destinations or beneficiaries.

Money laundering by settlements

1. Payment

The money launderer will usually have substantial amounts of cash to dispose of and will, as mentioned earlier, use a variety of sources to deposit the money. Cash settlement through a financial adviser or broker may not in itself be suspicious, however large or unusual settlements of securities deals in cash and settlements in cash to a large securities house will usually provide cause for further enquiry. Examples of unusual payment settlement are:

- a number of transactions by the same counterparty in small amounts of the same security, each purchased for cash and then sold in one transaction
- large transaction settlement by cash
- payment by way of cheque or money transfer where there is a variation between the account holder/signatory and the customer.

2. Registration and delivery

Settlement by registration of securities in the name of an unverified third party should prompt further investigation.

Bearer securities, held outside a recognised custodial system, are very portable and anonymous instruments which may serve the purposes of the money launderer well. Their presentation in settlement or as collateral should always prompt further enquiry, as should the following:

- settlement to be made by way of bearer securities from outside a recognised clearing system

- allotment letters for new issues in the name of the persons other than the client.

3. Disposition

As explained, money laundering is the cleaning of dirty money so that the clean funds can then be used by the criminal to invest in either legitimate business or further criminal enterprise. They need to remove the clean money from the jurisdiction where it is deposited and conceal the destination of those funds.

The following situations should provoke further enquiries:

- payment to a third party without any apparent connection with the investor
- settlement either by registration or delivery of securities to made to an unverified third party
- abnormal settlement instructions including payment to apparently unconnected parties.

Money laundering by e-mail and smart cards

The world wide web or internet is probably the fastest growing communication system ever, being used by commerce and the public to communicate, sell and purchase every type of commodity, and as a leisure tool. Currently there are 12.8 million host locations and 70 million+ users.

With this growth has been the development of electronic money transfers, particularly e-cash which will reduce the need for currency smuggling. The physical bulk of cash has been the main impediment to the money launderer, but new electronic systems can move vast amounts of money instantaneously and securely with a few computer key strokes. The speed of these transactions will hamper identification or tracking by the law enforcement agencies. It is estimated that there will be an e-cash market of some $10 billion worldwide by 2006 and the internet is already being used to perpetrate a wide variety of financial fraud.

Numerous countries are experimenting with e-cash as a replacement for traditional money, particularly the Scandinavian markets and, although it may liberate the economic markets and enhance personal privacy, it will pose a huge problem to those combating money laundering and organised crime.

E-cash owes its existence to three important developments:

- the legal authorisation to convert paper money into electronic data capable of transmission by electronic networks
- the internet
- increased confidence in payment systems through internet and e-mail systems, and increasingly on the internet.

These developments enable the transfer from a paper-based system to an electronic system. Unlike the inter-bank SWIFT system that only allows inter-bank money transfers, e-cash will permit secure electronic payments across the internet to all interested parties. The system is designed to link existing bank networks, merchants and customers worldwide to allow for global transactions. It allows merchants to obtain authorisation on-line and issue electronic receipts.

To use the system, the purchaser must first download an electronic wallet (e-wallet) from the site of an e-money issuer (the mint). This usually happens after the user registers with an e-cash supplier and has opened an account. The downloaded wallet can be installed on the user's PC or notebook. They then select a secret authorising number or code that allows digital identification, enabling the secure transfer of money from an e-money mint to the purchaser's e-wallet for spending with merchants.

The legitimate uses of e-cash are endless – on-line shopping, public transport, restaurants and so on – in fact anything that entails payment by cash or cheque. The system offers complete anonymity. Issuing banks do not link the anonymous e-cash numbers to a particular client, thus making it difficult to link payment transactions to the payer. The money launderers can protect themselves with anonymity.

Some experts have claimed that the problems of electronic money laundering are:

- The money laundered is electronic money because the ease of movement and storage of electronic money makes the launderer's task easier.
- The problem that is usually glossed over is – how does it happens that the criminal has a large amount of electronic money? Was it originally in electronic form or was it converted from hard cash?

Mark Bortner presented a paper on the law and the internet at the University of Miami School of Law where he gave the example of laundering drug money by e-cash. He theorises the situation where after smurfing the hard cash, the money is transferred out of the banks to internet banks that accept e-cash. To protect themselves, the drug traffickers keep the transfers below the reportable amount.

Once transferred, the money has become anonymous and untraceable. Whereas the physical smurfing of hard cash deposits is an offence under money laundering legislation, electronic smurfing is difficult to relate to current banking laws as cyberbanks are not necessarily registered or licensed and cybercash is not recognised as entering the marketplace of hard currency, thus affecting monetary supply or policy. Therefore the requirement for the cyberbank to report a suspicious transaction is probably not mandatory (especially if that cyberbank is registered in somewhere like Niue).

In other words, once the e-cash account is established, funds can be transferred from any computer connected to the internet. As Mark Bortner claims, a truly creative, if not paranoid, launderer could access funds via Telnet, the basic command that involves the protocol for connecting to another computer on the internet. The launderer sitting on a beach with his laptop can connect to his internet service provider in the USA or anywhere, and get the leased internet account to contact the bank or banks to transfer funds to wherever. The risk of identification of the launderer is practically zero. E-cash, being anonymous, allows the account holder total privacy to make internet transactions. Thus the bank holding the digital cash, as well as the seller who accepts e-cash, has virtually no means of identifying the purchaser.

As we all know, money is frequently laundered by the purchase of property or expensive items such as cars, aeroplanes and such like. Currently, there are very few vendors selling such items for e-cash so the launderer may still have to revert the money to hard cash at some stage, thus entering the proverbial spotlight of the alert money laundering reporting officer. However once the property market realise that there is money to be made by accepting e-cash, even if there is a mandatory report made by them that they sold a property for £2 million, the investigator will find it difficult to identify the purchaser. Subsequent enquiries may reveal ownership by some Niue-registered shell company, but the subsequent investigation will be difficult. One can only hope that the criminal follows the usual pattern of making a mistake, thus opening the doors to the investigators.

Until the patterns of abuse become apparent, all e-cash transactions should be dealt with extreme caution.

E-cash systems on the market are:

Cyber- Cash	www.cybercash.com
Digicash	www.digicash.com
Ecash, Net Chex	www.netc.hex.com
Net Cash	www.gost.isi.ed/info/netc.ash
NetBill	www.ini.cmu.edu/netbill
Mondex	www.mondex.com
Bitbux and VisaCash	www.visa.com

Smart cards are another innovation which may also provide the means for a money launderer to transfer funds without using the normal banking system. If no limit is placed on the amount of money that can be placed on a smart card, the criminal will be able to transfer funds from his card to another card via a computer. Launderers will become free of the two problems they currently face:

- there will be no need to enter the money into the banking system
- there will be no need to carry around bags of cash.

Even street level drugs deals could be completed by using smart cards. Despite conferences and discussion forums being held to discuss the weaknesses in the proposed smart card systems, the current proposals do not appear to have any in-built controls over individual smart card identification (i.e. card to registered user) thus stolen cards, or transferred cards will replace cash and an electronic card holding substantial funds that cannot be traced is a better risk than a suitcase of banknotes that needs washing.

Michael Levi, an academic, stated,

'The whole idea of a suspicion based system (suspect transaction reporting) is old fashioned, since unlike burglaries and robberies, most cross-border transactions are conducted purely electronically, without anyone physically seeing them: because of the legislation (and sometimes to guarantee that the transaction will be paid for) customers must be identified, but how are the bankers to know whether there is legitimate business case for the myriad transactions they undertake, and why should it be their business to 'shadow' their customers? Legislation does not require them to do these things, but they (and the 'informal banking' sector) would have to do so if they were to smoke out all the laundering and fraud.'

In Australia, there is a central system called AUSTRAC that is basically a computer forensic programme that looks for trends and patterns of electronic transfers thus enabling automated collection of objective data rather than the reliance of the subjective human judgment of bank tellers and their supervisors. Some experts are looking at self-regulation by the use of tailor-made detection systems that forensically examine transactions and only highlight those that are suspicious, thus eliminating those that are currently reported because of human interaction, when in fact they are quite innocent.

NCIS use a forensic analysis system to identify links between various individuals and companies but that system uses the suspicious incident reports as input data.

In October 2000, the US government enacted legislation that made an electronic signature valid in law with the same status as a written signature. Some experts claim that this law will make it easier for criminals to perpetrate fraud by theft of identity. Others claim that technological advances will make it more difficult to steal identities. It will be imperative the customer has appropriate software protection with encrypted digital signatures, such as a public key kept by a third party that guarantees that the key belongs to the individual, and a private key which is kept secret by the user/customer. However, this new marketplace will still require customer verification if money laundering is to be avoided. One company director whose company sells encryption technology to banks claims that investors will soon be able to sell stocks direct to each other, thus eliminating stockbrokers. The mind boggles and one wonders how the regulatory bodies will be able to legislate and control such trade.

There is no doubt that the whole area of electronic banking is open to abuse by the money launderer and, as I write this manual, an internet bank, and possibly others, has been hit with an attempted alleged industry-wide fraud by organised crime where the creation of multiple false loans, bank and credit cards on-line had taken place. Fortunately, the bank had crested software to identify multiple account applications which use false details. Anyone, according to current experience, making a false application usually uses the same address or employment and uses the same computer terminals. This type of control is essential when one considers the basic anti-money laundering rule of 'Know your Client'. I have no doubt that the clever criminal will overcome this problem by using corrupt individuals or companies as smurfs to launder their dirty money. The anonymity of the internet will help keep the money hidden.

The Hawalla money laundering system

In the previous chapters, we have detailed some case examples of how the criminal launders money through the world's banking systems and constantly looks for new ways and new technology to aid the legitimisation of his dirty money.

One system that has been very difficult to investigate is the Asian and Chinese underground banking systems. The Asian system is known as Hawallah and is based on a family concept using a world-wide network of ethnic Pakistani and Indian families providing efficiency and confidentiality for those wishing to avoid conventional banking channels.

Hawallah means 'reference' in Hindi, or 'transfer related money' in Arabic, and 'trust' in Urdu. The system is also called 'Chop' or 'Hundi' or by the Chinese 'fei ch'ien' which means flying money (see earlier comments in respect of the Triads).

The funds are layered through a complex chain of wire transfers, gold smuggling, and invoice manipulation. They are then usually integrated into legitimate business or investment in real estate.

The main elements of the Hawallah system are:

- **Confidentiality**

  This is crucial between client and the Hawallah dealer and a code of silence governs all transactions with dire consequences attached to the breach of trust. Should the code be broken, the dealer would put not only his business, but his life in jeopardy.

- **Convenience**

  Hawallah dealers often operate in rural areas of under-developed countries where there are no conventional banking services, and the dealer fills this void. They offer the same services as provided by conventional banks, such as cashier's cheques, money orders and currency exchange. Even where conventional banks exist, it is not uncommon to have Hawallah dealers working as tellers.

- **Efficiency**
  Banking transactions through the normal banking channels, especially in third world countries, can be slow and complex. However the Hawallah system can transfer large sums of money internationally within hours with little or no paperwork and no physical movement of funds.

The established, well known families who operate the Hawallah systems have earned a great deal of trust and respect within their communities. Many operate legitimate businesses with substantial cash flow and include travel agencies, carpet companies, gold dealerships, gem trading companies. Family members or associates of the same ethnic or religious group operate similar sister companies in foreign cities where there are large Indian or Pakistani communities.

Cost effectiveness

The economic incentive to use the Hawallah system rests upon favourable exchange rates and the low cost of Hawallah transactions. The exchange rate used in the Hawallah system is based on the Indian black market dollar price which is linked to the amount of gold being smuggled into the country. Therefore the exchange rate offered can be 10-25% better than the official exchange rate. It has been estimated that $10 billion a year passes through the Hawallah system in India.

The Hawallah dealer provides better rates and charges lower commissions because he makes additional profits through speculation in the money markets with the remittance funds and holds those funds in interest bearing accounts prior to transfer.

Operation

The most common method of Hawallah dealing is for the client who wishes to transfer funds overseas in secret to go to the Hawallah dealer who will agree the commission and exchange rate and take the cash from the client. This cash is usually in the currency of the client's home country. These funds are deposited locally by the Hawallah dealer being intermingled with the dealer's legitimate business.

The client is given a chit. This may be half of a playing card, a banknote or marked scrap of paper. During a money laundering investigation several years ago, I was searching the offices of an Asian accountant in London and in one of the desks found numerous blank sheets of paper all having been signed by customers in India. Obviously these pre-signed sheets enabled the accountants to write instructions to whoever to comply with their client's wishes. This of course would include money transfers, payments and so on.

During the Vietnam war, Hawallah dealers cashed American GIs' pay cheques at a favourable rate of exchange, sent the cheques to their opposite numbers in New York where the cheques were cashed, the cash then used to purchase gold which was then smuggled back to Vietnam and sold on the black market at a very good exchange rate realising good profits.

When the client's agent goes to the Hawallah dealer's opposite number in the country where the funds are to be sent, the agent produces the chit and it is matched to the other half by the Hawallah dealer. The funds, less the commission, are then paid to the agent.

Hawallah dealers maintain constant reconciliation accounts with other dealers, balances being settled by using Swiss bank accounts and interbank transfers again using the cover of legitimate business activity.

VIETNAM - HAWALLAH DEALS

5

Detection

With the ever increasing focus on money laundering throughout the United Kingdom, Channel Islands, Isle of Man and Gibraltar as well as the USA, EC and so on, there has been an increase in the sale of in-house training packages, including a number of computer-based training modules that staff can use to learn how to recognise the suspicious. In addition there has been a proliferation of money laundering seminars. The problem is to sort out the good from the bad. Being the eternal cynic, I do not believe that staff can be trained to recognise the suspicious transaction without the help of well planned systems. The Bank of New York case involved some 160,000 wire transfers over a short period of time. How on earth can anyone be expected to identify one suspicious transaction in so many? I have detailed in this chapter some of the controls and support systems that are available to help with the implementation of anti-money-laundering measures.

Suspicious wire transfers

Fortunately, some computer software designers have formulated systems that, by using customer history patterns, will identify the suspicious transaction, and any financial institution dealing with a large client base and associated money movements should consider using this type of software. Basically, the system installed on the bank's computer constantly scans the transactions passing through the various client accounts. Should a transaction fall outside the accepted customer trading/transaction pattern, the transaction is highlighted for investigation. The systems can also identify those multiple transactions that together may prove 'suspicious'.

Some of these systems are very expensive, but the cost should be assessed against the risk of handling dirty money and if not discovered, the potential financial penalties and loss of reputation. Many of the financial jurisdictions insist that there are controls in place to identify the suspicious transaction and if your business handles thousands of transactions, it is obvious that a computerised system is necessary to act as an appropriate filter. One of the leaders in this field are Americas Software in Florida, but there are others in the marketplace. There are also specialist contractors who can also examine data and can formulate procedures to identify suspicious transactions. I would certainly recommend that the prudent financial manager explore the use of such systems and/or forensic computer system specialists.

Should the cost of such systems be too high, I would recommend the smaller business should consider setting up a joint facility with other similar businesses, thus sharing the cost. I realise that such an arrangement may be against all client confidentiality agreements, but the data could easily be encoded so that the joint facility or bureau merely reports back to the appropriate participating financial institution the coded suspicious transaction report for decoding and subsequent reporting or investigation.

Office of Foreign Assets Control – (OFAC)

As discussed elsewhere in this book, the Americans are more bullish than most in respect of money laundering where their currency is involved. Whereas one could argue that drugs trafficking is mainly an American problem and that there are too many coke-heads in California, it is important that one recognises that the launderer will seek other jurisdictions and 'friendly' financial institutions to launder their dirty money. Added to their own internal laws and the fact that they will go anywhere in the world to prosecute those that launder greenbacks, they have also various acts of Congress that empowers OFAC to freeze assets and impose sanctions. OFAC has a blacklist of countries, companies and individuals where they will freeze and impound dollar transactions should such a transaction to any of those on the blacklist be noted. In simple terms, this means that should an honest customer of your bank request a dollar transfer to some freight company in what appears to be a non-suspicious jurisdiction, it is possible that the freight company may be on OFAC's blacklist. So when the dollars go through the American corresponding bank they have a good chance of being frozen by OFAC.

The blacklist is available to Financial institutions on CD-Rom, is updated frequently from FBI/CIA sources and includes details of individuals (including known passports) front companies for terrorist and drug organisations, and countries that the USA and United Nations have sanctions against. Certainly, if your client base includes a reasonable percentage of US dollar transactions, the use of this intelligence is important to protect your clients' funds. In addition, utility programs are available that filter your accounts and transactions before they are sent overseas thus highlighting potential risk transactions.

False documents and instruments

The use of computers, digital photography, scanners, and colour laser printing has made forgery a science available to many. As mentioned previously, passports, educational qualification certificates, and other dubious documents can easily be purchased on the web.

So how can the financial institution identify false documents or instruments? Again, it is impossible for the employee to identify such forgeries unless the forgery was obviously prepared using a John Bull printing kit. There are a number of forensic companies who, using the latest technology, can by various tests, establish the validity of a document, whether it be the identity of the printing ink and paper used, the integrity of the watermark or of any evidence of physical or chemical interference. For example, brake fluid is used to remove ink handwriting or rubber stamp marks. This is an old trick which I first came across when investigating MOT/Insurance fraud where out-of- date certificates were immersed in brake fluid to remove the ink handwriting so that new data could be written on the document.

Identification of the paper may prove that the particular type of paper was not produced at the time the alleged document was prepared. The infamous Jack the Ripper and Hitler Diaries were forensically examined to prove or disprove their authenticity. Similarly, certain inks may have been unavailable when the document(s) were written/printed and fingerprint or DNA tests may indicate possible interference by suspects.

Other forensic technology

In addition, signatures can be analysed, tape recordings of deals can be enhanced (I used this type of forensic service in a case where an independent foreign exchange dealer claimed that the deals that had gone wrong had not been made on his instruction, but by the bank acting independently on their own volition – by enhancing the back office tapes, we proved he was lying), video security tapes can similarly be enhanced and such technology is frequently used to provide evidence of an incident whether it be the failure to carry out an operation correctly or to identify a crime being committed.

There are also forensic companies that specialise in computers and, using systems designed for law enforcement agencies, they can, without damaging the evidence on a computer, locate deleted or hidden data. These systems can find those documents prepared by the dishonest or devious employee for personal gain. This type of equipment was used when we investigated an industrial espionage case where a director was selling industrial secrets to Japanese competitors. The first document we found was a deleted memo sent by the director to his Japanese contact. In the financial world, such forensics can trace computer data relating to unauthorised transactions that may have been deleted by the dishonest employee.

There is one very important message (unless you are an experienced computer forensic specialist) when you suspect any type of computer fraud or that a computer has been used for dishonest processes – unplug the suspect computer(s) and store in a secure environment or you may lose valuable evidence.

Employment vetting

This leads to an area where some of the major problems in respect of money laundering lie, pre-employment and ongoing staff vetting. The money launderer has the attitude that some expense is necessary to enable them to launder the money. As I write this book, amongst the latest news mentioned is that the Colombian drug cartels, working with Russian mafia members and others, have been building a submarine to use for the shipment of drugs into the United States. I await more details with interest. No doubt it was to be fitted with nuclear weaponry provided by the Russians to see off any law enforcement agencies that may have had the cheek to try and stop their voyages.

So the cost of bribing an employee is negligible in the scheme of things. At a fraud and money laundering seminar we held in Jersey, a senior police officer (in his opening address) highlighted the risks and problems of staff dishonesty, especially in the financial environment where staff are frequently transient and can exploit lack of vetting to their personal advantage. It is no use just vetting staff prior to their walking through your front door if the current incumbents are taking money out of the back door by accepting bribes. The question is whether you are aware of changes in employee lifestyle or addictions to gambling, drugs, alcohol, sex or whatever. So often I have investigated fraud and on the successful completion of the investigation the losers have made to me such classic comments as:

- 'I wondered how he could afford that holiday in the Seychelles.'
- 'He was always on the phone to the bookies.'
- 'He changes his cars for new more expensive models every year.'
- 'He is only a clerk yet his house and its upkeep must cost him thousands.'
- 'I don't believe it – she is a member of my family.'

Whereas some individuals have other sources of income or may have won the lottery, the majority live within their financial limits. The dishonest will usually flaunt their wealth in one way or another.

It is an interesting fact that one in four job applications are fraudulent and employee vetting has to be more than just taking out references. If an individual is prepared to lie to obtain employment, they may well be prepared to accept bribes to act dishonestly. The dishonest recruit may be either susceptible to bribery and/or corruption or be an experienced fraudster who has targeted your company.

There are a number of important facts to consider in respect of employment vetting:

- 30% of the cost of crime in the retail industry is due to employee dishonesty
- the dishonest applicant could be underqualified, fraudulent and dangerous
- if underqualified, this could mean not only poor performance but negligence
- people who have successfully lied will probably lie again
- long term consequences include bad publicity, industrial espionage, computer crime and low morale

It is important that the employer does not see pre-employment screening as the end of the need for vetting. Vetting in situations of promotions to high risk positions, and monitoring of staff lifestyle are essential management controls. Certainly there is a need to define the sensitivity of the various job positions in your organisation. Consideration should be given to:

- the potential damage to your organisation through fraud, sabotage, or dishonesty
- highest position attainable
- data which may debar employment or promotion
- legal agreements necessary
- agency or temporary staff

However you complete employee vetting, it is essential that you check original documents, not copies. A check must be made of consistency in employment, lack of details, gaps or discrepancies in the chronology of employment history, omissions, wording of statements and eligibility for employment.

In today's computer-related world, there are various databases that can provide details of an individual's background such as electoral roll, credit history, directorships and press articles. In addition, Land Registry, regulatory bodies, P45s and telephone directory enquiries can provide additional material.

Use specialist agencies for comprehensive employee screening but ensure that they are both reputable and experienced.

Training

Staff training is mandatory and different organisations either implement in-house training or use training organisations. Many of these programmes are excellent and include staff role-playing in various scenarios. Certainly examine the marketplace and select the best training programme that suits your needs. Unfortunately, I have found that frequently there is a blinkered approach to staff training. The usual response when invited to conferences where the latest trends and protective systems are to be related to the delegates is:

- we have our own training programme
- we know all we need to know
- we will stick with.......... for our training needs

I find that these responses indicate a blinkered approach and perhaps an indication of doing only what one needs to do to meet the minimum requirements as a reactive rather than proactive stance and a failure to face facts. Some of the organisations offering training have little or no investigative experience and it is very important to keep abreast of trends, new protective systems, and who is out there to help you.

Whoever is used should be vetted and be the right organisation for the job. Just because the prospective training provider is a big named company does not necessarily make them the best for the job.

Conclusion

I am not saying that one should try to become an ace investigator but one should accept that in-house resources and experience needed to cope with the problems of money laundering and fraud are rarely fully available and even the in-house security professional will need to seek expert assistance from outside the organisation. Certainly the use of these experts is recommended if the need arises.

6

Terrorist Funding

Terrorist activity has always been supported by crime whether fraud, corruption or robbery. The problems in Northern Ireland and the funding for both sets of terrorists was supported by smuggling, bank robberies, protection rackets and fraud.

Similarly the terrorism in other parts of the world (South Africa, Afghanistan, Sudan, etc.) was, and is supported financially by crime.

September 11 2001 suddenly highlighted the funding of terrorism that really had been going on for the past 100 years. In other words it was nothing new, just the scale of the act. Although it is estimated that the actual attack on the twin towers cost the terrorists less than £100,000 (flight school, hotels, air tickets etc) it identified that a number of wealthy Saudis were and continue to financially support Al Quaeda.

Intelligence reports show that the following terrorist attacks cost:

Attack	Date	Estimated cost
London transport system	7 July 2005	GBP 8,000
Madrid train bombings,	11 March 2004	USD 10,000
Istanbul truck bomb attacks	15/20 November 2003	USD 40,000
Jakarta JW Marriot Hotel bombing	5 August 2003	USD 30,000
Bali bombings	12 October 2002	USD 50,000
USS Cole attack	12 October 2000	USD 10,000
East Africa embassy bombings	7 August 1998	USD 50,000

Terrorist organisations, like other organised crime syndicates can be related to private enterprise, ranging from large, international organisations to small, decentralised and self-directed companies/partnerships. The terrorists financing requirements reflect this diversity, varying greatly between the type of organisation.

Financing is required to meet their requirements whether to;

- fund specific terrorist operations, or
- to meet wider costs of developing, promoting and maintaining a terrorist organisation.

As mentioned previously the direct costs of mounting individual attacks have been low in proportion to the damage caused, but maintaining a terrorist network is akin to running a commercial enterprise, as it needs to provide for ongoing recruitment (especially where suicide bombers are used), planning of current and future strategies, plus procurement of weapons and other essential equipment causes a considerable drain on resources.

A very strong infrastructure is required to promote international terrorist networks and achieve their goals. Any sophisticated organisation requires significant funds to create and maintain an infrastructure of organisational support, to sustain a propaganda programme spreading the ideology of terrorism, and to finance whatever legitimate business activities are used to conceal the true nature of the organisation.

Terrorists are using a wide variety of methods to move funds within and between organisations, including the financial sector, the physical movement of cash by couriers, and the movement of goods through the trade system, charities and alternative remittance systems (Hawallah) (as mentioned at the beginning of this book) are also used to disguise terrorist movement of funds. The adaptability and opportunism shown by terrorist organisations suggests that any method that currently exists to move money around the globe is at risk.

If terrorist funding is disrupted it causes serious problems, reducing the overall capabilities of the terrorists and helping frustrate their ability to execute attacks. Disrupting terrorist financing ideally involves both;

- systematic safeguards, which will protect the financial system from criminal abuse, and
- targeted economic sanctions based on information received from counter-terrorism intelligence.

However the alternative remittance systems continue to create problems. Whereas the major banks and regulatory bodies in some of the countries where terrorist organisations are actively endeavouring to implement anti-money laundering controls, the alternative remittance systems such as Hawallah continue to thrive and are extremely difficult to investigate and close down.

Terrorist requirement for funds

To consider ways of stemming the flow of funds to terrorist organisations one has to understand their financial requirements.

Funds are required to promote;

- militant ideology,
- pay operatives and their families,

- arrange for travel,
- training
- forged documents,
- pay bribes,
- purchase weapons,
- and finally plan and stage attacks.

Frequently, a variety of higher-cost services, including propaganda and what appear to be legitimate social or charitable activities are needed to provide a veil of legitimacy for organisations that promote their objectives through terrorism.

The nature of funding for both operational and broader support activities will vary by the type of terrorist organisation, with traditional, government supported terrorist organisations on one side of the spectrum and small, anarchist independently supported organisations on the other. At its extreme, this second category has involved small, self-directed networks seeking to meet their own funding requirements through means that differ little from their everyday activity.

Terrorist financing requirements are;

1. Funding specific terrorist operations, such as direct costs associated with specific operations and

2. Broader organisational costs to develop and maintain an infrastructure of organisational support and to promote the ideology of a terrorist organisation.

Direct costs – operational support

While the funding requirements of terrorist organisations vary too widely to be described in a single description there are some common themes;

The direct costs of terrorist attacks and conflict are *the materials necessary to stage specific attacks are highly diverse and include, for example, vehicles, improvised bomb-making components, maps, surveillance material, etc.*

Those terrorist organisations involved in geographical conflicts have a constant need of funds to support the organisation and their activities in territories they control or act in.

Salaries/subsistence and communications

Individual operatives need to cover their day-to-day expenses and perhaps also those of their dependents. A cell will also need to communicate with its members and perhaps the parent network. This will be a more significant commitment if there is no other source of income for the operatives (such as employment or welfare payments).

Training, travel, and logistics

Training of operatives continues to be an important investment for terrorists, both in terms of ideological indoctrination and practical skills. The financial costs of training and travel, which can include the procurement of false documentation, represents an important cost for many terrorist networks. Even in recent attacks where terrorist operatives were 'home grown' and largely operationally independent of any other leadership structure, many of these operatives still travelled to receive training or other forms of indoctrination prior to the operational phase of their plans.

Shared funding

Where a cell is part of a network or shares a common goal or ideological or religious background with another cell or network, it may be called upon or feel compelled to provide financial support.

Broad organisational requirements

Financially maintaining a terrorist network – or a specific cell – to provide for recruitment, planning and procurement between attacks represents the most significant drain on resources. Beyond the funds needed to finance terrorist attacks and provide direct operational support, terrorist organisations require funding to develop a supporting infrastructure, recruit members and promote their ideology.

In addition, this infrastructure spending may go to support charitable organisations and media owned or controlled by the terrorist organisation.

Charities

Terror networks often use compromised or complicit charities and businesses to support their objectives. For example, some groups have links to charity branches in high-risk areas and/or under-developed parts of the world where the welfare provision available from the state is limited or non-existent.

In this situation, groups that use terrorism as a primary means to pursue their objectives can also utilise affiliated charities as a source of financing that may be diverted to fund terrorist attacks and terrorist recruitment by providing a veil of legitimacy over an organisation based on terrorism.

Mass media outlets

In addition to the civilian or social welfare function of organisations committed to paramilitary violence, there is usually a sophisticated public relations and media operation that sustains the ideology of terrorism.

Terrorist groups such as al-Qaeda have been especially adept at manipulating television through the release of videos. In addition, virtually every terrorist organisation has a website dedicated to recruitment and spreading the message of bloodshed. These major mass media tools emit powerful propaganda for violence, suicide bombing, and the killing of innocent civilians, posing a direct threat to international stability.

Inciting terrorist violence via the Internet

Three British residents used illicit funds to pay for web sites promoting martyrdom through terrorist violence. In 2007 the three men were sentenced to jail terms ranging from six-and-a-half years to ten years. All three pleaded guilty to 'inciting another person to commit an act of terrorism wholly or partly outside the United Kingdom which would, if committed in England and Wales, constitute murder.'

These were the first people to be convicted in the UK of inciting terrorist murder via the Internet. Two of the men registered dozens of Internet domains through Web hosting companies in the US and Europe. The sites facilitated communications among terrorists through online forums, hosted tutorials on computer hacking and bomb-making, and hosted videos of beheadings and suicide bombings in Iraq. The sites were paid for with funds stolen from 'hacked' credit card accounts, with the money being laundered through online gambling sites.

This case demonstrates the full scope of terrorist exploitation of the Internet. The three men involved took advantage of the web's global reach and multimedia capability for terrorist recruitment, training, and tactical coordination. They also used the web for terrorist financing through online financial fraud and money laundering.

Terrorist-owned and operated television station

TV Station Al – Manah (the official television station of Group Hezbolah). With a stated purpose of waging 'psychological warfare', this TV Station is a potent instrument that incites violence to viewers in the Middle East, Europe, and elsewhere. The US Treasury blacklisted the broadcaster for serving as the media arm of Hezbolah and facilitating terrorist activity. The EU has stated that it is in breach of Article 22 of the Television Without Frontiers Directive – the directive that governs all audio-visual law – which states that 'Member States shall ensure that broadcasts do not contain any incitement to hatred on grounds of race, sex, religion or nationality.'

> *Television employees are members of the organisation and engage in pre-operational surveillance for Hezbolah operations under cover of employment by the station. The station also supports fundraising and recruitment efforts. The station has broadcast bank account numbers calling for donations specifically for the terrorist organisation and incites viewers to commit acts of violence. The station has repeatedly called for disrupting the public order and peace by promoting suicide bombing and terror. It also broadcasts videos encouraging children to become suicide bombers.*
>
> *The station has been removed from ten satellite providers in France, the Netherlands, Spain, Australia, China, Brazil, and the United States. The station is still being broadcast in Europe and the Middle East by two satellite providers.*

These diverse funding requirements indicate that although individual terrorist attacks can yield great damage at low financial cost, a significant infrastructure (even if relatively loosely organised) is required to sustain international terrorist networks and promote their goals over time.

These funding requirements are reflected in the financing of terrorist networks themselves. According to the National Commission on Terrorist Attacks on the United States, al-Qaeda is believed to have spent some USD 30 million per year prior to the September 11 attacks on funding operations, maintaining its training and military apparatus, contributing to the Taliban and their high-level officials, and sporadically contributing to related terrorist organisations.

Raising terrorist funds

In general, terrorist organisations may raise funds through: legitimate sources, including through abuse of charitable entities or legitimate businesses and self-financing, criminal activity, state sponsors and activities in failed states and other safe havens. The following examples focus on how terrorists raise funds, with some reference to how they move funds.

The sources of terrorist financing can be divided into two general types:

- financing from above, in which large-scale financial support is amassed centrally by states, companies, charities or permissive financial institutions; and
- financing from below, in which the terrorists fundraising is small-scale and dispersed, for example based on self-financing by the terrorists themselves using employment or welfare payments.

A single terrorist organisation may use a number of different financing methods.

Raising funds from legitimate sources

Terrorist organisations receive considerable support and funding from and through legitimate sources including charities, businesses, and through self-funding by terrorists and their associates from employment, savings, and social welfare payments. This includes the phenomenon known as 'black-washing' where legal funds, for example money stemming from collection by charities or governmental subsidies and social benefits, are diverted for purposes of radicalisation, recruitment or terrorism. In other words clean money becomes dirty.

Charities

Charities or non-profit organisations possess characteristics that make them very attractive to terrorists or vulnerable to misuse for terrorist financing. They usually enjoy public trust, have access to considerable sources of funds, and their activities are usually cash-intensive. Furthermore, some charities have a global presence that provides a framework for national and international operations and financial transactions, often in or near areas most exposed to terrorist activity.

Finally, charities have been, in some jurisdictions, subject to significantly lighter regulatory requirements than financial institutions or publicly-held corporate entities, (for example, for starting capital, professional certification or background checks for staff and trustees at registration, or for ongoing record keeping, reporting and monitoring), reflecting their principally non-financial role.

The FATF has found that 'the misuse of non-profit organisations for the financing of terrorism is recognised as a crucial weak point in the global struggle to stop such funding at its source'.

Charities have different sets of risk profiles and can vary in the types of unusual characteristics that may be detected and help to identify terrorist financing. Potentially there are three forms of abuse:

1. Diversion of funds through fraud – for example, donors are told that they are donating money for orphans, and the charity then uses the funds to fund terrorists. This can occur alongside charitable work and within an otherwise legitimate charity. In one case investigated, a legitimate charity was established and quickly raised large amounts of funds from the local community. A controller of the charity diverted a portion of these donations to terrorist training camps in Pakistan using a cash courier.

2. The use of an entirely bogus or sham organisation that poses as a legitimate charity as a front organisation for terror groups. While the funds of charities can, on occasion, be misappropriated by individuals with privileged access to them,

cases have arisen in which the entire charity is used as the vehicle to perpetrate fraud against donors in order to raise funds for terrorism.

Terrorist organisations have used sham organisations to pose as legitimate charities to disguise terrorist financing activity and provide apparently legitimate explanations for links with terrorist groups.

United Kingdom Charity

In the United Kingdom a charity raised significant sums over two years by fraudulently obtaining grants from a Government agency. British Intelligence associated the controllers of the charity with violent extremist groups in another country. Separately, there were indications – such as an unrealistic growth in the organisation's student numbers (and therefore its demands for funds) of possible fraud.

Russian Charity

A charity with an office in Russia came to the attention of the law enforcement agencies through the submission of suspicious transaction reports (STRs) by credit institutions because of an apparent discrepancy between the stated objectives of the charity and its actual expenditure. The charity also had a poor history of reporting to the authorities on tax issues.

The subsequent investigation revealed that funds were being transferred from the charity to apparently fictitious or shell entities and then being withdrawn in cash for onward transmission to illegal armed militants.

---

3. Broad exploitation – for example, the charity raises money to feed orphans and actually does so but does it through a designated terrorist organisation.

Charity funds diverted to terrorists

A suspicious transaction report (STR) was made following an attempt by an individual to deposit substantial amounts of cash into the account of a charity – over which he had power-of-attorney – with the instruction that it be transferred onward to a notary as an advance for the purchase of real estate. The subsequent investigation revealed that payments into the account consisted of multiple cash deposits (presumably donations) but also payments directly from the account of the individual. In turn, his personal account revealed multiple cash deposits that corresponded to donations from private individuals.

> *Analysis of the debit transactions consisted of transfers to the charity and international transfers to an individual who police sources revealed was known to be involved with terrorist activities, as with others that the individual transmitting the funds was known to have links with..*
>
> *The law enforcement investigation assessed that the charity, which continued to fulfil an important social function, was being exploited both as a 'front' to raise funds and as a 'means of transmission' to divert a portion of them to known terrorists. This case highlights the vulnerabilities to exploitation that arise with weak governance combined with high levels of cash deposits.*

There are major concerns in respect of the use of charitable organisations to raise funds for recipients in a third country who are part of an organisational structure that includes paramilitary violence. However establishing whether there are linkages between military and charitable aims of a charity can be difficult.

During my enquiries into an Islamic Charity Muwafaq (Blessed Relief) operating in Sudan and registered in Jersey I came across the name of a wealthy Saudi who had a number of international companies. He was suing a publication for printing that the charity was a front for terrorists. Further enquiries revealed that one of his companies had apparently supported another Islamic charity (Quronic Institute) in the USA (Illinois). This charity had invested in property and the profits were being used to finance arms supplies to Hamas in Israel. One of their operatives (Salah) was arrested in Israel and after imprisonment was deported back to Chicago where the FBI froze bank Accounts and assets.

Post September 11, the Saudi's bank accounts were frozen in the UK, USA and Canada and to date he has been only partially successful in getting the freezing orders lifted. In London when a national newspaper reported the Hamas connection just prior to an appeal hearing when he hoped to have the UK freezing order lifted, he did not bother to return to court.

Investigations into these two charities had revealed that in 1995 Bin Laden identified the Blessed Relief Society in Croatia as a supplier of aid, and that Yassin al-Kadi incorporated the Quronic Institute charity in Delaware (1992) and in five years it is estimated that he paid some $20 million of his own money into it.

An audit of the National Commercial Bank of Saudi Arabia revealed the transfer of $3 million to Osama Bin Laden from Saudi businessmen via the Blessed Relief charity. Obviously, the fact that this individual had decided to sue the publication revealed a link between him and Bin Laden.

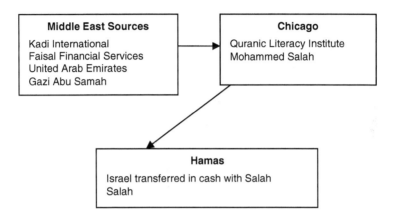

Funds destined to support the participation of terrorist and paramilitary groups in conflicts differ from other forms of terrorist exploitation of charities thus giving law enforcement agencies greater opportunities to detect them. The scale of funding required is usually larger, and transfers are concentrated on specific locations with funds raised where the same ethnic group are living and transferred to the territories the terrorist organisation controls.

Legitimate business

The proceeds of legitimate businesses can be used as a source of funds to support terrorist activities. This is a particular risk in sectors which do not require formal qualifications and where starting a business does not require substantial investments. The risk that a business will divert funds to support terrorist activity is greater where the business is cash intensive and the relation between sales reported and actual sales is difficult to verify

Note: Many religions operate a voluntary charitable tithe, normally of 1/40th of income, paid as a religious obligation and these funds can be used to fund terrorism especially where religious fanatics are involved at the place of worship.

Case study: Diversion of funds from legitimate business

The personal bank account of a restaurant manager was seen to regularly receive cheques drawn from wooden pallet company, as well as significant cash deposits. The account did not show any 'normal' financial activity such as payment for food, travel, etc. The bank account of the pallet company also showed significant cash withdrawals of between EUR 500000 and EUR 1 million.

The bank where the restaurant manager's account was held became suspicious because of the inconsistency between his profession and the nature of the pallet company's business (how many pallets can one get in a kitchen – maybe he was using them for fuel especially with the price of gas or perhaps he needed a good supply of toothpicks) and the bank submitted a suspicious transaction report to the financial intelligence unit. FIU analysis revealed that the individuals concerned were linked to terrorist movements, and the case was referred to prosecutors for wider investigation.

In another case routine monitoring of the bank account of a locksmith company revealed large-scale flow of funds that was disproportionate to the normal business activity of this kind of company. The company had also issued cheques to individuals involved in organisations defending prisoners detained for terrorist offenses.

FIU analysis revealed links between the locksmith company and radical movements; with individuals sending money orders between themselves as well as to prisoners and to other individuals registered in police databases. This prompted a wider investigation.

Self-funding

In some cases, terrorist groups have been funded from internal sources, including family and other non-criminal sources. The amounts of money needed to mount small attacks can be raised by individual terrorists and their support networks using savings, access to credit or the proceeds of businesses under their control.

Terrorist organisations can be highly decentralised, and self-funding can include cases in which a relatively autonomous external financial facilitator who is not directly involved in planning or carrying out an attack nevertheless contributes funding.

The official report into the 7 July 2005 attacks on the London Transport system stated that:

'Current indications are that the group was self-financed. There is no evidence of external sources of income. Our best estimate is that the overall

cost is less than £8,000.

The bombs were homemade, and that the ingredients used were all readily commercially available and not particularly expensive.

The group appears to have raised the necessary cash [for overseas trips, bomb making equipment, rent, car hire] by methods that would be extremely difficult to identify as related to terrorism or other serious criminality.

Terrorist A appears to have provided most of the funding. He had a reasonable credit rating, multiple bank accounts (each with just a small sum deposited for a protracted period), credit cards and a £10,000 personal loan. He had two periods of intensive activity – firstly in October 2004 and then from March 2005 onwards. He defaulted on his personal loan repayments and was overdrawn on his accounts.

Terrorist B made a number of purchases with cheques (which subsequently bounced) in the weeks before 7 July. Bank investigators visited his house on the day after the bombings.

Though Terrorist B was not specifically identified as a terrorist until after an attack took place, this case demonstrates that financial intelligence on its own was sufficiently accurate to prompt investigation by financial institutions.'

Raising funds from criminal proceeds

In the past, some terrorist groups derived much of their funding and support from state sponsors of terrorism. With increased international pressure, many of these funding sources have become less reliable and, in some instances, have disappeared altogether. Libya has allegedly stopped but Iran and North Korea appear to continue with this funding. In addition, newer decentralised, independent cells often do not have the same level of access to foreign funding as traditional terrorist groups. As a result, terrorist groups have turned to alternative sources of financing, including criminal activities such as arms trafficking, kidnap-for-ransom, extortion, racketeering and drug trafficking.

Terrorist use of criminal activity to raise funds ranges from low-level fraud to involvement in serious and organised crime. It is often difficult to determine whether the funds raised from these activities are destined for terrorist activities or are simply the proceeds of general criminal activity. Described below are criminal activities terrorists are known to have engaged in, including selling narcotics, credit card fraud, cheque fraud and extortion.

Drug trafficking

Drug Trafficking is an attractive source of funds for terrorist groups, enabling them to raise large sums of money. The degree of reliance on drug trafficking as a source of terrorist funding has grown with the decline in state sponsorship of terror groups. This trend has increasingly blurred the distinction between terrorist and drug trafficking organisations.

Both criminal organisations and terrorist groups continue to develop international networks and establish alliances of convenience. Globalisation has enabled both terror and crime organisations to expand and diversify their activities, taking advantage of the internationalisation of communications and banking systems, as well as the opening of borders to facilitate their activities.

Investigations and intelligence have revealed direct links between various terrorist and drug trafficking organisations that frequently work together out of necessity or convenience and mutual benefit. Due to tighter controls in Iran the drugs from the Afghanistan poppy fields are smuggled through the Balkans to Moscow where the Russian crime gangs export onto the West.

Terrorist organisation raises money through drug trafficking

Since 1990, Person A led an international heroin-trafficking organisation (the 'Organisation') responsible for manufacturing and distributing millions of dollars worth of heroin in Afghanistan and Pakistan. The Organisation then arranged for the heroin to be transported from Afghanistan and Pakistan into the United States, including New York City, hidden inside suitcases, clothing and containers. Once the heroin arrived in the United States, other members of the Organisation received the heroin and distributed the drugs. These co-conspirators then arranged for millions of dollars in heroin proceeds to be laundered back to Person A and other members of the Organisation in Afghanistan and Pakistan. To launder the funds, Person A used several import/export commercial enterprises to wire his funds. Funds were placed in the financial system as proceeds and/or expenses related to those diverse concerns and remitted under that cover.

The Organisation was closely aligned with the Taliban in Afghanistan. During the course of their cooperation, the Organisation provided financial support to the Taliban. More specifically, between 1994 and 2000, the Organisation collected heroin proceeds in the United States for the Taliban in Afghanistan. In exchange for financial support, the Taliban provided the Organisation protection for its opium crops, heroin laboratories, drug transportation routes, and members and associates.

Source: United States

Terrorist organisation raises money through drug trafficking

Paramilitary organisation F currently supplies more than 50 % of the world's cocaine and more than 60% of the cocaine that enters the United States. Organisation F initially taxed other narcotics traffickers involved in the manufacture and distribution of cocaine in areas it controlled. Recognising the increased profits available, from the 1990s up to the present, Organisation F moved to become directly involved in the production and distribution of cocaine. Methods include, among other criminal activities, setting the prices to be paid to farmers across Colombia for cocaine paste, the raw material used to produce cocaine, and transporting cocaine paste to jungle laboratories under its control where it was converted into ton quantities of finished cocaine and then shipped out of Colombia to the United States and other countries.

Organisation F leaders allegedly ordered the murder of Colombian farmers who sold cocaine paste to external buyers or otherwise violated its strict cocaine policies. Colombian farmers who violated rules were allegedly shot, stabbed, or dismembered alive, and the bodies of murdered farmers were cut open, filled with rocks, and sunk in nearby rivers. Organisation F Leadership also allegedly ordered members to kidnap and murder US citizens to discourage the US government from disrupting its cocaine-trafficking activities. In July 2007 a senior leader was convicted of conspiring to commit hostage-taking. Organisation F leaders allegedly authorised their members to shoot down US fumigation planes and plotted to retaliate against US law enforcement officers who were conducting the investigation into the organisation's narcotics activities.

Recognising that cocaine was the lifeblood of Organisation F, its leaders allegedly collected millions of dollars in cocaine proceeds and used the money to purchase weapons for terrorist activities against the government and people of Colombia.

Source: United States

Exchange of narcotics for weaponry

Nine persons were involved in a conspiracy to procure USD 25 million of weaponry in exchange for cocaine and cash.

High-ranking members of the group were arrested in a sting operation in Costa Rica, while they were preparing to inspect a purported cache of weapons. Simultaneous with that operation, the weapons broker was arrested in the United States.

> This case is an example of an attempt by a terrorist group to finance its activities, including the purchase of weaponry, through the sale of illegal narcotics. Seven defendants pleaded guilty to both providing material support to terrorists and to drug conspiracies. Three defendants pleaded guilty to the material support conspiracy only.
>
> Source: United States

Terrorist organisation extorts money from drug traffickers

An investigation and prosecution carried out by Turkish authorities revealed that drug trafficking is the principal source of funds for a terrorist organisation. Drugs are grown in Pakistan, Afghanistan and Iran; and sent from there to Europe, both through known members of the organisation, and through their associates and other non-designated militants.

In 2007, more than 10 members of the organisation terrorist group were arrested and large amounts of money seized. Investigation and testimony by these members revealed that the organisation extorts money from smugglers at points of entry in the North of Iraq in the form of 'taxes' worth around 7% of the value of smuggled items. The groups also collect money for each person or each car crossing their 'customs points'. One such 'customs point' earns USD 20,000 – 30,000 per week. One member of the group stated that the most important income for the group is the money collected from drug traffickers as 'taxation'.

Source: Turkey

Credit card fraud

The methods of making dishonest purchases through the use of someone else's credit card details are many – but one of the easiest ways to do so is to buy goods using the internet or by phone (carding). The following two cases related to credit card fraud shows the vulnerability of credit cards to misuse for terrorist financing purposes and other illegal activities.

There is a market for illegally obtained personal details, including credit card account numbers, as well as personal information such as the card holder's full name, billing address, telephone number, start and expiry dates, the security number on the rear of the card, etc.

Stolen card details purchased online

Person A frequented criminal Internet sites that specifically bought and sold credit card information (including shadowcrew.com, investigated by the United States Secret Service in 2003). Stolen credit card numbers were passed to Associate B, and then on to C, a computer expert specialising in facilitating the creation and management of websites that provided forums for extremists and downloads of highly violent material intended to incite attacks.

The associates were later found to be linked, via telephone and e-mail records to a terrorist cell in Bosnia, and were arrested on the brink of launching an attack.

This case illustrates how terrorists' need for funds can go far beyond those required to launch specific attacks. In this case, terrorist facilitators fully exploited the opportunities of new technology to acquire funds illicitly and anonymously – extending the distance between their identity and their actions. The case also highlighted how sophisticated forensic skills can be needed to recover financial data.

Source: United Kingdom

Credit card fraud

A North African terrorist funding group accumulated details of nearly 200 stolen cards and raised more than £200,000 to fund the al-Qaeda terrorist network through international credit card fraud. Twenty to thirty 'runners' collected the names and credit card details of almost 200 different bank accounts from contacts working in service industries such as restaurants. These details were not used in their country of origin (the UK) but sent on to associates in Spain and the Netherlands. These associates used the cards to fraudulently collect more than £200,000 for al-Qaeda cells around Europe. This case highlights the fact that the high returns achievable from credit card fraud are not lost on terrorists and that sophisticated arrangements can be put in place to operate a fraud ring linked to terrorism.

Source: United Kingdom

Cheque fraud

Several cases have been identified in which a basic bank fraud has been applied to generate funds for terrorism. These cases involved bank accounts being opened using false identity documents and fraudulent deposits.

Cheque books are then stockpiled; and when a large number have been accumulated, they are used to purchase goods from department stores costing under the amount that would trigger verification to ensure sufficient funds were available in the account. The goods are returned for a cash refund. This activity can be carried out by organised individuals, who draw on cheques from the same account simultaneously in several locations.

Cheque book fraud, which has figured in a number of terrorist finance cases, allows terrorists to raise and move significant amounts of cash quickly. There are often limited preventative measures in place to obviate what appears to be an 'ordinary' crime, rather than terrorist finance. It can be perpetrated alone or in concert with others to maximise the amount taken. However It is important to note that in many countries the use of cheques for payment is now redundant, many retail establishments no longer accepting cheques and requiring payment by credit/debit card.

Example

A network of North African terrorists used organised, low-level bank fraud against a number of UK banks to raise funds in support of terrorist activity. Using over 50 individuals the group raised at least £550,000 within 12 months. Once raised this money was used to support terrorist training, procurement, travel and subsistence costs incurred by terrorists and extremists across Europe.

Source: United Kingdom

Extortion

Supporters of terrorist and paramilitary groups exploit their presence within expatriate or immigrant communities to raise funds through extortion. A terrorist organisation would make use of its contacts to tax the immigrants on their earnings and savings. The extortion is generally targeted against their own communities where there is a high level of fear of retribution should anyone report anything to the authorities. They may also threaten harm to the relatives – located in the country of origin – of the victim, further frustrating any law enforcement action.

Extortion from immigrant communities can be a significant and consistent source of funds. Estimates state that before 2001 one terrorist group collected up to USD 1 million a month from expatriates in Canada, Britain, Switzerland and Australia, making it among the best funded terrorist groups in the world. One report outlined how extortion demands were made on expatriate businesses of up to CAD 100,000 and £100,000 in Canada and the UK respectively, with equally high demands made in France and Norway.

Extortion of a commercial organisation

In September 2007, An American company was sentenced to pay a USD 25 million criminal fine, placed on five years of corporate probation and ordered to implement and maintain an effective compliance and ethics program. Earlier in the year, the company pleaded guilty to one count of engaging in transactions with a Specially Designated Global Terrorist (SDGT) in that, from 1997 through 2004, the company made payments to a terrorist group.

The payments, demanded by the group, were made nearly every month and totalled over USD 1.7 million. The group was designated as a Foreign Terrorist Organisation in September 2001, and listed as an SDGT in October 2001.

Source: United States

Multiple types of criminal activity

The opportunism of terrorist financiers is particularly illustrated by cases where suspects move fluidly from one kind of crime to another. One group was found to be responsible for burglary, identity theft and credit card fraud in its drive for funds.

Example

A terrorist financier was a member of an enterprise that created a complex cigarette smuggling scheme in the US. This financier would purchase low-taxed cigarettes from one US State; apply forged 'tax stamps' to the goods; and then smuggle the untaxed cigarettes into Michigan (where State cigarette taxes are considerably higher) for resale.

In parallel with this exercise, the organisation defrauded retail and wholesale merchants with counterfeit credit cards. The cash garnered from these unlawful activities would then be laundered by members of the enterprise by purchasing businesses, buying additional cigarettes, and obtaining additional fraudulent credit cards.

The enterprise also committed acts of arson and attempted to engage in insurance fraud by burning down a cigarette shop that it owned on an Indian reservation in New York, and then attempted to recover on their fire insurance policy.

The terrorist financier used the profits from these activities to provide material support to a designated terrorist organisation.

This case demonstrates the wide range of fraudulent activities that terrorist supporters will engage in, such as trading in illegal contraband, and tax, credit card and insurance fraud, to generate funds to support terrorist groups.

Source: United States

The role of safe havens, failed states, and state sponsors

I have already mentioned Operation Safehaven (Nazi money laundering) but the word 'safehaven' is used to provide support for terrorist organisations. This can be through the absence of effective jurisdictional control, tolerance of terrorist organisations and their activities, or active support to terrorist organisations, safe havens, failed states and state sponsors create enabling environments or otherwise provide support to terrorist organisations.

Safe havens, failed states and state sponsors continue to represent crucial sources of support for terrorist organisations today, including from territories in Somalia, Iraq, and the Pakistan-Afghanistan border.

Safe havens and wider cases of weak jurisdictional control, state tolerance or support of terrorist organisations are also important in how terrorists move and use finance, in addition to their role in raising terrorist funds. The wider issues of how jurisdictional factors can enable terrorists to move funds are included in the following chapters.

When the Taliban regime swept to power in Afghanistan in late 1996, it became a critical safe haven and source of support for Osama bin Laden and al-Qaeda until it was removed from power by international coalition forces following the terrorist attacks against the United States on 11 September 2001.

On 15 October 1999, the United Nations Security Council unanimously adopted Security Council Resolution (UNSCR) 1267 against the Taliban regime in Afghanistan in response to the Taliban's continuing support for terrorist organisations and activity, including providing sanctuary to Osama bin Laden and al-Qaeda. In particular, UNSCR 1267 cited the continuing use of Afghan territory, especially areas controlled by the Taliban, for the sheltering and training of terrorists and planning of terrorist acts, and the safe haven provided by the Taliban to Osama bin Laden and al-Qaeda to allow the continued operation of terrorist training camps from Taliban-controlled territory and the use of Afghanistan as a base from which to sponsor international terrorist operations and the continued refusal of the Taliban to surrender them for trial,

The Taliban also facilitated the largest production of opium in the world as a means of financing their activities and providing further support for international terrorism and a war effort that devastated the humanitarian conditions of the people of Afghanistan.

Moving terrorist funds

There are three main methods by which terrorists move money or transfer value:

- Through the use of the financial system
- The physical movement of money (for example, through the use of cash couriers)
- through the international trade system.

Terrorist organisations will also

- abuse alternative remittance systems (ARS),
- charities, or other captive entities to disguise their use of these three methods to transfer value.

Terrorist organisations use all three methods to maintain ongoing operation of the terrorist organisation and undertake specific terrorist activities.

The multiplicity of organisational structures employed by terror networks, the continuing evolution of techniques in response to international measures and the opportunistic nature of terrorist financing all make it difficult to identify a favoured or most common method of transmission. Regular funding to maintain a group's capacity is best facilitated via the conventional banking system – as money sent from one country to another can be disguised behind false name accounts, charities or businesses to disguise the ultimate recipient; but other ways to move money are used for specific purposes, or to disguise terrorist financial trails.

The reports and expert evaluation by various experts on terrorist finance developed since 2001 has emphasised the great adaptability and opportunism that terrorists deploy in meeting their funding requirements.

In answer to the question 'How do terrorists raise and move funds?' is: **'Any way they can.'**

The following cases highlight how, in many situations, the raising, moving and using of funds for terrorism can be especially challenging and almost indistinguishable from the financial activity associated with everyday life.

The identification and the disruption of terrorist finance are naturally more difficult when authorities are confronted by 'informal' support networks that do not operate as part of well structured organisations with clear roles and lines of accountability. In such circumstances, the links between financial activity and terrorist activity become more opaque and the targets for disruption harder to identify.

Indeed, experience suggests that all of the mechanisms that exist to move money around the globe are to some extent at risk. This is illustrated by the list of known and historical techniques uncovered. An investigative challenge that appears common to them all is that the connections between funds and terrorism can be extremely difficult to determine in the country of origin, when the terrorist-related activity itself takes place elsewhere.

Formal financial sector

Financial institutions and other regulated financial service providers represent the formal financial sector and serve as the main gateway through which retail and commercial transactions flow. Additionally, the services and products available through the formal financial sector serve as vehicles for moving funds that support terrorist organisations and fund acts of terrorism. The speed and ease with which funds can be moved within the international financial system allow terrorists to move funds efficiently and effectively and often without detection between and within jurisdictions.

Combined with other mechanisms such as offshore corporate entities, formal financial institutions can provide terrorists with the cover they need to conduct transactions and launder proceeds of crime when such activity goes undetected.

Money and value transfer (MVT) mechanisms have proven to be particularly attractive to terrorists for funding their activities. MVT operations range from the large-scale and regulated funds transfer mechanisms available in the formal financial sector, to small-scale alternative remittance systems. Funds transfers refer to any financial transaction carried out for a person through a financial institution by electronic means with a view to making an amount of money available to a person at another financial institution..

Investigation and analysis of a number of terrorism cases by various researchers working for the FATF and other agencies has revealed that radical groups as well as persons related to terrorist organisations have used the network of the registered and world-wide operating money transfer companies to send or receive money. These transactions enabled authorities to develop a wider understanding of the main contacts of these people and the extent of their networks. Coordination and liaison between intelligence/law enforcement agencies and financial institutions has made it possible to gain a valuable source of financial intelligence on the operations of networks worldwide.

Money transfer offices are obliged to register identity-data of the person who sends the money from Country A and the person who receives the money in Country B – This data have proved to be excellent input for network analysis in regard to terrorist financing.

Terrorist organisation uses MVT mechanisms to move money

Person D, a leader of a terrorist organisation based in Country C and once a resident in Country A, was in hiding in Country B. The FIU in Country A found out though investigations that persons in Country A were sending money through money transfers to D's friends in Country B to financially support him. The money flow was detected because the transfers were made by nationals of Country C – which was unusual in Country A. Person D was later arrested in Country B on suspicion of terrorism. Money transfers from Country A to Country B were presented in court as supporting evidence of terrorist financing.

Source: The Netherlands

This case highlights the need to look for unusual transaction/transaction patterns.

Advances in payment system technology have had a twofold impact on the potential abuse by terrorist financiers and money launderers of such systems. Electronic payment systems allow law enforcement an increased ability to trace individual transactions through electronic records that may be automatically generated, maintained and/or transmitted with the transaction. However, these advances also create characteristics that may be attractive to a potential terrorist or money launderer. For instance, the increased rapidity and volume of funds transfers, in the absence of the consistent implementation of standards –for recording key information on such transactions, maintaining records, and transmitting necessary information with the transactions, could serve as an obstacle to ensuring traceability by investigative authorities of individual transactions.

Terrorist organisation uses wire transfers to move money across borders

A terrorist organisation in Country X was observed using bank wire transfers to move money in Country Y that was eventually used for paying rent for safe houses, buying and selling vehicles, and purchasing electronic components with which to construct explosive devices. The organisation used 'bridge' or 'conduit' accounts in Country X as a means of moving funds between countries. The accounts at both ends were opened in the names of people with no apparent association with the structure of terrorist organisation but who were linked to one another by kinship or similar ties. There were thus the apparent family connections that could provide a justification for the transfers between them if necessary.

Funds, mainly in the form of cash deposits by the terrorist organisation were deposited into bank accounts from which the transfers are made. Once the money was received at the destination, the holder either left it on deposit or invested it in mutual funds where it remained hidden and available for the organisation's future needs. Alternatively, the money was transferred to other bank accounts managed by the organisation's correspondent financial manager, from where it was distributed to pay for the purchase of equipment and material or to cover other ad hoc expenses incurred by the organisation in its clandestine activities.

Trade sector

The international trade system is subject to a wide range of risks and vulnerabilities which provide terrorist organisations the opportunity to transfer value and goods through seemingly legitimate trade flows. In recent decades, international trade has grown significantly: global merchandise trade now exceeds USD 9 trillion a year and global trade in services accounts for a further USD 2 trillion.

Terrorist use of the trade sector to move funds

An FIU received disclosures from several banks concerning account holders: Persons A and B and Company C, all active in the diamond trade. In the space of a few months, A, B and C's accounts saw a large number of fund transfers to and from foreign countries. Moreover, soon after the opening of his account, person B received several bank cheques in large amounts of US dollars.

Financial information collected by the FIU showed that Company C was receiving large US dollar transfers, originating from companies active in the diamond industry and debited by several transfers to the Middle East in favour of Person A, a European citizen born in Africa and residing in the Middle East. One of the directors of Company C, a Belgian citizen residing in Africa, held an account at a bank in Belgium through which transfers took place to and from other countries in Europe, Africa, North America, and the Middle East. Inward transfers from foreign countries mainly took place in US dollars. These were then converted to EUR and used to make transfers to foreign countries and to accounts in Belgium belonging to Person B and his wife.

Police information collected by the FIU showed that the prosecutor had opened a file related to trafficking in diamonds originating in Africa. The largest transfers of funds by the company trading in diamonds were mainly destined to the same person, A, residing in the Middle East. Police sources revealed that both Person A and Person B were suspected of having bought diamonds from the rebel army in Sierra Leone and of smuggling them into Belgium for the benefit of a terrorist organisation.

Moreover, it appeared that certain persons and companies linked with Persons A and B had already been referred to prosecutors by the FIU in other cases for money laundering derived from organised crime.

Source: Belgium

Cash couriers

The physical movement of cash is one way terrorists can move funds without encountering the AML/CFT safeguards established in financial institutions. It has been suggested that some groups have converted cash into high-value and hard-to-trace commodities such as gold or precious stones in order to move assets outside of the financial system.

Counter-terrorist operations have shown that cash couriers have transferred funds to a number of countries within the Middle East and South Asia. Direct flight routings are used for simple transfers; however, indirect flight routings using multiple cash couriers and changes in currencies take place within more sophisticated schemes.

The movement of cash across borders is prevalent in countries where the electronic banking system remains embryonic or is little used by the populace. Large parts of Africa and the Middle East have predominantly cash-based societies, and this naturally lends itself to cash flows using alternative remittance systems or by courier. Analysis of a number of terrorism cases has shown that money couriers are active even within Europe and between countries with a well functioning financial system. In most cases couriers are involved in moving funds generated outside the financial system and kept out of the financial system to avoid detection.

Terrorist financing using cash couriers – Bali bombings

The activities of Terrorist Organisation A in Southeast Asia clearly show the critical role of cash couriers in support of their terrorist operations. Organisation A avoided using the conventional banking system in order to evade safeguards and to avoid leaving an audit trail for law enforcement. The funding for the Bali bombings that took place in October 2002 were provided by Al-Qaeda's chief of operations to Person H, Organisation A's head of operations, who was hiding in Thailand in 2002. Person H passed USD 30,000 to the perpetrators of the Bali bombings in two batches using several cash couriers. The couriers took several weeks to complete the runs.

> The funding for the JW Marriott Hotel bombing in Jakarta was also provided by Person H from Thailand. Again, a total of USD 30,000 of Al-Qaeda's funds was sent to Indonesia in April 2003 through a string of couriers.
>
> Moving money using cash couriers may be expensive relative to wire transfers. As legitimate financial institutions tighten their due diligence practices, it has become an attractive method of transferring funds without leaving an audit trail. When cross border remittance of cash is interdicted, the origin and the end use of cash can be unclear. Cash raised and moved for terrorist purposes can be at very low levels – making detection and interdiction difficult.

> **Case study: Terrorists use Gold to Move Value**
>
> During the invasion of Afghanistan in 2001, it was widely reported that the Taliban and members of al-Qaeda smuggled their money out of the country via Pakistan using couriers that handled bars of gold. In Karachi, couriers and Hawalla dealers transferred the money to the Gulf Region, where once again it was converted to gold bullion. It has been estimated that during one three-week period in late November to early December 2001, al-Qaeda transferred USD 10 million in cash and gold out of Afghanistan. An al-Qaeda manual found by British forces in Afghanistan in December 2001 included not only chapters on how to build explosives and clean weapons, but on how to smuggle gold on small boats or conceal it on the body.

Gold is often used by Hawalla brokers to balance their books. Hawalla dealers also routinely have gold, rather than currency, placed around the globe. Terrorists may store their assets in gold because its value is easy to determine and remains relatively consistent over time. There is always a market for gold given its cultural significance in many areas of the world, such as Southeast Asia, South and Central Asia, the Arabian Peninsula, and North Africa.

Use of Alternative Remittance Systems (ARS)

As previously mentioned alternative remittance systems (ARS) such as Hawalla are used by terrorist organisations for convenience and access. ARS have the additional attraction of weaker and/or less opaque record-keeping and in many locations may be subject to generally less stringent regulatory oversight. Although the FATF have called for significantly strengthened controls over such service providers, the level of anonymity and the rapidity that such systems offer have served to make them a favoured mechanism for terrorists.

For some networks there are also cultural and pragmatic reasons for using these services: many have their origins or control structures in areas where the banking infrastructure is weak or practically non-existent. The role of ARS in terrorist financing may be primarily an 'end-user' gateway; i.e. the means by which new or stored funds are passed to operational cells.

Alternative remittance system used for terrorist financing

An African national, residing in Africa, held an account with a bank in European Country B. This account had been credited with significant sums transferred from companies that had their registered offices mostly in Western Europe. Shortly afterwards the client issued an order to transfer a large sum in favour of a company in the Middle East which held an account with a bank located there.

Analysis by the FIU revealed the following elements:

- *According to police information, it appeared that the beneficiary bank, located in the Middle East, was suspected of maintaining financial links with a terrorist group.*
- *According to the security services in Country B, this bank had collaborated with another bank in making transfers of funds on behalf of Hawalla operators. This latter bank was suspected of having links with an organisation with ties to a terrorist group.*
- *Analysis further revealed that the account of the African national, who had no known connections with Country B, was being used as a transit account for large funds transfers originating primarily with a European company involved in the sale of chemical products and destined for a company in the Middle East. There was no apparent reason why operations should be performed via an account in country.*

Source: Belgium

Use of charities and non-profit organisations

As previously mentioned terrorists use charity networks as a means to move funds some being set up as a cover for their true purpose. Many thousands of legitimate charitable organisations exist all over the world that serve the interests of all societies, and often transmit funds to and from highly distressed parts of the globe. Terrorist abuses of the charitable sector have included using legitimate transactions to disguise terrorist cash travelling to the same destination; and broad exploitation of the charitable sector by charities affiliated with terrorist organisations. The sheer volume of funds and other assets held by the charitable sector means that the diversion of even a very small percentage of these funds to support terrorism constitutes a grave problem.

Use of non-profit organisation for terrorist recruitment

A bank checked its customer database for matches with lists relating to terrorism; and found that a non-profit organisation which held an account with it, with its registered office in European Country B, was named on a terrorism list. The Bank submitted a STR based on this match.

The organisation's account had been opened a few years before and had seen low activity, then suddenly experienced a particularly intense bout of activity starting on 1 January 2002. The transactions on this account consisted of multiple cash deposits made by several different people for a large total amount. These funds were then withdrawn in cash.

Analysis by the local FIU revealed the following elements:

Based on information requested from the state security services in Country B, the FIU concluded that this non-profit body was one of a number of contact points in Country B established with the aim of recruiting and sending people to fight in the Middle East.

It also transpired that two or three of the signature authorities for the account of this organisation were linked to a terrorist group.

This case is the subject of an ongoing judicial investigation.

Source: Belgium.

Charity embedded in terrorist finance laundering network

FIU analysis of STRs identified substantial transfers of funds between an apparently small company and a charity working in the North Caucasus region.

Further investigation revealed that the company had itself received significant transfers from other charities, ostensibly for consultancy services received from the company. The company had also received funds from an individual based in a region with a high level of activity by extremist groups. The company appeared to be accumulating the income from these sources and then passing it on to the charity in the North Caucasus region.

Further concern arose from the discovery that the charity had another source of funding: a foreign citizen living in Russia, who routinely received transfers of funds of small amounts of cash below the statutory monitoring threshold which were then transferred in bulk to the charity. These small transfers originated from a region with a high level of activity by extremist groups.

> *The investigation of the charity's expenditures showed that funds were used in a variety of ways, including: cash withdrawal and couriering to the North Caucasus region; direct transfers to a 'welfare unit' within a known illegal militant organisation; and onward transfers to apparently legitimate charitable organisations in the North Caucasus region. As a result of the investigation, the authorities discontinued the activities of the charity concerned.*
>
> *Source: Russia*

Investigations and indicators

The following list sets out the types of activities that were most frequently reported as suspicious and the indicators that factored into the Canadian FIU's Terrorist Financing case disclosures:

- **Most frequently reported suspicious activity**
  - Unusual business activity
  - Unable to ascertain source of funds
  - Multiple deposits at different branches
  - Third party deposits in US cash
  - Wire transfers following cash deposits
  - Wire transfers to specific location/account on regular basis
  - Large cash deposits

- **Most frequently used indicators in terrorist funding case disclosures**
  - Sending or receiving funds by international transfers from and/or to locations of specific concern
  - Atypical business/account behaviour
  - Charity/Relief organisation linked to transactions
  - Large scale cash transactions
  - Media coverage of account holder's activities

Financial information is obviously now one of the most powerful investigative and intelligence tools available. As money moves through the financial system, it leaves a verifiable trail that can in many cases indicate illicit activity, identify those responsible, and locate the proceeds of criminality that can then be recovered. Through the development of internationally recognised Anti Money laundering and CFT standards, financial institutions and other designated non-financial entities have taken steps to know their customers and keep records. The value of financial information in counter-terrorist investigations has increased dramatically in recent years.

Other types of financial reports (including large cash transactions, wire transfers, and cross-border currency movements) can significantly increase the pool of financial information available to investigators.

Financial information is now used as part of the evidential case to hold criminals and terrorists to account. It also has a key intelligence role – for example by allowing law enforcement to have a 360 degree view of the suspicious financial activities, i.e;

Look backward, by piecing together how a criminal or terrorist conspiracy was developed and the timelines involved.

Look sideways, by identifying or confirming associations between individuals and activities linked to conspiracies, even if overseas – often opening up new avenues for enquiry.

Look forward, by identifying the warning signs of criminal or terrorist activity in preparation.

Financial information is particularly suited to these tasks in that it is relatively unambiguous, can be processed easily using technology, and easily accessed with little intrusion on the provider.

Looking backward: financial investigation following terrorist acts
Exploiting the 'financial footprint' left behind by terrorists can often give the investigators details of how, when and where terrorist attacks were conceived, planned, and executed. Financial information has proved to be a reliable source of historical intelligence, available to investigators even when all the terrorists have died during the commission of their attacks.

Analysing preparations for an attack

Following the series of suicide attacks in London investigators were able to exploit financial intelligence which identified vehicle hire, accommodation at hotels, procurement and overseas travel. This assisted in identifying the timescale for the planning and preparation for the attacks. Other investigative techniques were then used to exploit the financial intelligence and establish a comprehensive picture of the lead-up to the terrorist attacks.
Source: United Kingdom

Looking sideways: the role of financial intelligence in counter-terrorism enquiries

Conventional investigative techniques have come to rely heavily on identifying telecommunications contacts to establish where there are links between individuals and groups. Following the money can produce similar information: Financial intelligence can be used to identify a terrorist's activity and be used directly to trace links with other individuals and groups, or indirectly to compare methods and approaches. Exploiting this additional intelligence can identify those who may otherwise go undetected. This reduces the chances of successful terrorist attacks.

Financial investigation jump-starts a post-attack enquiry

The identity of one of four perpetrators of a multiple suicide attack across the London Underground was identified from two credit cards bearing the same name, but found at two different bomb scenes establishing an association between both of them. He was identified with an address that was used as the bomb factory.

Transaction analysis of associated accounts helped to establish the individual's activities in the months preceding the attack and the milestones in the attack-planning exercise, including the purchase of camping equipment associated with a pre-attack training event.

Interviews with shop staff revealed that these purchases had been preceded by others minutes beforehand, made by another person but for exactly the same amount. This was the first time that an association between two individuals, later confirmed as attackers, had been identified.

This case is symbolic of the integrated role that forensic financial analysis plays in a counter-terrorism investigation. Financial intelligence, recovered from forensic examination of a bomb scene, provided a leap forward for the investigative team's efforts to establish the identity of the attackers and the nature of the conspiracy, in the immediate aftermath of the attack.

Source: United Kingdom

Tactical intelligence sharing as basis for financial investigation

Group G operated a network of cells engaged directly in attack planning and the in the wider facilitation of terrorism. This latter activity included the transmission of funds to Country X to pay for the development of false documentation. In related cases, passport documents were stolen in armed robberies in Europe which were later found in the possession of several Group members in the UK, Germany and France.

> *With the serial numbers of many of these stolen and falsified documents established, and intelligence connecting these to a terrorist organisation, the FIU of country Y made these systematically available to financial institutions to enable them to cross reference against their 'know your customer' checks. In Country Y, 81 STRs were submitted in response relating to money transfers alone.*
>
> *Source: The Netherlands*

Look forward: identifying indicators of future attacks

It is challenging to identify a terrorist conspiracy in preparation solely from financial activity. Nevertheless, timely detection of financial factors can play a critical role in identifying indicators of future terrorist activity. The following case study highlights how financial intelligence has been essential in building the evidence suggesting a conspiracy was underway.

Identifying attack indicators

An individual suspected of involvement with Al-Qaeda used multiple accounts held in multiple identities to fund the supply of bomb components for use in another country. The conspiracy was revealed through extensive and forensic financial investigation, which allowed law enforcement to establish that:

- *to disguise the true destination the travel patterns were via various other jurisdictions to confuse any surveillance/investigation*
- *the various components for the improvised explosives were sent in small parcels, using an international courier, but over several months so as not to arouse suspicion.*
- *multiple financial transactions were made to various accounts, which were controlled by an associate of the suspect indicating a wider conspiracy.*

The associate's financial affairs were deliberately structured to hide the audit trail and it was established that he was acting closely with the first suspect and sending money to the target country via third parties in multiple countries. The intelligence revealed that the suspect components and funds were being sent to the same country. The original suspect was arrested by law enforcement agencies in a makeshift bomb factory.

7

Proliferation Financing

In the previous book I mentioned the black market for 'lost' nuclear weaponry and with the current war on terrorism the proliferation of weapons of mass destruction, especially those in the hands of fanatics, is of serious concern. Yes we all are aware that Saddam only had spud guns to play with but there is always going to be someone somewhere (probably the little man in North Korea) who would like to really push the button.

Whereas the problem is one of governments to resolve and their plans are probably on some cd-rom dumped in a waste bin somewhere, the various financial institutions need to be aware of the potential problems and possible areas where not only weapons but materials that are an important part of weapon construction can be traded.

Globally all States, in accordance with their national laws should adopt and enforce effective laws which prohibit any non-State individual to;

- manufacture,
- acquire,
- possess,
- develop,
- transport,
- transfer

or use nuclear, chemical or biological weapons and their means of delivery, in particular for terrorist purposes, as well as attempts to engage in any of the foregoing activities, participate in them as an accomplice, assist or finance them.

All jurisdictions should take and enforce effective measures to establish domestic controls to prevent the proliferation of nuclear, chemical, or biological weapons and their means of delivery, including by establishing appropriate controls over related materials and to this end shall:

1. Establish, develop, review and maintain appropriate effective national export and trans-shipment controls over such items.
2. Include appropriate laws and regulations to control export, transit, trans-shipment and re-export and controls on providing funds and services relate

to such export and trans-shipment such as financing, and transporting that would contribute to proliferation.

3. Establish end-user controls; and enforce appropriate criminal or civil penalties for violations of such export control laws and regulations.

Now you are probably asking what the hell has this to do with money laundering, this is not a financial institution, lawyer, accountant etc problem. Hopefully the following will identify your potential participation in the process.

Assessing the threat of proliferation financing

The threat of proliferation is significant and the consequences are severe. Proliferation has many guises but ultimately involves the transfer and export of technology, goods, software, services or expertise that could be used in nuclear, chemical or biological weapon-related programmes, including delivery systems; it poses a significant threat to global security. If appropriate safeguards are not established, maintained and enforced for sensitive materials, technology, services and expertise, they can become accessible to individuals and entities seeking to profit from the acquisition and resale, or for intended use in WMD programmes.

They can also find their way into the hands of terrorists willing to employ WMD in acts of terrorism. There is evidence that terrorist organisations continue to pursue chemical, biological, radiological or nuclear (CBRN) capabilities, and it is worrying that their efforts are increasing. In such circumstances, terrorism financing as it relates to providing financial support to terrorist organisations that endeavour to acquire and/or deploy CBRN weapons is then by its nature also contributing to proliferation.

Proliferation financing is an element for the movement of proliferation-sensitive items and as such, contributes to global instability and potential catastrophic loss of life if WMD are developed and deployed. As with international criminal networks, proliferation support networks are using the international financial system to carry out transactions and business deals.

Proliferation is the transfer and export of nuclear, chemical or biological weapons; their means of delivery and related materials.

This could include, inter alia, technology, goods, software, services or expertise, i.e.;

- Means of delivery: missiles, rockets and other unmanned systems capable of delivering nuclear, chemical, or biological weapons that are specially designed for such use.
- Related materials: materials, equipment and technology covered by relevant multilateral treaties and arrangements, or included on national control lists, which could be used for the design, development, production or use of nuclear, chemical and biological weapons and their means of delivery.

Proliferation financing is providing financial services for the transfer and export of nuclear, chemical or biological weapons; their means of delivery and related materials.

It involves, in particular, the financing of trade in proliferation sensitive goods, but could also include other financial support to individuals or entities engaged in proliferation.

Whereas I accept that this problem is a government one and involves the intelligence services in various countries bound by pacts and agreements, research has identified that the financial system has been used by criminals/terrorists to finance WMD proliferation.

Although Governments have established numerous multilateral arrangements to detect and prohibit proliferation including the Nuclear Non-Proliferation Treaty; traditional arrangements have not focused on proliferation financing. The detection of even one proliferation related case should raise concern, in particular, given the consequences that the use of or threat of using a biological, chemical, radiological or nuclear weapon can have on the international community, including the international financial system.

Governments have established and maintained extensive export controls and safeguards to prevent the acquisition of the required goods, services, technology and expertise by proliferators or their supporters. These controls, including safeguards such as the registration, licensing and pre-approvals for the manufacture and export of a broad range of designated goods, are fundamental in preventing proliferators from acquiring important goods, services, technologies and expertise. **However, these controls are not uniform across jurisdictions, and some jurisdictions have yet to implement the requirements mentioned in several international treaties to detect and restrict trade in proliferation sensitive goods and items.**

In addition, trade globalisation and steady advances in technology are obviously providing fresh challenges for the maintenance of effective export controls. Trade volumes continue to rise and trade patterns are less discernable.

Dual use goods/technology

Further, there is a growing range of goods and technology that have commercial applications as well as applications for WMD and WMD delivery systems (i.e. 'dual use' goods), and while proliferators previously attempted to buy or sell whole manufactured systems with the effective control systems, there is an increasing trend to purchase or sell more elementary components. Proliferation networks will continuously seek out and exploit weaknesses in the global export control system and international financial system.

Export controls are used to inter alia prevent dual use and other sensitive goods (listed and unlisted) from being exported to known individuals and entities that are involved in WMD proliferation-related activities. However, it is challenging for authorities to designate and monitor trade in all relevant 'dual use' goods.

One or two decades ago financial institutions were in a better position to collect and scrutinise information regarding the ultimate end–use of potentially sensitive proliferation items. However, procurement networks have become more complex over time, increasing:

- the number of individuals involved;
- the trade in sub-components; and
- the indisputable probability that the true end-users of proliferation sensitive goods will avoid detection.

This implies, inter alia, the acquisition of technology with the aim of shifting the production capacity to their own country or to generally unwitting production facilities in other countries.

With changes to the procurement process and a significant increase in the number of normally innocuous items that now have potential proliferation-sensitive applications, it has become far more difficult to assess with a sufficient degree of certainty whether an item will truly be used for civilian purposes.

While information that is held by intelligence services has not changed significantly, information held by other entities, including suppliers and financial institutions is greatly diminished. For example, it is common today for suppliers to only have information on intermediary players in the procurement chain.

Suppliers deliver dual use products and other critical items that are often not subject to export controls, to traders, brokers and other entities responsible for forwarding on the items as inputs to other facilities where proliferation sensitive goods are then produced.

Today, financial institutions have far less information about end-users and ultimate end-uses of items underlying financial transactions. Apart from information that is collected concerning their clients, information in transactions that describe items is generally too vague and/or would require a significant amount of technical knowledge to determine if they were sensitive or not.

Proliferation networks operate globally. Advances in economic integration and in the volume and speed of international travel and trade, facilitate the global transfer of sensitive items by proliferators.

Proliferators mask their acquisitions as legitimate trade. They exploit global commerce, e.g. by operating in countries with high volumes of international trade or utilising free-trade zones, where their illicit procurements and shipments are more likely to escape scrutiny. However, in reaction to this phenomenon, jurisdictions with a highly developed and efficient export control system make enhanced efforts to control these transactions.

In contrast to trafficking in nuclear or radiological material, these purchases are mostly settled using a range of financial transactions, normally through the formal financial sector.

Dual use goods are items that have both commercial and military or proliferation applications. This can include goods that are components of a weapon, or those that would be used in the manufacture of a weapon (e.g. certain machine tools that are used for repairing automobiles can also be used to manufacture certain component parts of missiles).

Export control systems are continuously updated and expanded to incorporate new goods and technologies. This has forced proliferators in some cases to adopt a different strategy to select, where feasible, elementary components rather than complete subassemblies to elude authorities. However, a high level of technical expertise is often required to integrate various elementary goods into a full assembly, and as such, proliferation networks may continue to attempt to illegally purchase subassemblies or complete systems. They may even attempt to acquire the manufacturing company.

Dual use goods destined for proliferation use are difficult to identify even when detailed information on a particular good is available. Regardless of the amount of information provided for a particular good, highly specialised knowledge and experience is often needed to determine if a good may be used for proliferation. The table below includes a small list of the kinds of items – with only minimal information – that are often classified as dual use by jurisdictions, it is by no means an exhaustive list of dual use items, as national dual use goods lists often contain hundreds of items, as well as the technology used to design, manufacture or use such items.

Dual use items can be described in common terms with many uses – such as 'scrubbers' – or in very specific terms with more specific proliferation uses – such as metals with certain characteristics. Further, many of the goods listed in this table are only regarded as dual use if they measure-up to very precise performance specifications.

Examples of general dual use items

- Nuclear
- Chemical
- Biological
- Missile and delivery
- Centrifuges
- Scrubbers
- Bacterial strains

- Accelerometers
- High-speed cameras
- Mixing vessels
- Fermenters
- Aluminium alloys
- Composites
- Centrifuges

- Filters
- Aluminium powders
- Maraging steel
- Elevators
- Mills
- Gyroscopes
- Mass spectrometers
- Condensers
- Presses
- Isostatic presses
- Pulse generators
- Connectors
- Pumps
- Composites
- X-ray flash apparatus
- Coolers
- Spray dryers
- Maraging steel
- Pressure gauges
- Precursors
- Tanks
- Homing devices
- Ignition
- Pumps
- Growth media
- Oxidants
- Vacuum pumps
- Reactors
- Machine tools
- Heat exchanges

A foreign trade pattern abused for proliferation

An importer may arrange for the shipment of goods directly with an exporter or could use a front company, broker or both a front company and a broker.

Similarly, payments may be settled with a manufacturer's bank either: directly; using a front company; using a broker; or the manufacturer may arrange for payment using Letter of Credit or other payment method.

Proliferators rely on support structures that exploit a number of channels to facilitate the purchase, sale, export or import of sensitive goods. As with most illicit trafficking, proliferation networks work to conceal the end-user of traded goods, the goods themselves as well as the entities involved and associated financial transactions.

To ensure that authorities do not detect the real end-use of sensitive goods being exported, networks may use intermediaries and front companies to arrange for the trade and export of goods by witting or unwitting companies. However, the use of intermediaries is not in itself an indication for proliferation financing. Exporters employ intermediaries for legitimate purposes. When exporting out of or through jurisdictions with well-developed export control regimes, intermediaries and front companies may use fraudulent documents, such as false end-use certificates, forged export and re-export certificates. Couriers or other facilitators may be used to ensure that the transfer of goods, in particular at main transit points, avoids inspection to ensure safe entry of the goods by land, sea, or air.

The theft of high value materials from authorised storage facilities with the intention of resale must also be considered a proliferation-relevant activity.

Trans-shipment and diversion

Trans-shipment centres, commonly known as 'hubs' are cargo-sorting and redistribution destinations through which much international trade is routed. Examples of major international hubs include the Netherlands (Rotterdam), the UK (Felixstowe), Hong Kong, Singapore, and Malaysia (Port Klang).

Free trade zones are destinations where goods pass through on route to their final destination. Free trade zones, while not always trans-shipment hubs, are sometimes used by exporters as the landing post for goods destined for end-users in nearby jurisdictions. Examples include the United Arab Emirates (Jebel Ali free port), Malta and Cyprus.

Routing goods through trans-shipment hubs offers a number of advantages to those seeking to facilitate international trade. It is common practice amongst cargo shippers and helps lower shipping costs by reducing the number of ship movements required. Although trans-shipment routes are often highly complex, with goods travelling through many hubs, they provide the opportunity to link up with other vessels going directly to the end-user destination and do not require specially charted ships to be commissioned or to travel empty – cutting the cost to the importer. Goods travelling through a hub may be small volume – single packages or containers. Many hubs, like free trade zones, have the additional advantage of being close to their eventual cargo destination.

For the procurer of illicit goods seeking to avoid detection, the advantages of Free Trade Zones and Trans-shipment Hubs are that less stringent export controls are often applied by states to goods being transhipped or routed through free trade zones than to goods entering their territory through other means. As goods do not officially enter the economy in question they may be beyond effective customs and police control.

The final journey may be by smaller cargo vessel or it may be completed by land or air. Although certain destinations maintain accurate data for cargo passing through their ports for commercial reasons the constant rerouting of goods can make effective tracking of cargo difficult.

Diversion occurs when the supplier, broker or end-user deliberately tries to conceal the eventual destination of a particular shipment. For instance, when diverted goods pass through a third country, an individual in that country who is aware of the true destination of the goods seeks to establish himself as a false end-user. Entities or persons seeking to conceal the true end-user have the best chance of doing so by diverting or routing goods through third countries with weak (or non-existent) controls. Diversion points used by proliferators will often be ports where national shipping carriers call and where goods can be passed on to other cargo shippers on route to their final destination.

While trans-shipment and diversion make traditional counter-proliferation controls harder to enforce it can result in a financial intelligence trail for investigators and customs authorities to follow breaches of export control law. Financial flows required to move goods from one place to the next could provide authorities with supplementary information to link up entities of concern with transport routes and ultimate end-users.

Proliferators' use of the formal financial sector

Some elements of proliferation support networks may operate for financial gain and the formal financial sector can be abused by networks to carry out transactions and business dealings worldwide. Apart from transaction and business activities in the informal financial sector, proliferation financing can involve traditional trade finance products and transactions.

There have been incidences where proliferation-related transactions are settled through opaque cash or 'barter-like' settlements involving goods such as oil, sensitive military goods or other proliferation sensitive goods. Cash may be used by proliferators to avoid detection by financial monitoring systems. Further, the cash used in payments may have been obtained through illegal activity. Cash payments for goods do not create financial (paper or electronic) trails and therefore do not contribute financial information that may be useful in identifying and combating proliferation activity.

However, it is important for proliferators to have access to the international financial system under most circumstances. Purchases must appear to be legitimate if proliferators are to elude suspicions and they often exploit commercial companies with legitimate businesses.

While there are cases where proliferators have exchanged suitcases of cash, this is not cost effective or efficient and is certainly suspicious. Companies being used unwittingly are aware of the sensitivities surrounding their products and are often required to exercise due diligence with purchasing parties. It would be quite suspicious, for example, if an individual tried to purchase a piece of machining equipment with cash.

International trade has well established instruments to facilitate imports and exports while mitigating business risks, including the general level of trust between parties engaged in a transaction. Trust is exploited by proliferators to ensure the minimum amount of scrutiny. Traditional trade financing contracts clearly define the specific terms of trade and ensure each party that the other will follow through on their end of the arrangement. The most common payment methods include open account payment, pre-payment, documents against payment and letters of credit. Trade can also be financed through more direct means via credit. These are discussed in more detail below.

Proliferation networks also use financial flows to pay intermediaries and suppliers outside the network. Similar to actors that supply proliferation networks, financial institutions are usually unwitting facilitators of proliferation, as a consequence of the complexity of dual use goods, the involvement of illicit intermediaries, front companies and illegal trade brokers.

Disrupting and deterring proliferation and proliferation financing

The most significant risk factors include:

- laws or enforcement capacity,
- its size, openness, industrial make-up
- and volume of trade with respect to the economy and/or geography.

Specific factors raised include:

- Weak or non-existent export control regime and/or weak enforcement of existing export control regime.
- Non-party to relevant international conventions and treaties regarding the non-proliferation of weapons of mass destruction.
- Lack of implementation of relevant UNSCRs.
- The presence of industry that produces WMD components or dual use goods.
- A relatively well-developed financial system or an open economy.
- The nature of the jurisdiction's export trade (volumes and geographical end-users).
- A financial sector that provides a high number of financial services in support of international trade.
- Geographic proximity, significant trade facilitation capacity (e.g. trade hub or free trade zone), or other factors causing a jurisdiction to be used frequently as a trans-shipment point from countries that manufacture dual use goods to countries of proliferation concern.
- Movement of people and funds to or from high-risk countries can provide a convenient cover for activities related to proliferation financing.
- Lack of working coordination between the customs authority and the export licensing authority of a specific jurisdiction.
- A jurisdiction that has secondary markets for technology.

Financial institutions providing trade finance services are at risk of being abused for proliferation financing with financial services and products such as letters of credit (or documentary credits), loans and electronic funds transfers. The Hawalla and money remittance services and the insurance sector are also at risk for proliferation financing and proliferation networks may also use cash couriers to finance proliferation.

Witting and unwitting participants

Proliferators will abuse typical trade structures to facilitate their activities, this includes supporters, financiers, logistical support, front companies, assets, shippers and facilitators. Entities that are knowingly engaged in proliferation, such as a front company, may also be involved in legitimate business. Other participants used by a network may knowingly support proliferation, be 'wilfully blind' that they are being used for illicit purposes, or are truly unwitting participants. When an entity is engaged in both legitimate and illicit trade it may be less likely for financial institutions to suspect illegal activity.

Front and other companies

In individual cases, proliferation networks have employed companies to conceal the true end-use or end-user of traded goods. Most front companies are sensitive to public exposure and disruption of legitimate activities.

Front companies established by proliferators conduct transactions similar to those of companies engaged in legitimate business. **Front companies used by proliferators may be similar to those established by money launderers. As is the practice of other criminal organisations, proliferators create companies for a seemingly legitimate commercial purpose and co-mingle illegal funds with funds generated by legal commercial activity.**

In some cases, front companies established by proliferators do not engage in any legal activity at all. Front companies may use fraudulent accounting practices and establish various offshore entities in jurisdictions with lax controls to disguise illegal operations. Proliferators are also known to change the names of front companies, or to use multiple names for the same front company, to prevent the detection of the companies' association with proliferation – or other illicit activity.

Front companies used by proliferators are often located in a major trading hub of a foreign jurisdiction with lax export controls but may also be found in jurisdictions with more established controls. They can be shell corporations with a fictitious business and physical location or can have normal commercial and industrial operations.

Front companies can arrange shipping services, routing or re-routing goods acquired by the importer or its intermediary. The same and/or additional companies can also be located in jurisdictions with weak financial controls, enabling related financial transactions to settle the underlying trade without detection.

In exceptional cases, front companies may seek complicity within a particular jurisdiction's government for signoff by national authorities, by production of false cargo manifests to misdirect customs, law enforcement, and intelligence as to the true nature of the goods being exported and their end-use.

Brokers

Brokers are involved in the negotiation or arrangement of transactions that may involve the transfer of items (often between third world countries) or who buy, sell or arrange the transfer of such items that are in their ownership.

In addition they may also become involved in ancillary activities that facilitate the movement of items such as, but not limited to:

- providing insurance;
- marketing;
- financing; and
- transportation/logistics.

Illicit brokers illegally participate in proliferation by circumventing existing controls and obfuscating trade activities.

Brokers used by proliferation networks are often individuals relying on simple commercial structures, who are very mobile (financially and geographically) so that they can operate from any jurisdiction.

Other intermediaries

Intermediaries may include companies and individuals that purchase or sell sensitive goods for further manufacture or redistribution. Intermediaries may have a particular knowledge of a jurisdiction's commercial infrastructure. Intermediaries that are knowingly engaged in proliferation will use this knowledge to exploit vulnerabilities in export control systems to the advantage of the proliferator.

Use of Financial Institutions

Proliferation networks may:

- use financial institutions to hold and transfer funds, settle trade and pay for services.
- use both private and public financial institutions for international transactions.

States seeking to acquire WMDs may also use foreign branches and subsidiaries of state-owned banks for proliferation finance-related activities, giving these institutions the responsibility of managing funds and making and receiving payments associated with proliferation-related procurement or other transactions. These subsidiaries may be engaged in both legitimate and illegitimate transactions.

Financial institution settlement of international trade transactions

Financial institutions support international trade in three main ways:

- A financial institution's products and services are used to settle international trade transactions. These products and services range from payment transfers from the importer to the exporter to more sophisticated financial products, such as a letters of credit, documentary collections and guarantees.
- The financial sector provides export finance to bridge the time between the need of funds for production, transportation etc. and the payment for such products by the importer. Banks and other export credit agencies provide loans and credit to traders to enable them to purchase and resale goods or equipment.
- The financial sector may provide insurance against certain risks involved in the trading process. Insurance instruments can protect exporters against the non-payment of buyers and insure against non-compliance by the seller and risks arising from government policy changes (i.e. political risk).

The role of financial institutions in trade finance is not limited to the provision of financial products. In addition, financial institutions provide valuable information to investors and traders depending on the financial service they provide to their client. They may inform their clients about present and future money and capital market conditions.

They operate through established international banking relationships with correspondents, which give their clients greater assurance about the legitimacy of their trading partners. While correspondent banks are used to facilitate trade transactions, the use of these banks does not provide legitimacy to the commercial parties to a transaction. Depending on the trade finance process used, it may provide a greater assurance of payment, however, it does not account for the legitimacy of a trading partner.

Trade settlement

In all business transactions, there is some commercial risk. However, in the international context, this risk can be magnified, as information about foreign companies (e.g. importers, foreign banks, economic conditions and foreign laws) would likely be less familiar to the exporter and his bank, than in respect of domestic clients. This applies equally to both exporters and importers.

For the exporter, commercial risks include the importer not accepting the merchandise or not paying for it once it is accepted. The importer risks that the exporter does not deliver the products at the agreed quality and time. In both cases, the capital invested in the purchase or sale – be it out of companies' own funds or through a credit facility – is at risk.

A key consideration in mitigating commercial risk is the choice of trade financing instrument. Traders typically choose from three main methods for settling trade transactions, depending on the extent of commercial risk:

- Clean Payments (open account and payment in advance),
- Documentary Collections, and
- Letters of Credit.

Research shows that It is estimated that about 80% of global trade is conducted not by using the traditional process of letters of credit and collections, but may be simply clean payments processed through financial institutions. Of the remaining 20% of global trade it is estimated that as much as ten percent may be transacted completely outside the traditional financial system.

The following is a description of the three main methods of settling trade transactions.

Clean payments

Clean Payments are typically limited to transactions between well-established, ongoing trading partners or other partnerships where significant trust exists between the importer and exporter. In clean payment transactions, the role of the financial institutions is limited to the transfer of funds. Documents, such as title documents and invoices, are transferred between trading parties without a financial institution acting as the intermediary. Clean payments may be used for any purpose and are not specific to transactions between an importer and exporter.

As mentioned, the use of open account transactions by entities engaged in international trade is most commonly used. The decline in use of letters of credit or other trade finance vehicles is in relation to the overall growth in world trade. The actual transaction volume for letters of credit has remained relatively stable over time while the volume of world trade has grown.

A significant advantage of clean payments is that the administrative costs, including the time required to settle the transaction and the fee paid to a financial institution, are minimal.

The two most common types of clean payments are open account and payment in advance.

Open account

An open account transaction involves the exporter shipping the goods and sending the trade documents directly to the importer. Once the goods are received, the importer arranges through its financial institution to forward payment to the exporter. In this arrangement, the exporter bears all risk and, in the absence of other financial arrangements, cannot access the funds until payment is received from the importer.

Payment in advance (full or partial)

A payment in advance transaction reverses the order of an open account transaction. The first step involves the importer providing payment to the exporter as agreed. Once the exporter receives payment, the goods are shipped and the documents sent to the importer. In this arrangement, the importer bears all risk. In addition, there is an opportunity cost to the importer of using the funds prior to the goods being received.

Financial institutions participating in open account transactions will monitor transactions in accordance with domestic anti-money laundering and counter-terrorist financing regulations. This typically involves undertaking the appropriate customer due diligence and record keeping as outlined in local regulatory requirements.

The level of scrutiny and information available on the underlying transaction will depend on the financial institution's exposure to credit and reputation risk associated with the nature of the customer relationship or its participation in the transaction. For example, because an institution's risk exposure when participating in an open account transaction is low, it is quite possible that it would not scrutinise (or even see) the documents supporting the transaction (e.g. bills of lading or invoices).

Documentary collections

Documentary Collections involve the exporter transferring documents (such as an invoice and transportation documents) through exporter's bank to the bank designated by the importer. The importer is able to retrieve the documents once it has made payment or accepted drafts for future payment and obtain release of the goods. In simple terms, banks act as intermediaries to collect payment from the buyer in exchange for the transfer of documents that enable the holder to take possession of the goods. In a typical collections transaction, the bank does not have title or control over the goods.

As in the case of an open account transaction, there is a risk of non-payment by the importer, because financial institutions involved in the transaction do not guarantee payment or assume credit risk. The role of financial institutions is to act as an intermediary to forward documents from the exporter to the importer upon receipt of payment (Documents against Payment) or the importer's promise of payment at a later date (Documents against Acceptance). The banks are under no obligation to authenticate documents.

Documentary collection process

The documentary collection procedure involves the step-by-step exchange of documents giving title to goods for either cash or a contracted promise to pay at a later time. The diagram following the description below illustrates by way of example only each numbered step.

1. Contract for the purchase and sale of goods
The Buyer and Seller agree on the terms of sale of goods:

- specifying a documentary collection as the means of payment,
- naming a Collecting Bank (usually the buyer's bank), and
- listing required documents.

2. Seller ships the goods
The Seller ships the goods to the Buyer and obtains a transport document from the shipping firm/agent. Various types of transport documents (which may or may not be negotiable) are used in international trade and only where required by the underlying transaction is a negotiable document.

3. Seller presents documents to Remitting Bank
The Seller prepares and presents a document package to his bank (the Remitting Bank) consisting of:

- a collection order specifying the terms and conditions under which the bank is to hand over documents to the Buyer and receive payment, and
- other documents (e.g. transport document, insurance document, certificate of origin, inspection certificate, etc.) as required by the buyer.

4. Remitting Bank sends documents to Collecting Bank
The Remitting Bank sends the documentation package by mail or by courier to the Collecting Bank in the Buyer's country with instructions to present them to the Buyer and collect payment.

5. The Collecting Bank reviews and provides documents to Buyer
The Collecting Bank

- reviews the documents making sure they appear to be as described in the collection order,
- notifies the Buyer about the terms and conditions of the collection order, and
- releases the documents once the payment or acceptance conditions have been met. Acceptances under documentary collections are known as 'Trade

Acceptances' which, when accepted (by the Buyer), only carry the obligation of the buyer as opposed to a 'Bankers Acceptance' commonly used under a letter of credit which carries the obligation of a bank.

While a collecting bank may be in the buyer's country it need not be.

6. Buyer provides payment to Collecting Bank
The Buyer
- makes a cash payment, or if the collection order allows, signs an acceptance (promise of the Buyer to pay at a future date) and
- receives the documents and takes possession of the shipment.

7. Collecting Bank provides payment to Remitting Bank
The Collecting Bank pays the Remitting Bank either with an immediate payment or, at the maturity date of the accepted bill of exchange if it receives payment from the Buyer.

8. The Remitting Bank pays the Seller.

Letters of credit

A letter of credit (also known widely as a documentary credit) is the written and almost always irrevocable promise of a bank to pay a seller the amount specified in the credit, subject to compliance with the stated terms. The fact the seller is relying on the promise of a bank rather than the buyer for payment is the biggest distinction between a letter of credit and a documentary collection transaction.

Documentary credits provide a high level of protection and security to both buyers and sellers engaged in international trade. The seller is assured that payment will be made by a bank so long as the terms and conditions of the credit are met. The buyer is assured that payment will be released to the seller only after the bank has received the documents called for in the credit and those documents comply with the terms and conditions of the credit.

Although documentary credits provide good protection and are the preferred means of payment in many international transactions, they do have limitations. They do not, for example, ensure that the goods actually shipped are as ordered. It is up to the parties to settle questions of this nature between themselves. Documentary credits will also have higher transaction costs than other settlement methods. A letter of credit is an international established practice offering the best level of legal/contractual certainty, and therefore constitutes one of the most reliable payment methods for international transactions. A core element of the letter of credit is the concept that banks deal with documents and not with goods, services or performance to which the documents may relate and banks examine documents presented under letters of credit 'on their face' in compliance with international standards banking practice.

While this covers the traditional commercial letter of credit, standby letters of credit and bank guarantees are often frequently used for the purchase of goods and services internationally.

Revocable credits are rarely used today and are no longer included in international rules such as the International Chamber of Commerce Unified Customs and Practise (UCP).

Basic documentary credit procedure

The documentary credit procedure involves the step-by-step exchange of documents required by the credit for either cash or a contracted promise to pay at a later time. There are four basic groupings of steps in the procedure:

- Issuance;
- Amendment, if any;
- Utilisation; and
- Settlement.

A simplified example follows:

(a) Issuance

Issuance describes the process of the buyer's applying for and the issuing bank opening a documentary credit and the issuing bank's formal notification of the seller either directly or through an advising bank.

Contract – The Buyer and Seller agree on the terms of sale:

- specifying a documentary credit as the means of payment,
- naming an Advising bank (usually the Seller's bank), and
- listing required documents.

The naming of an Advising Bank may be done by the buyer or may be chosen by the issuing bank based on its correspondence.

Issue credit – The Buyer applies to his bank (Issuing Bank) and the issuing bank opens a documentary credit naming the Seller as beneficiary based on specific terms and conditions that are listed in the credit.

Documentary credit – The Issuing Bank sends the documentary credit either directly or through an advising bank named in the credit. An advising bank may act as a bank nominated to pay or negotiate (nominated bank) under the credit or act as a confirming bank where it adds its undertaking to the credit in addition to that of the issuing bank. Only in those cases where an advising bank is not nominated to negotiate or confirm the credit is the role of that bank simply an advising bank.

Credit advice – The advising, nominating or confirming bank informs (advises) the seller of the documentary credit.

(b) Amendment
Amendment describes the process whereby the terms and conditions of a documentary credit may be modified after the credit has been issued.

When the seller receives the documentary credit, it may disagree with the terms and conditions (e.g. the transaction price listed in the credit may be lower than the originally agreed upon price) or may be unable to meet specific requirements of the credit (e.g. the time may be too short to effect shipment).

If the seller wants to amend the terms prior to transacting, the seller can request these from the buyer. It is at the discretion of the buyer to adopt the proposed amendments and request an amendment to be issued by the issuing bank. An amended letter of credit would be issued by the issuing bank to the seller through the same channel as the original documentary letter of credit.

Title only transfers if a document of title is required under the credit.

Amendments to a letter of credit require the agreement of the issuing bank, confirming bank (if any), and the beneficiary to become effective.

(c) Utilisation
Utilisation describes the procedure for the seller's shipping of the goods, the transfer of documents from the seller to the buyer through the banks (presentation), and the transfer of the payment from the buyer to the seller through the banks (settlement). For example:

Seller ships goods – The seller (beneficiary) ships the goods to the buyer and obtains the documents required by the letter of credit.

Seller presents documents to Advising or Confirming Bank or directly to the Issuing Bank – The seller prepares and presents a document package to his bank (the advising or confirming bank) consisting of

- the transport document if required by the credit, and
- other documents (e.g. commercial invoice, insurance document, certificate of origin, inspection certificate, etc.) as required by the document package.

Nominated or Confirming Bank reviews documents and pays Seller – The nominating or confirming bank

- reviews the documents making certain the documents are in conformity with the terms of the credit and
- pays the seller (based upon the terms of the credit) which may mean that payment does not occur until after. An advising bank does not normally examine the documents, but simply **forwards them on to the issuing bank**

Advising, Nominated or Confirming Bank transfers documents to Issuing Bank – The Issuing Bank

- reviews the documents making certain the documents are in conformity with the terms of the credit, under advice to the Buyer that the documents have arrived, and
- pays the beneficiary through the advising bank

Buyer reimburses the Issuing Bank – The Buyer immediately reimburses the amount paid by the issuing bank

Buyer receives documents and access to goods.

(d) Settlement

Settlement describes the different ways in which payment may be effected to the seller from the buyer through the banks. The form of payment is specified in the original

The Sight Credit (Settlement by Payment) – In a sight credit, the value of the credit is available to the exporter as soon as the terms and conditions of the credit have been met (as soon as the prescribed document package has been presented to and checked by the issuing, nominated or confirming bank and found to be conforming to the terms and conditions of the credit) or once the advising bank has received the funds from the issuing bank (unconfirmed). Payment may be affected directly by the nominated bank or confirming bank upon their examination of the documents and they are reimbursed for that payment by the issuing bank.

The Usance Credit (Settlement by Acceptance) – In a Usance Credit, the beneficiary presents the required document package to the bank along with a time draft drawn on the issuing, nominated or confirming bank, or a third bank for the value of the credit. Once the documents have been found to be in order, the draft is accepted by the bank upon which it is drawn (the draft is now called an acceptance) and it may be returned to the seller who holds it until maturity.

The Deferred Payment Credit – In a deferred payment credit the issuing bank and/or the nominated or confirming bank accepts the documents and pays the beneficiary after a set period of time. The issuing, nominated or confirming bank makes the payment at the specified time, when the terms and conditions of the credit have been met.

Negotiation is the term used where a bank other than the issuing bank agrees to advance funds or discount drafts to the exporter before the issuing bank has paid. Discounting an accepted draft has the same effect.

A *letter of credit* will normally require the presentation of several documents including a Draft Commercial Invoice, Transport Document, Insurance Document, Certificates of Origin and Inspection, Packing and Weight Lists.

Export financing

Through a variety of sources and structures, exporters can obtain financing (working capital) to facilitate their trading activities and bridge the time from which they spend money on an export activity (for example, securing an export order) until the moment of payment. Working capital financing can be applied to the manufacture and development of goods prior to shipment, or be applied to business activities following shipment but prior to receipt of payment.

The following section briefly describes the following types of trade finance:

- Direct Loans or general credit facility.
- Note Purchases (also known as forfaiting).
- Factoring.
- Guarantees.

Direct Loans
Acting independently or as part of a syndicate, financial institutions and other entities offer loans to facilitate export transactions. There are two basic types of loans. Buyer credit involves an arrangement to finance exports generally related to a specific contract. Supplier credit transactions are structured to provide the exporter with the ability to provide its buyer with extended payment terms. These loans may also be backed by export or buyer credit guarantees provided by the governments of the countries involved.

Drafts are not always required by a credit.

Note Purchases/Forfaiting
Financial entities can purchase promissory notes or bills of exchange issued by foreign buyers to exporters for the purchase of goods and services, freeing up cash for the exporter.

Factoring

In international trade, factoring is the purchase or discounting of a foreign account receivable for cash at a discount from the face value. While factoring is primarily undertaken by non-bank financial entities, banks may participate in factoring if the exporter has obtained accounts receivable insurance that guarantees the liquidity of the accounts.

Guarantees

Guarantees are provided to or by financial institutions on behalf of exporters. Two popular types of export guarantees are pre-shipment and performance guarantees.

Pre-shipment Guarantees encourage other financial institutions to advance pre-shipment loans to fund the upfront costs associated with an export contract.

Performance Guarantees providing contract performance cover to buyers on behalf of the exporter.

It should be noted that both guarantees and standby letters of credit may be used in various ways to generate the purchase or sale of goods or services. In those cases many of the documents outlined in the steps above may or may not be utilised as part of the transaction.

Transaction risks for importers vs. exporters

Importers and exporters consider these transactional risks in conducting legitimate trade transactions. The product choice will depend on the level of trust between the buyer and seller. Proliferators will also consider transactional risks when deciding how to sell/purchase and receive payment for/send payment for goods.

Risk management and customer due diligence (CDD)

All financial institutions involved in trade finance, no matter what their business line, have both commercial incentives and legal obligations to conduct CDD and potentially account monitoring. But the nature and depth of CDD undertaken, and how it is organised, can vary significantly between financial institutions, from transaction to transaction and based on the regulations in the local jurisdiction.

Some elements of CDD are universal: CDD processes include the identification and, in a risk-based manner, the verification of the identity of customers and reasonable measures to identify and verify the identity of beneficial owners, obtaining information on the purposes and intended nature of the business relationships and conducting ongoing due diligence. Of these components, the identification and verification of identity of customers are requirements that need to be completed in all situations.

The implementation of other components of CDD is variable, depending on the risks associated with the transaction and the legal requirements in the jurisdictions involved. A reasonably implemented risk-based approach may allow for a determination of the extent and quantity of information required, and the mechanism used to meet these standards.

The CDD process that a financial institution will perform before they act or an international trade transaction will be dependent upon a number of factors, these include:

- Specific regulatory requirements or guidance to which it is subject.
- The role which it will be required to perform in the transaction.
- The institution's own exposure to financial or reputational risk through the transaction.
- Its assessment of the risk posed by the country in which the instructing party is based or operates.
- Its assessment of the risk nature of the underlying trade business (i.e. the goods, products or services being traded.).
- Whether any other higher risk parties appear to be involved as owners or intermediaries.

Appropriate CDD measures, relying in particular the factors above, are a critical first step for a financial institution to mitigate the risk of proliferation financing.

Where the financial institution is granting any form of credit to the party from whom instructions are expected, then more extensive information would be requested as part of the CDD process, focused particularly on the client's financial standing, credit risk, and ability to repay. Equally where the financial institution assesses a customer to be higher risk then it may well employ 'enhanced CDD' to the extent that a risk-based approach is allowed by the relevant regulatory authority.

In a letter of credit transaction, for example, financial institutions view different parties in the transaction as their customers for CDD purposes. As an issuing bank the applicant of the credit will be their customer, as an advising, nominating or confirming bank the issuing bank will be their customer. In some cases the beneficiary of a credit may be the customer of the advising, nominated or confirming bank and they may have done CDD on that beneficiary, however in most transactions the banks look to the issuing bank as their customer.

Customer Due Diligence is, depending on the type of internal organisation, conducted at the relationship management area rather than in the trade operations. This area may be a specific relationship manager, a relationship management group, a client coverage area, a compliance group or other area designated by the bank. Depending on the bank's internal policies and procedures the actual point of review, investigation, notification, determination, decision or reporting may vary..

Each financial institution has its own organisational structure for conducting CDD, an element of which may include outsourcing to employees that are located in different countries and undertake transactions that are not local to them. The same obligations for CDD apply no matter what arrangements are in place for implementing them.

Correspondent banks

In the context of trade finance it is important to note that no one financial institution will undertake all aspects of CDD related to a specific transaction; and as discussed, different financial institutions will be responsible for individual elements depending on their role.

Since financial institutions in foreign countries do not necessarily have a presence in all countries or a relationship with all financial institutions, financial institutions are sometimes used as correspondents in the payment chain. Payment transactions are ordered in a foreign country, transit through one or more financial institutions and finally are received by the beneficiary located in a second foreign country. Such transactions may also occur when designated financial institutions in a country are prohibited from conducting financial transactions with institutions from another country, and therefore a correspondent financial institution in a third country is used as an intermediary.

With banks undertaking international financial transactions for themselves and for their customers in jurisdictions where they have no physical presence, correspondent banks must rely on the respondent bank's due diligence and monitoring controls. However, a financial institution would not normally initiate a transaction on behalf of a party it does not know.

A primary objective for any financial institution when agreeing to accept instructions from a correspondent should be to ensure that the correspondent conducts satisfactory CDD on its own customers. Establishing a correspondent relationship might involve an understanding of the customer and documenting that the associated CDD obligations are undertaken.

As part of due diligence which is performed on a potential correspondent it is critical for the financial institution to agree and establish the types of accounts, if any, they will operate and the means of exchanging authenticated (bank to bank) messages. These mechanics are necessary for the handling of international trade transactions.

Although many financial institutions have procedures to ensure that the respondent institution's controls are adequate to mitigate the risk of money laundering and terrorist financing, most do not specifically assess whether a respondent institution has adequate controls to detect and prevent proliferation financing. Such assessments may rely on information that is not currently reviewed as part of correspondent banking procedures, such as information related to a respondent financial institution's trade finance controls or its association with a state proliferator.

Reviewing and monitoring transactions

Financial institutions manage a wide range of risks in the processing of international trade business. In practice risk management will normally include credit risk, including cross border or country risk, and the operational risk. Exposure to money laundering and terrorist financing form part

Customer Due Diligence for correspondent banks is usually conducted in a centralised relationship management area within financial institutions. This area may be a specific relationship manager, a relationship management group, a client coverage area, a compliance group or other area designated by the bank..

If there is potential exposure to proliferation financing, financial institutions consider whether parties involved in payments are named in UN or relevant local sanctions lists or are considered to pose other risks. For example, if the transaction is subject to any export licensing requirements or trade embargoes.

All financial institutions are expected to have a form of financial transaction monitoring in place. The form of monitoring varies between (and within) institutions, including automated or manual checking, or a mixture of both, in order to monitor the transactions handled. This may involve reviewing customers' accounts or patterns of activity.

The information presented to a financial institution will vary according to the nature and complexity of the transaction. The extent to which this information needs to be verified will also vary. In general a financial institution will normally examine trade instructions received to establish whether:

- They have CDD on the instructing party;
- The instruction is consistent with what would normally be expected from the instructing party.

Financial institutions will also check the documents presented to them in accordance with relevant International Chamber of Commerce (ICC) rules and accepted banking practice. Furthermore, where letters of credit are concerned, the vast majority of transactions will be subject to commercial expectations and ICC standards which determine the time allowed for processing the various stages during the lifespan of the letter of credit.

It should be noted that in processing trade finance transactions, financial institutions deal with documents, not the physical goods to which they relate. Any physical inspection of goods will only occur in exceptional circumstances and would tend to relate to wider credit issues where the underlying goods are pledged as security. However, commercial parties to the underlying transaction may use other agencies to independently verify a particular shipment. Consequently inspection and verification measures in relation to physical goods are relatively rare as the vast majority of trade transactions are conducted legally between parties who willingly disclose all the information needed to conclude such transactions.

However, some existing transaction monitoring controls currently employed by financial institutions may result in the detection of proliferation finance. Financial institutions may currently detect transactions associated with proliferation activity by screening transactions against proliferation-related United Nations sanctions lists,(for example the list of individuals and entities designated pursuant to S/RES/1737 (2006), or other local proliferation sanctions lists), to detect the presence of an individual or entity involved in proliferation in the transaction. In some cases, financial institutions may also attempt to verify whether a transaction is subject to any export licensing requirements or trade embargoes by requesting additional verification or documentation, such as export control licenses.

Identifying suspicious activity

There are several points in the trade finance cycle at which financial institutions could potentially detect suspicious activity if provided sufficient information by their customer and/or relevant government authorities. For example, CDD processes can establish risks: whether a customer is a producer or buyer of goods or services which the institution regards as high risk, including ongoing monitoring of transactions, as described above, can also identify activity which may be intended to obscure the ultimate counterparties to the transaction or the eventual destination of goods.

If suspicious activity is suspected, the role of financial institutions is not to determine the underlying criminal activity; but to report suspicious activity in line with their domestic legal framework and relevant local regulations (including data privacy laws).

Financial institutions rely on export control regimes and customs authorities to police the activities of exporters which are its customers, in part as financial institutions are unlikely to have staff technically qualified to understand whether an apparently legitimate or innocent trade transaction is subject to such a control or whether in any event it is actually part of a proliferation finance scheme.

The ability of financial institutions to detect suspicious activity in their trade finance operations is constrained by several factors:

- The description of goods may be too vague and/or technical for a financial institution to determine if it is proliferation-sensitive or not.
- The fragmented nature of the trade cycle and the involvement of different financial institutions in a single transaction.
- The systems used to monitor transactions and volume of transactions will also influence the ability to review information and identify potential suspicious activity. Even where only a single financial institution is involved in a transaction, the organisational complexity of the institution may mean

that no one individual examines all elements of CDD and monitoring associated with a transaction. This can make it difficult to identify complex or large-scale patterns which might indicate suspicious activity.

The detection of fraud or money laundering by financial institutions is based on well-understood indicators and profiles, developed from a substantial case history. Proliferation financing has only recently gained attention and consequently has not necessarily been incorporated into financial institutions' due diligence processes.

Indicators or 'red flags' invariably only become evident after the event when a transaction has already been completed.

The availability of specific information regarding suspicious or high-risk entities is critical, as the factors noted above limit financial institutions' capacity to detect generic patterns associated with proliferation financing. **Therefore, the ability of a financial institution to detect and identify potential proliferation financing is dependent on clear guidance or specific intelligence provided by authorities**.

Money services businesses

Apart from supervised payment services, illegal, informal or registered money services businesses or alternative remittance systems (e.g. Hawallas) can also be used to transfer funds. Entities involved in proliferation financing activity may also use this sector if there is strong detection or monitoring measures in place for financial institutions in the formal sector.

Authorities relevant for export control in most jurisdictions are invariably government agencies.

Ideally, licensing authorities, financial institutions and exporters should work together to ensure compliance with this legislation.

Case studies

The following examples illustrate some of the common techniques used by proliferators to transfer and export technology, goods, services or expertise that contribute to the proliferation of weapons of mass destruction.

These cases indicate that the international financial system is being used to facilitate proliferation and also frequently use letters of credit to settle trade in sensitive goods. In some of the cases there are more simple examples of wire transfers and large cash transactions that are used to move funds in efforts to facilitate proliferation.

While the majority of the cases mentioned illustrate traditional means of trade financing such as letters of credit, there is no evidence that suggests that these financial instruments are more susceptible to potential abuse by proliferators. It would have been very difficult for the financial institution to detect proliferation financing based on evidence provided in the cases that illustrate links to the international financial system.

There is no doubt that proliferation background is more difficult to detect if other financial instruments, such as clean payments, are used. These cases studies describe features of the transactions, which were discovered through subsequent investigation, which would not at the time have provided a meaningful basis for financial institutions to report suspicions. They nevertheless highlight the financial features associated with the underlying acts of proliferation.

Cases involving letters of credit

Letters of credit and front company

In Jurisdiction A, Company A requests that Bank A draw up Letter of Credit (1) and arranges payment for goods from a Front Company.

Bank A issues Line of Credit (1) to the Front Company.

The Front Company then requests Letter of Credit (2) from Bank B in Jurisdiction B and arranges payment using Letter of Credit (1).

Bank B issues Letter of Credit (2) to Company B located in Jurisdiction B.

Company B arranges for shipment of goods to Front Company, arranges documents and tranships goods.

Company B presents documents to Bank B and receives payment.

Front Company receives documents from Bank B, presents for Letter of Credit (1) and alters shipping instructions.

Front Company gets documents and finalizes payment to Bank A.

Company A receives goods at port.

Source: United States

Purchase of magnets through front companies and intermediaries

A proliferator set up front companies and used other intermediaries to purchase magnets that could be used for manufacturing centrifuge bearings.

False declaration documents

Front Company 1 signed documents with the foreign jurisdiction's manufacturing company concerning the manufacturing and trade of magnets, however, it was not declared in these documents, nor was it detected by authorities, that these components could be used to develop WMD.

Diversion

The magnets were transhipped through a neighbouring third jurisdiction to Front Company 2. This jurisdiction was typically used as a 'turntable' for goods i.e. goods are imported and re-exported. The proliferator used an intermediary to arrange for the import and export of the magnets in this third jurisdiction. The intermediary had a sound understanding of the strength and weaknesses of the jurisdiction's export and commercial controls and used this knowledge to conceal the nature of the goods.

Using banks with poor AML/CFT controls

The intermediary also conducted financial transactions to settle trades. The intermediary had accounts with several banks in the third jurisdiction and used these banks to both finance the acquisition of goods and launder the illegal funds used for these transactions. A combination of cash and letters of credit were used to pay for the trade of the magnets, which totalled over 4 million USD.

Source: Gruselle, Bruno, (2007)

Pizzas as weapons of mass destruction (The Thyratron case in Halmstad)

In the spring of 1999 the Swedish Customs found out that a person (P) in Halmstad, via a pizzeria, had exported a thyratron to Iran that was classified as a strategic product and therefore was subject to export control. After an audit and interview with P, suspicions grew that it was a question of smuggling.

A search was made of P's apartment of P and a seizure of a thyratron was made at Arlanda Airport. It was on its way to a jurisdiction of proliferation concern. Earlier another thyratron had already been exported.

P stated that he had been contacted by his cousin in the jurisdiction of proliferation concern in the spring of 1998 who worked at a university in that jurisdiction. The cousin wanted P to get a thyratron to the university.

The producer of the thyratron in the United States directed P to the branch in Sweden. P then falsely stated that he would use it as a degree project at a Swedish university. He subsequently forged an end user statement in order to buy the thyratron.

P paid the company 22,000 SEK and delivered the product to Halmstad. P contacted a forwarding company in order for them to export the thyratron to a university in the jurisdiction of proliferation concern. P wrote a pro forma invoice in the name of the pizzeria (whether it was deep pan or otherwise *has not been determined). The buyer was the university in the jurisdiction of concern. The thyratron was then exported.*

In November 1998 P ordered one more thyratron after an order from another university in the jurisdiction of concern (obviously he was known by then to be able to facilitate the purchase an export of such equipment/components. P ordered the goods and in 27 May 1999 the thyratron was delivered to P in Halmstad.

The forwarding company got an assignment to send it to the jurisdiction of concern. The product was not exported because P had not paid the forwarding company for the cost of the freight terminal. P claimed during interviews that he was under the impression that Iran Air would once again be responsible for all expenses like last time.

During the preliminary investigation the Swedish Customs found documents like dispatch notes for payment from abroad, inter alia, from the jurisdiction of proliferation concern.

Source: Sweden

Letter of credit and front company

A Front Company in a Middle-Eastern jurisdiction of proliferation concern, used the following method in order to obtain goods.

The Front Company represented several large companies located in the jurisdiction of concern that were also established in Europe and other Western countries.

The Front Company stood surety for the delivery of the needed goods to the companies in the jurisdiction of concern and executed eventual after sales services.

The Front Company also has the first contact with the true End User.

The End Users order the needed goods from the Front Company.

The Front Company orders the goods of the different Western companies from ' A', that is to say, only on the basis of the article numbers in the catalogue and informs 'A' about the supplier the goods have to be bought from.

At request a Letter of Credit is opened in favour of 'A'. It also happens that 'A' itself has to look for a supplier on the basis of an article number or article description. This happened worldwide.

'A' orders the goods after having received the order (pro-forma invoice) from the Front Company and the Letter of Credit from the Middle Eastern client or end user.

The goods that were bought outside the Netherlands came in transit to the airport of Schiphol and were delivered at a forwarding agent. The goods were sent from Schiphol airport to the jurisdiction of concern. ('A' did not see the goods itself).

'A' placed the payment received from the end users through the Letter of Credit at the disposal of the Front Company by means of a bank account with a Dutch bank and after deduction of a commission. The suppliers were paid by the Front Company.

Source: The Netherlands

State-owned entities

I have included three known instances of procurement for WMD programmes routed through state-owned banks whose overseas branches and correspondent banking partners facilitate business with foreign suppliers:

Company A, a well-known front company for one of the entities responsible for country Z's ballistic missile programme, in order to buy 'special items' from country X, opened a Letter of Credit at a branch of a state-owned bank in Z's capital. The London branch of the same state-owned bank was named as the Advising Bank and in due course transferred payment to the supplier of the 'special items'.

A branch of the same state-owned bank in another European capital was instructed to transfer over $100,000 to the account of a company in country U, a near neighbour of Z and a known diversionary destination. The company is owned by a well-known procurement agent who asked for the money to be transferred to a specific UK bank in order to cover the purchase of goods associated with a Letter of Credit opened with a branch of the same state-owned bank in Z's capital.

In country Y, a state-owned bank known as the X Commercial Bank was known to have close relations with country Y's main arms exporters. In the past it had routed transactions through European banks. Recently it sought correspondent bank relationships with several banks in a large Asian country, seeking to open Euro and US dollar accounts.

Use of a UK bank in a Diversionary Destination

Trading company B in country Z dealt in laboratory test-equipment for university and research centres and also for the energy sector. It is also known to have procured dual use items for country Z's WMD programmes.

Company B has bank accounts in a number of countries and has a UK account with a UK bank in country U, a known diversionary destination.

Source: United Kingdom

Infringement of export controls and Letter of Credit

This case concerns the infringement of export controls. Strategic goods were exported without the obligatory authorization. The Dutch producer was contacted by a Front Company, in an Asian jurisdiction of proliferation concern, to provide certain strategic goods, carbon fibre with special characteristics. The Dutch producer ordered the materials from two suppliers in other European countries. Payment took place through a Letter of Credit. The bank of the true Asian end user actually issued the letter of credit to the Dutch bank of the producer.

Finally the prosecutor decided to no longer pursue this suspect, since during the pre-trial the testimony of the expert stated that after the specific production performed by the Dutch producer, the end result of the carbon fibre no longer contained the characteristics for which it qualifies as a strategic good.

Source: The Netherlands

Pakistan & Asher Karni

Asher Karni was the principal in an import/export business known as Top-Cape Technology. In July 2003, agents from the US Commerce Department (Commerce) and the Department of Homeland Security (DHS), US Immigration and Customs Enforcement learned that Karni was in the process of acquiring 200 triggered spark gaps from a company in Massachusetts and that he planned to have the triggered spark gaps sent to Top-Cape in South Africa, from where the items, at his instruction, would be re-exported to Pakistan. (Triggered spark gaps are high-speed electrical switches that are capable of sending synchronized electronic pulses. They can be used as detonators of a nuclear device).

US export laws and regulations required the issue of a license for the export of triggered spark gaps to Pakistan. At the request of investigating agents, the manufacturer agreed to disable the triggered spark gaps before they were shipped to Karni's company in South Africa through a broker.

In October 2003, Karni's company illegally sent the triggered spark gaps to Islamabad, Pakistan via Dubai, UAE. Karni was arrested on January 1,

2004, in Denver, CO, when he arrived for a ski vacation. He was detained pending trial. In September 2004, Karni pleaded guilty and cooperated. Karni acted as a middle man for Khan, a Pakistani, in illegally shipping both triggered spark gaps and oscilloscopes to Pakistan. Khan was indicted in April 2005. Karni received credit for his cooperation and was sentenced to 36 months in prison in August 2005.

Financial elements
The triggered spark gaps shipment was financed via letter of credit opened by Khan at the National Bank of Pakistan with the Standard Bank of South Africa.

Source: United States

Thiodiglycol

Immigration and Customs Enforcement, Office of Investigations, through its predecessor agency the United States Customs Service, conducted an investigation into the illegal export of thiodiglycol, which is a precursor for sulphur-containing blister agents found in Mustard Gas. Thiodiglycol is a Chemical Weapons Convention schedule 2 chemical used in the production of sulphur-based blister agents such as mustard gas.

The investigation had revealed that Alcolac International, a United States based company, was shipping large amounts of thiodiglycol out of Baltimore to several trans-shipment countries with a final destination to Iran. During the investigation, agents discovered a large shipment of thiodiglycol with a declared final destination to a 'Far East country.' Federal agents substituted the chemical with water and tracked the shipment from the United States through two trans-shipment countries and ultimately to Iran.

The investigation led the agents to multiple bills of lading for shipments to other companies with one marked 'Trans-shipping is allowed.' A review of the financial documents and related bank records revealed multiple Alcolac Letters of Credit noting preference for immediate payment in cash. They also discovered that individuals attempted to open new accounts under shell companies in the US to facilitate the exportation through a letter of credit.

Alcolac International pleaded guilty to two counts related to the illegal export of thiodyglycol. As a result the company was fined $437,594. Several additional individuals who took part in the illegal exportation of thiodyglycol were also found guilty.

Source: United States

Cases involving other payment methods such as wire transfers and cash transactions

The following show how proliferators have used wire transfers and cash transactions to support their activities. One case actually reveals an example where a proliferator under-valued the shipment in an effort to disguise the true nature of the goods being transferred.

Sponsoring of students by a known WMD procurement entity

Voluntary information received from a Canadian intelligence agency indicated that Individual 1's education in Canada was sponsored by a known WMD procurement entity located in Country X and that Individual 1 was possibly a procurement agent.

Analysis of the intelligence information revealed that Company A, located in Country X, sent Electronic Funds Transfers (EFTs) to Individual 1 and three other individuals (Individuals 2, 3 & 4). For some of the EFTs, the transaction was noted to be for 'cost of study'. All EFTs were sent to personal bank accounts and totalled about $140,000 US.

Other than all receiving funds from Company A, no apparent connections between the four individuals were identified. Individuals 1 & 2 were found to be located in two different Canadian provinces, while no address was found for either Individual 3 or Individual 4.

During the same period, a Large Cash Transaction Report (LCTR) received from a depository financial institution indicated that Individual 2 who appeared to be a student, deposited about $10,000 US into his/her personal account.

It was unknown why Company A would be funding the education of these four individuals. However, the research field in which Company A was apparently involved indicated a possible association to a WMD program. In addition, at the time, Country X was known to sponsor students who agreed to study overseas in science and engineering programs. It was suspected that Country X's objectives were to gain knowledge and expertise in some areas that could be useful for its WMD program.

Source: Canada

AMLINK

R. David Hughes was the president of an Olympia, Washington-based company, AMLINK, a medical supply company, but it was involved in export of commodities that did not match its business profile.

> In June 1996, the US Customs Service began an investigation of the exportation of nuclear power plant equipment by Hughes and AMLINK from Seattle to Cyprus. According to a confidential source, the nuclear power plant equipment was to be shipped from Cyprus to Iran via Bulgaria, in violation of the US embargo on Iran.
>
> The equipment in question was nuclear power plant equipment that had been purchased in an auction by a Washington company, LUCON. The origin of the equipment was a Washington-based power company that led a consortium in the 1970s to develop a nuclear power station in Burlington, Washington.
>
> The power plant was cancelled in 1983, and the equipment was subsequently sold. Hughes worked with another individual, Habib T. Abi-Saad, a Lebanese national with permanent US resident status, to purchase the equipment from LUCON, export it to Cyprus and attempt to find buyers for the equipment. Hughes used a freight-forwarding company to assist in arranging the shipment.
>
> The equipment was transported in three shipments from Seattle in 1995, which transited Rotterdam, before arriving in Cyprus. Although the documentation regarding the shipment did not indicate it included nuclear equipment, Cypriot authorities who inspected the cargo determined that it was nuclear-related equipment. The equipment was controlled by the Nuclear Regulatory Commission and required a license to export. Hughes did not request or receive such a license. Further, documentation/bills of lading were marked 'for re-export only,' but there was no end destination or consignee was provided and the exporter provided vague/incomplete information to the freight forwarder on commodities involved.
>
> Hughes was indicted and convicted of export of nuclear equipment without a license.
>
> Payment for the deal was made via wire transfer from Abi-Saad into Hughes US bank account; Hughes then paid for the equipment with a cashier's check. The declared value of the shipment was **under-valued** with ten containers being exported with a declared value at $20,000, even though it would cost $2,000 to ship an empty container out of the country.
>
> *Source: United States*

Research shows many similar cases and with the proliferation of nuclear weapons in Iran and North Korea, plus the 'missing ' nuclear technology from the old Soviet Bloc, one cannot over emphasize the urgent need to monitor and investigate such trade as there is no doubt that the fanatical terrorist will use such weapons to support the aims of the ideology.

Bank branches

The following investigation shows the difficulties in discerning the true purpose of trade when an authorization request is separated from the actual delivery of the goods.

The Dutch Supplier 1 was contacted by two separate front companies, both located in an Asian jurisdiction of proliferation concern. The invoice was sent to one Front Company A in the jurisdiction of proliferation concern but the Dutch Supplier 1 received the quotation and the actual confirmation of the order from another front company, Front Company 2 (Front company 1 and Dutch Supplier 2 had personal contact with the End User in the jurisdiction of concern about the orders and payments.

This intelligence could be deduced from administrative information (emails and other documents) found during the investigation at Dutch Supplier 2.

Dutch Supplier 2 also contacted and confirmed that it could acquire goods form an additional supplier, Supplier 3, a branch located in Europe.

The goods were then shipped directly by a regular Dutch shipping agent company to Front Company 2. The shipping agency was unaware of the order confirmation and the invoice that was sent to the US Supplier, since it received a proforma invoice of Dutch Supplier 2 directly.

The payments were received via wire transfers form the End User's Bank in the jurisdiction of concern, through a separate branch on the bank account of Dutch Supplier 2.

By using different companies (both in The Netherlands as in the jurisdiction of concern) that acted separately in different phases of the process, parties tried to disguise the actual circumstances of the trade transaction.

Source: The Netherlands

Pakistan/France

A French businessman was contacted by Pakistani nationals for the supply of dedicated electronic equipment for missile and/or drone tracking and guidance. He decided to acquire this equipment from an American intermediary, who would in turn order the components from an American manufacturer.

Exportation of this sensitive equipment from the United States to France is authorised, provided that the latter country is the final destination. This planned operation was therefore subject to a prohibition on re-exportation from France.

The equipment would not even be cleared from customs on arrival in France but remain in transit until immediate re-exportation to the United Arab Emirates, destined for a local front company acting on behalf of the Pakistani principal, which is affiliated with the Department of Defence (DoD) in Islamabad.

Contracts

A Pakistani purchasing network operating on European territory contacted a French industrialist to acquire electronic components that could be incorporated into tracking – ballistic control equipment for missiles or drones.

The French industrialist, who did not carry such equipment, contacted an American intermediary, which in turn placed an order with an American electronic equipment manufacturer. On receipt, the intermediary decided to export the equipment to France, taking advantage of an export authorisation subjected to a restrictive condition prohibiting re-exportation from France.

Meanwhile, a front company based in the United Arab Emirates, acting on behalf of the Pakistani principal linked with the Department of Defence, officially places an order with the French supplier.

Logistics

The equipment leaves the US for France by express air freight.

It was not be cleared through customs in France. While in transit in Marseille, it was immediately re-exported to the front company in the United Arab Emirates, which then delivered the equipment to Pakistan.

Financial elements

This involved a direct financial transfer from Dubai (branch of a Dutch bank) to one of the French company's two banks (French branch of a Spanish banking group + branch of a French banking group).

One bank (branch of the Spanish bank) received the money from Dubai and the other paid the American supplier, which itself had two banks, both domiciled in New York.

The transactions were split, both in France and in the US, between two banking institutions, seemingly unrelated because they belonged to separate groups.

Source: France

160

French customs investigation

Subsequent to the action described in the previous example the Pakistani intermediaries acting on European territory established contact with a company specialised in designing and selling ballistic testing and programming equipment for missiles and drones.

This firm, very small (three employees) yet capable of designing and producing high technology customised to satisfy its customers' needs, bought components from a Norwegian manufacturer specialising in the space industry (in which the firm had acquired financial interests) to then incorporate them into equipment exported to Pakistan.

The shipments were split up to prevent inspection services from getting a comprehensive picture of the equipment (declared to Customs as electrical testing equipment), its characteristics and its sensitivity.

The equipment was exported without authorisation:

- *either directly to Pakistan, destined for an import-export company fronting for the Department of Defence (DoD);*
- *or via an intermediary company based in the United Arab Emirates.*

Searches were launched by French Customs at the firm's main office and at its employees' homes after an attempt to export one of the batches of equipment destined for Pakistan was intercepted at Roissy airport. These investigations confirmed the extreme sensitivity of all of the equipment (classified war materiel by the French Ministry of Defence) and the substantial involvement of the French company's director in the operations of the Pakistani military-industrial complex. The French company was declared dormant by its director. A claim was lodged by French Customs with French judicial authorities.

Contracts

This contract was divided between two separate but complementary orders. The first order was placed by a company based in Pakistan (55% of the system). A contract and letter of credit were drawn up for this order. The other part of the contract (45%) was fulfilled through a succession of single orders by a front company based in the United Arab Emirates.

The two companies (Pakistan and UAE) both acted on behalf of the same principal, i.e. Pakistan's Department of Defence (DoD). Down the purchasing chain, the French contact procured part of the components required to develop the system from a Norwegian manufacturer who specialised in aeronautics and space technology and supplied the Norwegian army. The French contact secured this procurement by investing in the Norwegian supplier's company (purchased shares).

The financial arrangements in this deal are very interesting because they show the range of financing possibilities behind an act of organised proliferation. The Pakistani principal went through two separate financing networks:

- One network put money into its front company in the United Arab Emirates and transferred the payments for single orders through Chinese/Pakistani banks. (The investigation revealed that the Pakistani customer indicated to the French seller that an American bank in London is to receive the kickback payments); and
- the Pakistani buyer used letters of credit destined for a single French bank, where the French seller had domiciled its accounts.

These letters of credit passed through four branches of the same Pakistani banking group (other than the one used by the front company in the United Arab Emirates) located in Islamabad, Karachi, London and New York, respectively.

The advantage of this scheme divided into two distinct parts was that the left hand did not know what the right hand was doing.

However, all of the operations (left hand and right hand) were linked to a single French bank, a connection that helped the French Customs' investigations. In addition, the French bank effected the payment of the electronic component orders placed with the Norwegian manufacturer via a Norwegian bank in Oslo.

Logistics
Upstream, the Norwegian manufacturer delivered the electronic subsystems to its French customer, which exported them directly in its name, one part to Pakistan and the other to the United Arab Emirates.

It is important to note that, as is generally the case in such affairs, the real nature of the goods and their sensitivity were obscured by the innocuous-looking commercial wording of the customs declaration (e.g. electrical equipment).

Source: France

Elements that may indicate proliferation financing
The following investigative indicators can serve as a starting point to assist financial institutions in understanding the risk that customers, transactions or other account activity may be associated with WMD proliferation.

I would comment that;

- Given that the sources of funding for WMD proliferation can be legal or illegal, well-known indicators or 'red flags' for money laundering may be relevant in cases where the source of funds is illegal. However, the risk of proliferation financing is more likely to be present in cases where the source of funds is legal but the end-user or type of goods involved is intended to be obscured. The structural differences between **money laundering and proliferation financing** should therefore be taken into account when considering how indicators could be used.
- Specific information on the risk posed by the end-user or counter-party involved, or technical expertise to evaluate the possible WMD use of goods involved, will generally be needed to fully understand the risk of proliferation financing for a transaction or a customer.

Proliferators will use a range of sophisticated schemes to obfuscate their activities. For example investigations into the financing shows that proliferators have used layered letters of credit, front companies, intermediaries, brokers etc. However, existing investigations have not enabled the identification of any single financial pattern uniquely associated with proliferation financing, though indicators, if available, may help to identify some of the modus operandi used by proliferators.

I must stress that in this trade individual financial institutions rarely deal with all of the counterparties involved, and may not be aware of the activities highlighted below.

Some of the indicators also presume that there is access to information, e.g. on customers of concern, which may not be routinely available to financial institutions, or which financial institutions lack the capacity to use.

The list includes;

- both indicators which could provoke initial suspicion of a transaction or customer, and
- also indicators which would be useful to remove 'false positives' through further investigation, but which are not themselves a basis for suspicion.

Finally, specific indicators may only be useful at particular stages of the transaction process i.e. during initial CDD, during transaction processing ('real time screening'), and after the transaction monitoring post transaction review in investigation of already-suspect activity. The opportunities and capacity to use indicators may therefore vary according to when they can be practically used.

It is important to note that where particular individuals, organisations or countries are the subject of WMD proliferation-finance sanctions programmes or export controls, the obligations on institutions to comply with those sanctions and export controls are determined by jurisdictions and are not a function of identifying potential risk. Violations of such sanctions (the Iraqi super gun comes to mind) may result in a criminal offence or sanctions in some jurisdictions if funds or financial services are made available to a target, directly or indirectly.

Indicators of possible proliferation financing

- Transaction involves individual or entity in foreign country of proliferation concern.
- Transaction involves individual or entity in foreign country of diversion concern.
- Trade finance transaction involves shipment route (if available) through country with weak export control laws or weak enforcement of export control laws.
- Transaction involves individuals or companies (particularly trading companies) located in countries with weak export control laws or weak enforcement of export control laws.
- Transaction involves shipment of goods inconsistent with normal geographic trade patterns (e.g. does the country involved normally export/import good involved?).
- Transaction involves shipment of goods incompatible with the technical level of the country to which it is being shipped, (e.g. semiconductor manufacturing equipment being shipped to a country that has no electronics industry).
- Transaction involves financial institutions with known deficiencies in AML/CFT controls and/or domiciled in countries with weak export control laws or weak enforcement of export control laws.
- Based on the documentation obtained in the transaction, the declared value of the shipment was obviously under-valued vis-à-vis the shipping cost.
- Inconsistencies in information contained in trade documents and financial flows, such as names, companies, addresses, final destination etc.
- Customer activity does not match business profile, or end-user information does not match end-user's business profile.
- Order for goods is placed by firms or individuals from foreign countries other than the country of the stated end-user.
- Customer vague/incomplete on information it provides, resistant to providing additional information when queried.
- New customer requests letter of credit transaction awaiting approval of new account.
- The customer or counter-party or its address is similar to one of the parties found on publicly available lists of 'denied persons' or has a history of export control contraventions.

- Circuitous route of shipment (if available) and/or circuitous route of financial transaction.
- Transaction demonstrates links between representatives of companies exchanging goods i.e. same owners or management.
- Transaction involves possible shell companies (e.g. companies do not have a high level of capitalisation or displays other shell company indicators).
- A freight forwarding firm is listed as the product's final destination.
- Wire instructions or payment from or due to parties not identified on the original letter of credit or other documentation.
- Pattern of wire transfer activity that shows unusual patterns or has no apparent purpose.

This indicator may also be apparent through credit-risk or other know-your-customer assessments, particularly if a customer is moving into a new line of business.

At the transactional level, a transaction involving a product whose capabilities do not fit the buyer's line of business, such as an order for sophisticated computers for a small bakery, should raise concerns.

In many cases, end-users may not be identified in documentation supporting a transaction. Additionally, wholesale companies routinely have this type of activity as a business model. In cases involving wholesalers, geographic or other factors should be considered in identifying risk.

8

Real Estate – Risks and Compliance

Since the highlighting of money laundering as a tool of criminals and terrorists, various reports over the last few years have made reference to the fact that the real-estate sector may be one of the many vehicles used by criminal organisations to launder their illicitly obtained money. Hopefully the following chapter will present a clearer picture of the way that real estate activity can be used for money laundering or terrorist financing. (Since 2001 the United Kingdom laws in respect of the proceeds of crime and money laundering have extended to other businesses including estate agents.)

This chapter has three primary goals:

- To identify the means by which illicit money is channelled through the real-estate sector to be integrated into the legal economy.
- To identify some of the control points that could assist in combating this phenomenon.
- Adoption of a risk-based approach

One of the most effective ways to understand how the sector is abused is to examine actual cases.

Several characteristics of the real estate sector make it attractive for potential misuse by money launderers or terrorist financiers. Several basic techniques have been identified:

- the use of complex loans or credit finance,
- the use of non-financial professionals,
- the use of corporate vehicles and so on

In almost all of the cases wire transfers to channel the money were identified to have been involved at some stage. Also emerging markets seem to be more vulnerable to misuse of the real estate sector. Due to the worldwide market growth of real estate-backed securities and the development of property investment funds, the range of options for real estate investments has also grown. This effect has not gone without notice in emerging markets. Money laundering transactions can be easily camouflaged in genuine commercial transactions among the huge number of real estate transactions taking place. Complicating the situation is the fact that often the less developed economies do not have an average market price for real estate, but rather prices varying across sectors and districts. To complete real estate transactions in some stage of the process involvement of a legal expert is inevitable. The case examples have shown this category, when not covered by anti-money laundering obligations, often becomes the weakest link in the process.

As I complete this new edition the real estate market has imploded but will no doubt bounce back.

Given that the purchase or sale of a property is one of the largest financial transactions a family or individual may undertake, changes in property prices have a substantial impact on the considerations taken into account by potential buyers and sellers of properties. Fluctuations in property prices have an impact on decisions about where to live and work in addition to affecting an owners net worth. Moreover, to the extent that property values influence rents, the effect is manifested in the distribution of wealth between landlords and tenants. In the Times newspaper recently it was reported that the USAF are renting properties in Italy where the landlord is the local Mafioso, the properties having been purchased with the proceeds of crime.

Finally, property prices significantly influence the building industry and as mentioned in my previous book most construction work projects in the Far East pay 'fees' to criminal organisations such as the Triads.. Combined these factors fluctuations in property prices can influence economic activity and price stability by affecting aggregate supply and demand, the distribution of income, and the debt decisions undertaken by households.

Nevertheless, it is difficult to monitor and explain variations in property prices due to a lack of reliable and uniform information. Property markets are geographically segmented and numerous factors shape the local price of real-estate.

Historically there exists a commercial and residential real-estate market, and the property in both types of market may be bought and sold, managed and/or developed. More recently, new investment vehicles have emerged, including property investment funds (PIF) and real estate investment trusts (REIT). Such instruments allow average citizens to invest in markets. In the United Kingdom the buy to rent market has expanded with many individuals jumping on the bandwagon.

Investment in the real-estate sector offers advantages both for law-abiding citizens and for those who would misuse the sector for criminal purposes. Real property has historically appreciated in value, and many countries offer incentives to buyers, including government subsidies and tax reduction. Most importantly for misuse by criminals the facility the property sector provides for obscuring the true source of the funds and the identity of the (ultimate) beneficial owner of the real asset, which are two key elements of the money laundering process.

The real-estate sector is therefore of extraordinary importance to the economy in general and the financial system in particular. The widespread use of mechanisms allowing households to access the property market, the elimination of personal limitations on property ownership, the economic development and growth of tourism in many regions have all led to considerable growth of financial transactions linked to real-estate hence the growth of property deals in the Costa del Crime (Southern Spain) and the multi-million pound properties purchased in London and other prime locations by the Russians. The extraordinary range of possibilities for misusing these processes also allows suspected criminals to integrate and enjoy illegally obtained funds.

In order to misuse the real-estate sector, a number of methods, techniques, mechanisms, and instruments are available. Many of these methods are in and of themselves illegal acts; however, certain of them might be considered perfectly legal if they were not associated with a money laundering or a terrorist financing scheme (or if this association could not be detected..

Use of complex loans or credit finance

Intercompany loans have become a frequent instrument used as a means for raising funds. The ease with which such loans can be arranged makes them popular with the general public. These loans are also used in the real estate sector. Where an instrument is frequently used, misuse of the instrument becomes a possibility as well. Depending on the way in which the loan is structured, two different schemes have been detected.

1. Loan-back schemes

Loan-back transactions are used by suspected criminals to buy properties, either directly or indirectly, through the purchase of shares in property investment funds. Essentially, suspected criminals lend themselves money, creating the appearance that the funds are legitimate and thus are derived from a real business activity. The purpose of the loan is to give the source of the money an appearance of legitimacy and to hide the true identity of the parties in the transaction or the real nature of the financial transactions associated with it.

The lack of information caused by the globalization of these funds and their specific structure make it difficult to understand the true relationship between the various corporate vehicles involved in the loan structure and to be sure of the real origin of the funds, and thus determine whether they are linked to criminal activities or not. In several cases, offshore company loans are used.

Proceeds of drug trafficking laundered into real estate

An individual set up three companies. For one of the companies he held bearer shares. To hide his involvement in the companies he used a front-man and a trust and company service provider as legal representatives. For each of the companies, the legal representatives opened bank accounts with three different banks in different jurisdictions. The individual used the three companies to set up a loan-back scheme in order to transfer, layer and integrate his criminal money. He then co-mingled the criminal funds with the funds that originated from the legal activities of one of his companies.

Next the front man then bought real estate. To finance that transaction he arranged for a loan between the two companies.

Investigation of the scheme identified that:

- *The source of the funds used to finance the real estate transaction was from abroad, in particular from offshore jurisdictions and jurisdictions with strict bank secrecy.*
- *The lender of the money, an offshore company, had no direct relation with the borrower of the money*
- *A financial institution was not involved in the loan structure.*
- *There was no loan agreement between the lender and borrower.*
- *The loan agreement was legally invalid.*
- *The information in the loan agreement was inconsistent or incorrect.*
- *The conditions in the loan agreement were unusual (for example, no collateral was required).*
- *No payment of interest or repayment of the principal.*

Transaction monitoring by financial institutions showed payable-through accounts, by which incoming payments from abroad were immediately transferred abroad without a logical reason.

The criminal set up companies A and B and made use of trusts/company service providers in each location with power of attorney to act as legal representatives. Accounts were opened in Bank L and DA the companies being explained as part of an international structure who wished to take tax advantages by inter-company loans.

Drugs money was deposited into company A but by use of intercompany loans the funds were intermingled with the drugs money and used to purchase real estate. The profits from the property deals were used to finance further criminal activity.

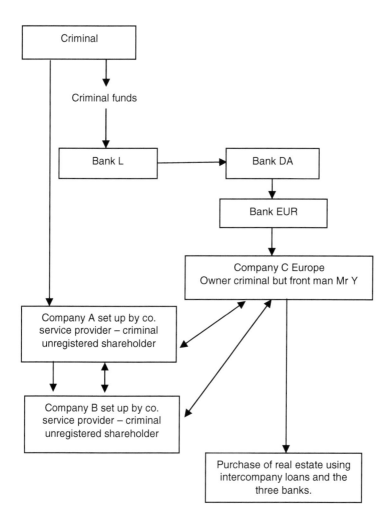

2. Back-to-back loan schemes

As with loan-back schemes, back-to-back loans are also known to have been used in real-estate related money laundering schemes. In this example, a financial institution lends money based on the existence of collateral posted by the borrower in the usual way. However, the collateral presented to the financial institution originated from criminal or terrorist activities.

Although financial institutions are obligated to disclose the existence of these funds on a risk dossier, there are occasions where this analysis may contain shortcomings. Instances where the collateral posted is not specified in the loan agreement or unreliable information as to the nature, location and value of the collateral make it very difficult to recognise a back-to-back loan.

Back-to-back loan used to launder funds

An individual set up two companies in different jurisdictions. He used a front man and a trust and company service provider as legal representatives to hide his involvement. One of the companies, led by the front-man, owned real estate and generated income through rental activity. He set up a back-to-back loan structure to use his criminal money for his real estate investments. He then arranged a bank guarantee between two banks in case of a default of the loan. The bank was willing to provide the bank guarantee with the pledged deposit of one of his companies as collateral. The money placed as a deposit was generated by the individuals criminal activity.

Investigation of the scheme revealed that;

- *there was no reference in the loan agreement to the underlying collateral.*
- *the collateral provided was not sufficient*
- *the collateral provider and other parties involved in the loan structure were not known.*
- *the borrower of the money was not willing to provide information on the identity and background of the collateral provider and/or the other parties involved in the loan structure.*
- *the complex nature of the loan scheme could not be justified*
- *there was an unexpected loan default.*

The role of non-financial professionals

When governments take action against certain methods of money laundering, criminal activities tend to migrate to other methods. In part, this reflects the fact that more aggressive policy actions and enforcement measures increase the risk of detection and therefore raise the economic cost of using these methods.

In recent years that money launderers have been increasingly forced to develop elaborate schemes to work around AML/CFT controls. This has often meant seeking out the experience of professionals such as lawyers, tax advisors, accountants, financial advisors, notaries and registrars in order to create the structures needed to move illicit funds unnoticed. These professionals act as gatekeepers by providing access to the international financial system, and knowingly or not, can also facilitate concealment of the true origin of funds.

Obtaining access to financial institutions through gatekeepers

A number of cases identified by various agencies reveal that criminals and terrorists have used non-financial professionals or gatekeepers to access financial institutions. This is especially important during the process of determining eligibility for a mortgage, opening bank accounts, and contracting other financial products, to give the deal greater credibility. It has also been documented that bank accounts are opened in the name of non-financial professionals in order to carry out various financial transactions on their behalf. Examples include depositing cash, issuing and cashing cheques, sending and receiving international fund transfers, etc., directly through traditional saving accounts or indirectly through correspondent accounts.

Misuse of a real estate agent to gain introduction to a financial institution, possible link to terrorist financing

A trustee for a trust established in an offshore centre approached a real estate agent to buy a property in Belgium.

The real-estate agent made inquiries with the bank to ask whether a loan could be granted. The bank refused the application, as the use of a trust and a non-financial professional appeared to be deliberately done to disguise the identity of the beneficial owner. The bank submitted a suspicious transaction report.

Following the analysis of the financial intelligence unit, one of the members of the board of the trust was found to be related to a bank with suspected links to a terrorist organisation.

The subsequent investigation identified that the scheme was initiated to purchase real estate with a loan using a bank, trust, and real-estate agent.

However it was apparent that the client was an offshore customer, the real estate agent was a non-account holder and the offshore customer was from a high risk jurisdiction.

Assistance in the purchase or sale of property

Non-financial professionals such as notaries, registrars, real-estate agents, etc., are sometimes used by suspected criminals on account of their central role in carrying out real-estate transactions. Their professional roles often involve them in a range of tasks that place them in an ideal position to detect signs of money laundering or terrorist financing.

Until relatively recently, however, these professionals have not been obligated under international standards to report suspicious activity to their national financial intelligence units (FIUs). In some countries where non-designated financial professionals fall under the scope of anti-money laundering legislation, these systems are still in the initial stages of implementation, so that the level of co-operation and the effectiveness of their suspicious transaction reporting have not yet been extensively tested.

In fact when one looks at the United Kingdom accountancy market/estate agent anyone whether qualified or not can act as agent or accountant, many are unaware of money laundering/proceeds of crime legislation.

Operational problems have also arisen. In some cases, these have resulted from difficulties in centralising information gathered from various domestic authorities, and in others it stems from differences in legal systems between jurisdictions (common law and civil law, for example).

Several cases have come to light revealing that the role of non-financial professionals in detecting illegal activity can also be significant in this area. There have been examples of notaries and registrars detecting irregularities in the signing of the property transfer documents (for example, using different names or insisting on paying a substantial part of the cost of the transaction in cash). Other examples include buying land designated as residential through a legal person and then reclassifying it a short time later for commercial development. Professionals working with the real-estate sector are therefore in a position to be key players in the detection of schemes that use the sector to conceal the true source, ownership, location or control of funds generated illegally, as well as the companies involved in such transactions.

Use of a notary when buying a real estate

An East European was acting under a cover name as the director of a company for which he opened an account with a Belgian bank. Transfers were made to this account from abroad, including some on the instructions of one of our clients.

The funds were then used to issue a cheque to a notary for the purchase of a property. The attention of the notary was drawn to the fact that some time after the purchase, the company went into voluntary liquidation, and the person concerned bought the property back from his company for an amount considerably above the original price. In this way the individual was able to insert money into the financial system for an amount corresponding to the initial sale price plus the capital gain. He was thus able to use a business account, front company customer, purchase of real estate, cross border transaction and wire transfers to launder money,

---

> that according to police sources, came from activities related to organised crime.
>
> It appeared that the company acted as a front and was set up merely for the purpose of carrying out the property transaction.

Trust accounts

A trust account is a separate bank account, which a third party holds on behalf of the two parties involved in a transaction. Funds are held by the trustee until appropriate instructions are received or until certain obligations have been fulfilled. A trust account can be used during the sale of a house, for example. If there are any conditions related to the sale, such as an inspection, the buyer and seller may agree to use a trust account. In this case, the buyer would deposit the amount due in a trust account managed by, or in the custody of, a third party. This guarantees the seller that the buyer is able to make the payment. Once all the conditions for the sale have been met, the trustee transfers the money to the seller and the title to the property is passed to the buyer.

> **Use of a solicitor to perform financial transactions**
>
> *An investigation of an individual revealed that a solicitor acting on his behalf was heavily involved in money laundering through property and other transactions.*
>
> *The solicitor organised conveyancing for the purchase of residential property and carried out structured transactions in an attempt to avoid detection. The solicitor established trust accounts for the individual under investigation and ensured that structured payments were used to purchase properties and pay off mortgages.*
>
> *Some properties were ostensibly purchased for relatives of the individual even though the solicitor had no dealings with them. The solicitor also advised the individual on shares he should buy and received structured payments into his trust account for payment.*

Management or administration of companies

There have been documented cases of non-financial professionals approached by money launderers and terrorists not just to create legal structures, but also to manage or administer these companies. In this context, these professionals may have been generally aware that they are taking an active role in a money laundering operation. Their access to the company's financial data and their direct role in performing financial transactions on behalf of their clients make it almost impossible to accept that they were not aware of their involvement.

Every week newsagents sell publications that advertise where one can buy limited company's off the shelf. These are available on the internet and unless the individual is barred from being a director it is simple to set up a company. As long as mandatory annual reports/accounts are submitted very few questions are asked.

Abuse of a notary's client account

A company purchased property by using a notary's client account. Apart from a considerable number of cheques that were regularly cashed or issued, which were at first sight linked to the notary's professional activities, there were also various transfers from the company to his account.

By using the company and the notary's client account, money was laundered by investing in real estate in Belgium, and the links between the individual and the company were concealed in order to avoid suspicions.

Police sources revealed that the sole shareholder of this company was a known drug trafficker.

Corporate vehicles

Corporate vehicles, that is, legal persons of all types and various legal arrangements (trusts, for example), have also been found to have been misused in order to hide the ownership, purpose, activities and financing related to criminal activity. Indeed the practice is so common that it almost appears to be normal practice in money laundering cases. The misuse of these entities seem to be most acute in tax havens, free-trade areas and jurisdictions with a strong reputation for banking secrecy. It may occur, however where the transparency of corporate vehicles can be exploited.

Apart from obscuring the identities of the beneficial owners of an asset or the origin and destination of funds, these corporate vehicles are also sometimes used in criminal schemes as a source of legal income.

In addition to shell companies, there are other specialised companies that carry out perfectly legitimate business relating to real estate, which have sometimes been misused for money laundering purposes. This aspect is illustrated by the use, for example, of property management or construction companies. The use of corporate vehicles is further facilitated if the company is entirely controlled or owned by criminals.

Offshore companies

Legal persons formed and incorporated in one jurisdiction, but actually used by persons in another jurisdiction without control or administration of a natural or legal resident person and not subject to supervision, can be easily misused in money laundering transactions. The possibilities for identifying the beneficial owner or the origin and destination of the money are at times limited. In these scenarios actors with wrongful intentions have the distinct advantage of extra protection in the form of bank secrecy.

Use of an offshore company to buy real estate.

A bank reported a person whose account had remained inactive for a long period but which suddenly was inundated with various cash deposits and international transfers. These funds were then used to write a cheque to the order of a notary for the purchase of a real estate.

It appeared that the party involved had connections with a company in insolvency and acted in this way to be able to buy the property with a view to evading his creditors.

The final buyer of the real estate was not the natural person involved but an offshore company. The party involved had first bought the property in his own name and subsequently had passed it on to the aforementioned company.

Legal arrangements

The use of some legal arrangements such as trusts can play an important role in money laundering. Under certain conditions these legal arrangements can conceal the identity of the true beneficiary in addition to the source and/or destination of the money.

The nature and/or structure of certain trusts can result in a lack of transparency and so allow them to be misused. Certain trusts may exist without the need for a written document constituting them.

Although there may be a deed defining the trust, in some cases it does not need to identify the depositary and/or a specific beneficiary.

There may be no obligation to register decisions regarding the management of a trust, and it may not be possible to disclose them in writing to anyone.

In some types of trust, such as discretionary trusts, the beneficiary may be named or changed at any time, which makes it possible to safeguard the identity of the beneficiary at all times up until the moment the ownership of the assets is transferred.

Trusts set up to protect assets may protect the depositary against decisions to freeze, seize or attach those assets.

Trusts may be set up to manage a company's shares, and they may make it more difficult to determine the identities of the true beneficiaries of the assets managed by the trusts.

Certain legislation may expressly prohibit the freezing, seizure or attachment of assets held in trust.

Certain clauses commonly referred to as escape clauses, allow the law to which the trust is subject to be changed automatically if certain events arise. Such clauses make it possible to protect the assets deposited in the trust from legal action.

These conditions may create a significant obstacle for the authorities charged with applying anti-money laundering and counter terrorist financing laws, especially in relation to international co-operation. This significantly slows down the process of collecting information and evidence regarding the very existence of the trust and identifying its ultimate beneficiary. Under these circumstances it may be very difficult, if not impossible, for a bank or other financial institution to comply with the know-your-customer policies applicable in the country or territory in which it is located.

Use of trusts to buy real estate

Two trusts were established in an offshore centre by a law firm. The trustee had been requested to accept two payment orders in favour of a bank in order to buy real estate. The communication between these trusts and their trustee always took place through the law firm. It appeared that the trust had been used to conceal the identity of the beneficial owners.

Information obtained by the FIU revealed that the beneficiaries of the trusts were individuals A and B, who were managers of two companies, established in Belgium that were the subject of a judicial investigation regarding serious tax fraud. Part of the funds in these trusts could have originated from criminal activity of the companies.

Shell companies

A shell company is a company that is formed but which has no significant assets or operations, or it is a legal person that has no activity or operations in the jurisdiction where it is registered. Shell companies may be set up in many jurisdictions, including in certain offshore financial centres and tax havens. In addition, their ownership structures may occur in a variety of forms. Shares may be held by a natural person or legal entity, and they may be in nominative or bearer form. Some shell companies may be set up for a single purpose or hold just one asset. Others may be set up for a variety of purposes or manage multiple assets, which facilitates the co-mingling of legal and illicit assets.

The potential for anonymity is a critical factor in the use of shell companies. They may be used to hide the identity of the natural persons who are the true owners or who control the company. In particular, permissive practices regarding the form of the shares, whether corporate, nominative or bearer, together with the lack of co-operation on the collection of information, represent a significant challenge when seeking to determine the ultimate beneficial owner.

Use of a shell company to buy real estate

This scheme involved the purchase of real estate which was then sold for a considerably higher price than it was worth. In this particular case the financial institutions informed the Financial Intelligence Unit (FIU) only about the initial transfer amount in respect of the initial property purchase by Shell Company A.

So as to carry out a full investigation it was necessary to interview various "gatekeepers" an registrars of real estate. The Ukrainian FIU checked a suspicious transaction report submitted by the auditor of the property buyer. Information from the state registries revealed that;

The building was then sold by Shell Company A to Company B.

Company B sold the property to a Mr S. Investigation into this individual showed that he was linked to the various shell companies/companies in this scheme, and that his income did not support the purchase of a building for $500,000. (He would have had to work for 200 years) This valuation of the building was confirmed by the state registrar.

However Mr S received the $500,000 in his bank account on the day of completion of the purchase from Shell company C.

Shell Company C then purchased the building from Mr S but cancelled the deal after three months.

Mr S then sold the building to Company D for $5.9 million (quite an increase and profit within a very short period)

It is believed the individual Mr S used his bank account to launder $5.4 million.

Source: MONEYVAL (Ukraine)

Property management companies

When using the real-estate sector, the purchase or construction of properties is a commonly used as a means by which criminals carry out financial transactions. However, a property that is bought or constructed using illegally obtained funds may subsequently be rented out to provide an apparently legal source of income in order to camouflage movements of funds between various jurisdictions (for example, the tenant and the landlord are located in different jurisdictions).

In cases where a company is owned or controlled by a criminal group, a possible way to use the property for money laundering is to mix cash of illegal origin with legitimate rental income. It then appears to be the result of the company's legitimate profits. In other cases, criminals seem to use the company's property management services to create a veil of legitimacy over other transactions they conduct.

Those cases that showed the active involvement of property management companies in criminal activity revealed that the level of their participation can vary widely both in what kind of property is involved and how the property management company is being misused. The company may be an integral part of the organised criminal group or it may provide a part of the criminal business activity, basically money laundering.

Use of property management companies

The FIU received a suspicious transaction report from notary A on one of his clients, person B, a foreigner without an address in Belgium, who in his office had set up a company for letting real estate. The sole manager and shareholder of this company was a family member of B, who also resided abroad.

Shortly after its creation the company bought a property in Belgium. The formal property transfer was carried out at notary A's office. The property was paid for through the account of notary A by means of several transfers, not from company X, but from another foreign company about which individual B did not provide any details. The establishment of a company managed by a family member with the aim of offering real estate for let and paid by a foreign company disguised the link between the origin and the destination of the money.

Police intelligence revealed that the individual was known for financial fraud. The investment in the property was apparently financed by the proceeds of these funds.

Non-trading real estate investment companies

Several characteristics of these companies make them especially vulnerable to abuse by suspected criminals. First, it is often very difficult to identify the real owner or controller. Second, the company can be created very easily with no minimum initial capital and without an authentic deed. Additionally, these entities are only recorded at the trade register. Finally, the shares of such companies can be sold without certification so that the true owner is not easily identified.

Misuse of non trading real estate investment companies

Two French non-trading real estate investment companies managed by two residents of a western European country successively bought two high value properties for a significant amount (more than EUR 20 million) with a single payment (not a loan).

The analysis of the FIU revealed that beneficial owner of the two properties was a resident of an Eastern European country. Further analysis showed that offshore Company A had moved the funds used to purchase the properties through SWIFT wire transfers. This offshore company was well known for holding shares of Company B registered in the very same country as the beneficial owner of the properties. Company B itself was known for its links to organised crime. Analysis also showed that the two managers of the real estate investment companies were senior staff of Company B.

Manipulation of the appraisal or valuation of a property

Manipulation of the real value of properties in relation to real estate involves the overvaluing or undervaluing of a property followed by a succession of sales and purchases. A property's value may be difficult to estimate, especially in the case of properties that might be considered atypical, such as hotel complexes, golf courses, convention centres, shopping centres and holiday homes. This difficulty further facilitates the manipulation when such property is involved.

Overvaluation or undervaluation

This technique consists of buying or selling a property at a price above or below its market value. This process should raise suspicions, as should the successive sale or purchase of properties with unusual profit margins and purchases by apparently related participants.

An often-used structure is, for example, the setting up of shell companies to buy real estate. Shortly after acquiring the properties, the companies are voluntarily wound up, and the criminals then repurchase the property at a price considerably above the original purchase price. This enables them to insert a sum of money into the financial system equal to the original purchase price plus the capital gain, thereby allowing them to conceal the origin of their funds.

Successive Sales and Purchases

In the case of successive sales and purchases, the property is sold in a series of subsequent transactions, each time at a higher price. Law enforcement cases have shown that these operations also often include, for example, the reclassification of agricultural land as building land. The sale is therefore fictitious, and the parties involved belong to the same criminal organisation or are non-financial professionals in the real-estate sector who implicitly know the true purpose of the transactions or unusual activity.

In addition to placing obstacles to discovering the true identity of the owners of the property and the real origin of the funds used in the transaction, these transactions usually have a significant tax impact, as they generally avoid the liability for capital gains tax.

Use of a lawyer when buying a real estate

A lawyer created several companies the same day (with ownership through bearer shares, thus hiding the identity of the true owners). One of these companies acquired a property that was an area of undeveloped land. A few weeks later, the area was re-classified by the town hall where it is located so that it could be urbanised.

The lawyer came to the Property Registry and in successive operations, transferred the ownership of the property by means of the transfer of mortgage loans constituted in entities located in offshore jurisdictions.

With each succeeding transfer of the property, the price of the land was increased. The participants in the individual transfers were shell companies controlled by the lawyer. Finally the mortgage was cancelled with a cheque issued by a correspondent account. The cheque was received by a company different from the one that appeared as acquirer on the deed (cheque endorsement). Since the company used a correspondent account exclusively, it can be concluded that this company was a front company set up merely for the purpose of carrying out the property transactions.

After investigation it was learned that the purchaser and the seller were the same person: the leader of a criminal organisation. The money used in the transaction was of illegal origin (drug trafficking). Additionally, in the process of reclassification, administrative anomalies and bribes were detected.

Monetary instruments

The use of monetary instruments in real estate transactions has traditionally dealt primarily with the use of cash. Although methods of payment continue to evolve, cash continues to be one of the main ways of obtaining and handling funds at the early stages of the process in many of the cases that ultimately involve funds of illegal origin.

Other monetary instruments used by criminals in their real-estate activities are cheques and wire transfers through conduit or correspondent bank accounts.

Cash

The purchase of high-value properties in cash is one way in which large sums of money can be integrated into the legal financial system. Some jurisdictions have observed that there has been a marked increase in demand for high denomination banknotes in their territory, which seems to be inconsistent with the progressive change in public preferences towards other means of payment.

Specific geographic and financial concentrations of demand and cross-border movements have also been detected (specific locations, banks, ports, etc.). Although this demand also arises for reasons not strictly considered to be money laundering or terrorist financing activities, such as tax avoidance, evasion or fraud, it does seem to be clear that the real estate sector may be a key contributing factor in the increase in this demand for some jurisdictions, as the black economy tends to grow during a property boom.

As well as being used to buy real estate, cash is also used in currency exchange and to structure deposits. It is common to structure cash transactions involving funds from criminal or terrorist sources and then to use these funds to buy, build or renovate a property. When the improved property is finally sold, the transaction has the advantage that it is difficult, or even impossible, to relate it to a specific individual or a criminal activity.

Cash is also used in rental or financial leasing transactions. These processes may be used by money launderers or terrorists to obtain the use of a property without having to fear losing it through its being seized or frozen if their criminal activity is discovered by the authorities. Moreover, it can also be used directly by criminals to settle contracts close to the start of the operation, receiving a reimbursement from the leasing company in the form of a cheque, for example, thus giving the transaction an air of legitimacy. It should be noted that a large share of the market remains in the hands of legal entities which are independent from the banks and financial institutions, thus creating a different channel for funds and making investigation and analysis difficult given the fragmentation of the information.

Use of cash to buy real estate

A criminal organisation operating in the Americas and Europe, laundered resources generated from drug trafficking through the misuse of bureaux de change and exploitation of apparently legitimate real-estate businesses in different countries. The criminal organisation led by Mr B, sent cocaine from South America to Europe, disguising it in rubber cylinders that were transported by air. The money generated from the trafficking was collected in Europe and forwarded in the same way back across the Atlantic.

In Latin-American Country 1, Mr B acquired an existing bureau de change; he changed its name and became its main shareholder and general director. With the purchase of an already constituted financial institution, the criminal organisation avoided the strict controls implemented by the regulatory authorities as regards to the constitution and operation of financial entities.

In European country 2, the criminal organisation acquired companies, created real estate corporations managed by citizens of Latin-American Country 1 and opened bank accounts in various financial institutions, declaring as commercial activity being the trade in jewels, financial intermediation and real estate activities, among others.

Those companies performed unusual transactions, such as cash deposits in amounts above EUR 500,000 and immediate transfer orders for the same amounts to foreign accounts belonging to Mr B's bureau de change in Latin-American Country 1 and American Country 2; allegedly for investments in the real-estate sector; money was deposited in low denomination currency and some counterfeit notes were identified as well.

Intelligence information revealed that the account of the bureau de change located in American Country 2, received during a year and a half period, deposits for more than USD 160 million.

Cheques and wire transfers

A number of cases investigated has revealed that criminals frequently use what might be termed payable-through accounts to channel large sums of money, generally through a series of transactions. In many cases sums are initially paid into these accounts in cash, cheques or via international wire transfers. The money never stays in the account for long, the rate of turnover of the funds is high, and the funds are then used to purchase real estate. There appears to be no commercial or economic justification for using these accounts. The same ld applies to correspondent accounts when used as a transit account. Suspicion about a legitimate use can be appropriate, when the account has high turnover, it appears to deal exclusively with wire transfer payments or cheques and the account appears to have no commercial or economic justification for such use.

Use of a transit account to buy real estate and launder the funds from human being trafficking

A bank's suspicions were raised after a bank cheque was issued to the order of a notary upon request of an Asian national for purchasing real estate. Analysis of the account transactions showed that the account received several transfers from Asians residing abroad and was known through an investigation regarding a network of Asian immigrants.

The analysis showed that the account had been used as a transit account by other Asian nationals for the purchase of real estate.

Mortgage schemes

Mortgage loans used to comprise one of the main assets on the balance sheets of banks and other financial institutions. Notwithstanding the current worldwide banking crisis an additional risk in this activity arises from the fraudulent or criminal use of these products. Through this misuse of the mortgage lending system, criminals or terrorists mislead the financial institution into granting them a new mortgage or increasing the amount already lent. This use constitutes part of the financial construction established to carry out criminal activities.

In many instances financial institutions consider these mortgage products to be low risk. A risk-based approach to monitoring subjects related to money laundering and terrorist financing, similar to those based on customer due diligence or 'know your customer' principles, could mitigate some of the risk of this activity.

Illegal funds in mortgage loans and interest payments

Criminals obtain mortgages and then the illegal funds obtained subsequently are then used to pay the interest or repay the principal on the loan, either as a lump sum or in instalments. The tax implications of using these products should also not be overlooked (for example, eligibility for tax rebates, etc.).

Front men are also sometimes used to buy properties or to apply for mortgages. The analysed cases seem to indicate that this misuse of mortgages goes hand in hand with a simulated business activity and the related income so as to deceive the bank or other financial institution when applying for the mortgage. On occasion the property is apparently purchased as a home, when in reality it is being used for criminal or terrorist activities (for example, selling or storing drugs, hiding illegal immigrants, people trafficking, providing a safe house for members of the organisation, etc.).

Use of illegal funds in mortgage loans and interest payments

An individual used a front-man to purchase real estate. The value of the real estate was manipulated by using a licensed assessor (real estate agent) to set up a false higher but plausible assessment of the market value of the property after renovation. The bank was willing to grant a mortgage on the basis of this false assessment. After the disbursement of the loan the real estate was paid for. The remaining money was then transferred by the owner to bank accounts in foreign jurisdictions with strict bank secrecy. The renovation took never place. The company finally went into default and the loan could not be reimbursed.

Undervaluation of real estate

Criminals often omit a part of the price from the purchase contract. In other words, the amount listed on the contract of sale is less than the real purchase price paid. The price shown on the contract is paid for with a mortgage loan; whereas the part not appearing on the contract is paid in cash produced by the criminal organisation or terrorist group's criminal activities and is paid to the seller under the table.

When the property is sold at fair market price the criminal converts illegal income into seemingly legitimate profits. The proceeds might remain available in the bank account of the criminal organisation or terrorist group in the jurisdiction in which the property is located and thus constitute a critical starting point for an investigation.

If the criminal organisation or terrorist group is unable to find a seller willing to accept money under the table or is unable to influence the valuation of the property by the independent appraiser, it may still pay for part of the price set in the contract in cash from illegal activities, with a sum of money left over from not using the whole of the mortgage granted to it. In all of these scenarios, it should be obvious to the bank or other financial institution that part of the purchase price is being paid via an alternative route, and it should verify whether this is consistent with the known profile of the customer in relation to the customer's pattern of income and expenses.

Overvaluation of real estate and used of third parties launder funds

(Predicate offence: money laundering, forged loan agreement)

The parents of Mr 'Smith' (Mr and Mrs 'SM') purchased a residential property and secured a mortgage with a Canadian bank. In his mortgage application, Mr 'SM' provided false information related to his annual income and his ownership of another property. The property he had listed as an asset belonged to another family member.

Mr and Mrs SM purchased a second residence and acquired another mortgage at the same Canadian bank. A large portion of the down payment came from an unknown source (believed to be 'Mr Smith'). The monthly mortgage payments were made by Mr 'Smith' through his father's bank account. This was the primary residence of 'Mr Smith'. Investigative evidence shows that Mr Smith made all mortgage payments through a joint bank account held by Mr and Mrs SM and Mr Smith.

Mr Smith then purchased a residential property and acquired a mortgage from the same Canadian bank. Mr Smith listed his income (far higher than the amounts he had reported to Revenue Canada) from Company A and Company B. Mr Smith made the down payment and monthly payments. Over two years, Mr Smith paid approximately C$130,000 towards the mortgage. During this time his annual legitimate income was calculated to be less than C$ 20,000.

Mr Smith also used his brother Mr B Smith as a front man (nominee) on title to purchase an additional property. Investigators discovered that Mr Smith had stated an annual income of C$ 72,000 on his mortgage application listing his employer as Mr B Smith although Mr Smith had never worked for his brother, and his total income for two years was less than C$ 13,000.

Mr Smith made the down payment on this property, and his tenants, who were members of Mr Smith's drug trafficking enterprise, paid all the monthly mortgage payments. A total of C$ 110,000 was paid towards this property until Mr Smith and his associates were arrested.

Mr Smith and his father purchased a fifth property. The origin of the down payment, made by Mr SM, was unknown but is believed to be the proceeds of Mr Smith's drug enterprise. Monthly payments were made by Mr Smith.

The use of real estate was one of many methods Mr Smith employed to launder the proceeds from his drug enterprise. Recorded conversations between Mr Smith and his associates revealed that he felt it was a fool-proof method to launder drug proceeds.

Mr Smith was convicted in 2006 of drug trafficking, possession of the proceeds of crime and laundering the proceeds of crime in relation to this case.

The question I would ask is what was the bank doing? Was this yet another mortgage advisors greed for bonuses?

What level of due diligence was used?

I understand that many of the properties purchased had been sold and the proceeds secured in a lawyers trust account which could not be restrained under any proceeds of crime legislation. It is believed that this fund may have held as much as C$ 500,000.

Investment schemes and financial institutions

Direct or indirect investment in the real estate sector by banks and other financial institutions is significant as recent events in the United States and the United Kingdom have revealed. However, the volume of investment by insurance companies and pension fund managers is also significant, as these institutions place a large part of their long-term liabilities in the property sector at both national and international levels. Bank and other financial institution investment policies over the past decade demonstrate that investment in property gained ground relative to other direct investments.

In the majority of countries, on the balance sheets of banks and financial institutions in most countries, the asset item referred to as credit investments mainly consists of mortgage lending transactions. This means that at times the evolution of the financial system is highly correlated with that of the real-estate sector and as we now know has resulted in recession.

Indirect investments are those considered to be limited or in which there is no direct control over the assets of the fund or investment vehicle. Moreover, real estate investment funds may or may not be publicly listed. If funds are unlisted it means that some or the entire fund or investment vehicle is capitalised by the financial institution. The number of co-investors generally ranges from two to ten.

The legal structures used for real estate investment funds vary:

- Investment trusts in the real estate sector, either listed or unlisted.
- Companies operating in the real estate sector, either listed or unlisted.
- Associations and unlisted limited companies.

A number of cases investigated in various jurisdictions have revealed that criminal organisations can influence property investment funds in various ways, depending on their degree of involvement by being;

- Partners in limited companies.
- Co-investors in property investment funds.
- Managers with direct or indirect control over the investment decisions made by property investment funds.

Institutions frequently outsource the management of their real estate assets to advisors or intermediaries, who, if they are managers of assets held in trust, may also outsource this task. Thus, several counterparties may be involved in the investment process, beginning with the investment policy set by the financial institution and ending with the investment ultimately made. The criminal organisation or terrorist group may operate or be situated at any point along this chain.

Through investment schemes in the real estate sector, the bank or other financial institution may, whether wittingly or not, facilitate or involve itself or become a vehicle for third parties to launder money.

Investments in hotel complexes through a front-man

On the French west seacoast, an individual presented a project to a district planning authority which involved several real-estate project management companies to develop a golf course with a hundred villas and apartments on property owned by the authority.

The total cost of the operation was very high and was to be funded mostly with funds originating from abroad. The analysis of the FIU revealed that the individual as well as close members of his family had already been involved in previous cases transmitted to the judicial authorities, in which the family had been implicated in the laundering of funds originating from Eastern Europe.

Note: These investment vehicles are known as real estate investment trusts (REIT), or real estate operating companies (REOC), in the US, and property investment funds (PIF) in the UK.

Concealing money generated by illegal activities

The use of real estate to launder money affords criminal organisations the following advantages;

- it allows them to introduce illegal funds into the system,
- earning additional profits and
- obtaining tax advantages (such as rebates, subsidies, etc.).

Some areas within the real-estate sector are more attractive than others for money laundering purposes, since the financial flows associated with them are considerable. This makes the task of hiding the funds of illegal origin in the total volume of transactions easier. The real estate sector offers numerous possibilities for money laundering:

- hotel businesses,

- construction firms,
- development of public or tourist infrastructure (especially luxury resorts),
- catering businesses.

Analysis of these activities show that they depend on different regional characteristics: for example, more cases occur in coastal areas (Costa del crime, south of France), in areas with a pleasant climate, and where non-resident foreign nationals are concentrated, etc (London, New York Los Angeles). Countries which have regions of this kind have become more aware of the problem and have increasingly begun to establish appropriate measures and controls in the real-estate sector. However weak links in due diligence will keep the proverbial door open.

Investment in hotel complexes, restaurants and similar developments

Real estate is commonly acquired in what is known as the integration or final phase of money laundering. Buying property offers criminals an opportunity to make an investment while giving it the appearance of financial stability. Buying a hotel, a restaurant or other similar investment offers further advantages, as it brings with it a business activity in which there is extensive use of cash.

Purchase of real-estate in order to establish a restaurant

An Asian national had purchased real estate in order to start a restaurant that he had financed by a mortgage at Bank A. This mortgage was repaid by transfers from an account opened with Bank B in name of his spouse. Within one year his spouse's account was credited by cash deposits and debited by cash withdrawals, as well as transfers to Bank A.

On the debit side of the account there were also various transfers to China in favour of a natural person. The repayment of the mortgage by transfers from an account opened with another bank in name of his spouse.

The main individual involved was known to be part of network that illegally smuggled foreign workers to Belgium.

Early warnings

Because the international standard on money laundering in real estate primarily focuses on prevention, it is essential to emphasise two types of measures:

- detection of suspicious transactions before they are completed, so as to avoid the funds being fed into the system; and
- analysis of these transactions in cases where it is impossible to detect

suspicious activity in order to detect such activity in the future.

Real estate agents in particular are involved in the vast majority of real estate transactions and therefore can play a key role in detecting money laundering and terrorist financing schemes, because they are in direct contact with buyers and sellers.

Real estate agents generally know their clients better than the other parties in the transactions. Therefore, they are well placed to detect suspicious activity or identify red flag indicators (see page 192).

Specific indicators within the industry

Wire transfers still constitute the best way to allocate money between countries. Although some controls have been established within the financial sector and for certain actors within it, settlement systems are still not included in the ML/TF legislation in most countries.

Finally, as they are key figures within the real estate sector and its transactions, designated non-financial businesses and professions (DNFBPs) legislation needs to be implemented to ensure the application by them of AML/CFT measures.

Emerging markets

The worldwide market growth of real estate-backed securities and the development of property investment funds over the past decade has meant that the range of options for real estate investments has also grown. Emerging markets in particular which can offer attractive returns at low prices with considerable room for growth have not gone unnoticed by many suspected criminals.

As a result of a the property boom in emerging markets, it has come to light that many money launderers believe that it is easier to camouflage genuine commercial transactions and these intermingled with the proceeds of crime are lost among the huge number of transactions taking place. Complicating matters is the fact that often these less developed economies do not have an average market price for real estate but rather prices varying across sectors and districts. Examining each and every transaction is impossible, and obtain a clear valuation of its real price is therefore also impossible.

At times this situation is made worse by the fact that the banking sector is insufficiently developed, in terms of its financial products and conditions, resulting in financial and company structures that make the tasks of supervision or investigation yet more difficult.

Emerging markets contain several characteristics that are highly favourable for money laundering, including:

- A high level of state intervention as a result of private sector financial structures and banking systems still at the embryonic stage.
- Absence, or limited development, of AML/CFT legislation and absence of indicators of the seriousness and social impacts of money laundering on the economy
- Lack of foreign capital in sectors other than raw materials.
- Banking and competent authorities (i.e. police, tax authorities, courts, etc.) lack training and the means necessary to detect and combat money laundering and terrorist financing.

Wire transfers

This method is without doubt one of the most accessible and widely used methods by criminals. The growing introduction of new technologies in financial markets and their increasing globalisation have meant that borders are disappearing and there are fewer obstacles to both legal and illegal activities.

As a result of their growing use, the regulatory standards applicable to the financial markets regarding wire transfers are scant as regards preventing money laundering and terrorist financing, focusing almost exclusively on the standardisation of the data fields used in order to automate and speed up transactions.

One must not forget that wire transfers can be performed by highly regulated financial institutions and also through by less regulated institutions, such as alternative remittance systems. Also other institutions providing message services and settlement services (e.g. FEDWIRE, CHIPS, SWIFT, etc.) should be mentioned.

Therefore differentiating between the providers of the wire transfer activity on a risk-based assessment is very important. Also, one needs to take into consideration the system and instrument used in each institution to perform their transactions in relation to the regulation level. This in effect means that there is a need not only consider the institutional regulation, but also if the money flows go through saving accounts, correspondent accounts, cheques, etc that can be considered as wire transfers.

The minimal information customers are required (or in some cases never requested) to provide in some jurisdictions to prove their identity facilitates the abuse of the system by criminal organisations and terrorist groups enabling them to be almost undetectable while moving large sums of money between countries in seconds.

The speed of execution, whether in person or not, the minimal documentation required and the high level of anonymity mean that they are commonly used by money launders abusing these regulatory loopholes. The facts are that in only a few countries are the wire transfer offices being supervised and subject to anti money laundering and counter terrorist financing requirements. This of course makes the offices even more vulnerable for misuse.

Wire transfer systems move billions every day in domestic and international transfers, and although some countries have introduced limited standards for their surveillance, they are extremely difficult to control.

Various experts have concluded from their research that there are no effective international controls on wire transfers, particularly as regards international transfers.

As an essential tool in the investigation and anti-money laundering controls it is important to review the current standards for the applicable to the parties involved and the reliable identification of those parties (payer, payee, etc.) in wire transfer as such information is indispensable to any effective effort to combating money launderings.

Notaries, registrars and similar figures

As previously mentioned, notaries and registrars seem to be the weakest link in the chain of real estate transactions. However they may be able to play a role in the detection of high risk transactions relating to the real estate sector.

Due to their central position in the legal system in relation to real estate transactions, they could potentially also perform a role in centralising and filtering information. However according to the legal professions in various countries it is not clear what their due diligence requirements are in complying with such legislation. Some jurisdictions have charged prevention bodies within the professional associations, to which notaries and registrars belong, with providing information to the authorities (both judicial and administrative) with powers in relation to money laundering and terrorist financing under the authority of national laws.

Red flag indicators

There are a number of common characteristics that, when detected individually or in combination, might indicate potential misuse of the real estate sector for ML/TF purposes. These red flag indicators can assist financial institutions and others in the conduct of customer due diligence for new and existing clients. They also may help in performing necessary risk-analysis in the more general sense for the sector. Thus, valid indicators may help in identifying suspicious activity that should be reported to competent national authorities according to AML/CFT legislation.

It should be remembered that activities related to money laundering or terrorist financing are always carried out with the aim of appearing to be normal.

The criminal nature of the activity derives from the origin of the funds and the aim of the participants. However one must not forget that some of the money laundering, especially in relation to terrorist activity, is of clean money invested by supporters.

Natural persons

- Transactions involving persons residing in tax havens or risk territories, when the characteristics of the transactions match any of those included in the list of indicators.
- Transactions carried out on behalf of minors, incapacitated persons or other persons who, although not included in these categories, appear to lack the economic capacity to make such purchases.
- Transactions involving persons who are being tried or have been convicted for crimes or who are publicly known to be linked to criminal activities involving illegal enrichment, or there are suspicions of involvement in such activities and that these activities may be considered to involve money laundering.
- Transactions involving persons who are in some way associated with the foregoing (for example, through family or business ties, common origins, where they share an address or have the same representatives or attorneys, etc.).
- Transactions involving an individual whose address is unknown or is merely a correspondence address (for example, a PO Box, shared office or shared business address, etc.), or where the details are believed or likely to be false.(it is important to note that in the middle east the majority of individuals have an address that consists of a PO box.
- Several transactions involving the same party or those undertaken by groups of persons who may have links to one another (for example, family ties, business ties, persons of the same nationality, persons sharing an address or having the same representatives or attorneys, etc.).
- Individuals who unexpectedly repay problematic loans or mortgages or who repeatedly pay off large loans or mortgages early, particularly if they do so in cash. (Yes, I know he/she won the lottery yet again.)

Risk Territory

The definition of a risk territory according to the FATF could be either one that is determined by the financial institution or another entity applying the indicator directly or else one that has been defined by the national authorities of the country in which the institution or entity is located. As many of the major money laundering cases have been within jurisdictions that appear to be well operated with good anti money laundering controls, one only has to look at recent reports of major financial institutions financing corrupt governments/individuals and laundering funds through offshore investment funds to deviate from local controls. **Therefore in my opinion everywhere is a risk territory.**

Legal persons

- Transactions involving legal persons or legal arrangements domiciled in tax havens or risk territories, when the characteristics of the transaction match any of those included in the list of indicators.
- Transactions involving recently created legal persons, when the amount is large compared to their assets.
- Transactions involving legal entities, when there does not seem to be any relationship between the transaction and the activity carried out by the buying company, or when the company has no business activity.
- Transactions involving foundations, cultural or leisure associations, or non-profit-making entities in general, when the characteristics of the transaction do not match the goals of the entity.(charities are an ideal example)
- Transactions involving legal persons which, although incorporated in the country, are mainly owned by foreign nationals, who may or may not be resident for tax purposes.
- Transactions involving legal persons whose addresses are unknown or are merely correspondence addresses (for example, a PO Box number, (see previous comments re PO box numbers) shared office or shared business address, etc.), or where the details are believed false or likely to be false.
- Various transactions involving the same party. Similarly, transactions carried out by groups of legal persons that may be related (for example, through family ties between owners or representatives, business links, sharing the same nationality as the legal person or its owners or representatives, sharing an address, in the case of legal persons or their owners or representatives, having a common owner, representative or attorney, entities with similar names, etc.).
- Formation of a legal person or increases to its capital in the form of non-monetary contributions of real estate, the value of which does not take into account the increase in market value of the properties used.
- Formation of legal persons to hold properties with the sole purpose of placing a front man or straw man between the property and the true owner.
- Contribution of real estate to the share capital of a company which has no registered address or permanent establishment which is open to the public in the country.
- Transactions in which unusual or unnecessarily complex legal structures are used without any economic logic.

Natural and legal persons

- Transactions in which there are indications that the parties are not acting on their own behalf and are trying to hide the identity of the real customer.
- Transactions which are started in one individual's name and finally completed in another's without a logical explanation for the name change. (For example, the sale or change of ownership of the purchase or option to purchase a property which has not yet been handed over to the owner, reservation of properties under construction with a subsequent transfer of the rights to a third party, etc.).
- Transactions in which the parties:
- Appear to be completely disinterested, despite the investment cost, in the characteristics of the property (e.g. quality of construction, location, date on which it will be handed over, etc.) which is the object of the transaction.
- Are so laid back that they do not seem particularly interested in obtaining a better price for the transaction or in improving the payment terms.
- Show a strong interest in completing the transaction quickly, without there being good cause.
- Show an over keen interest in transactions relating to buildings in particular areas, without any apparent concerns about the price they have to pay.
- Transactions in which the parties are foreign or non-resident for tax purposes and:
- Their only purpose is a capital investment (that is, they do not show any interest in living at the property they are buying, even temporarily, etc.).
- They are interested in large-scale operations (for example, to buy large plots on which to build homes, buying complete buildings or setting up businesses relating to leisure activities, etc.).
- Transactions in which any of the payments are made by a third party, other than the parties involved. Cases where the payment is made by a credit institution registered in the country at the time of signing the property transfer, due to the granting of a mortgage loan, may be excluded.

Intermediaries

- Transactions performed through intermediaries, when they act on behalf of groups of potentially associated individuals (for example, through family or business ties, shared nationality, persons living at the same address, etc.).
- Transactions carried out through intermediaries acting on behalf of groups of potentially affiliated legal persons (for example, through family ties between their owners or representatives, business links, the fact that the legal entity or its owners or representatives are of the same nationality, that the legal

entities or their owners or representatives use the same address, that the entities have a common owner, representative or attorney, or in the case of entities with similar names, etc.).

- Transactions taking place through intermediaries who are foreign nationals or individuals who are non-resident for tax purposes.

I should comment that these transactions may be completely genuine but it is important to ensure that know your client diligence is not just good but beyond reproach.

Means of payment

The following could be suspicious;

- Transactions involving payments in cash or in negotiable instruments which do not state the true payer (for example, bank drafts), where the accumulated amount is considered to be significant in relation to the total amount of the transaction.
- Transactions in which the party asks for the payment to be divided into smaller parts with a short interval between them.
- Transactions where there are doubts as to the validity of the documents submitted with loan applications.
- Transactions in which a loan granted, or an attempt was made to obtain a loan, using cash collateral or where this collateral is deposited abroad.
- Transactions in which payment is made in cash, bank notes, bearer cheques or other anonymous instruments, or where payment is made by endorsing a third-party's cheque.
- Transactions with funds from countries considered to be tax havens or risk territories, according to anti-money laundering legislation, regardless of whether the customer is resident in the country or territory concerned or not.
- Transactions in which the buyer takes on debt which is considered significant in relation to the value of the property. Transactions involving the transfers of mortgages granted through institutions registered in the country may be excluded but one should be aware that the 'know your client' procedures completed by the institution granting the mortgage may be flawed.

Nature of the Transaction

- Transactions in the form of a private contract, where there is no apparent intention to notarise the contract, or where this intention is expressed, but it does not finally take place.

- Transactions which are not completed and completely disregard any contract clause penalising the buyer with loss of the deposit if the sale does not go ahead.
- Transactions relating to the same property or rights that follow in rapid succession (for example, purchase and immediate sale of property) and which entail a significant increase or decrease in the price compared with the purchase price.
- Transactions entered into at a value significantly different (much higher or much lower) from the real value of the property or differing markedly from market values.
- Transactions relating to property development in high-risk urban areas, where in the judgement of the company the number of buildings required to be under construction is high relative to the number of inhabitants, etc.
- Recording of the sale of a building plot followed by the recording of the declaration of a completely finished new building at the location at an interval less than the minimum time needed to complete the construction, bearing in mind local building regulations and the characteristics of the building.
- Recording of the declaration of a completed new building by a non-resident legal person having no permanent domicile indicating that the construction work was completed at its own expense without any subcontracting or supply of materials.

Use of Illegal Funds in Mortgage Loans and Interest Payments

Mr X was the owner of Company A and the individual controlling its activities.

Mr X hired Mr Y as front man of Company A. Company A had some low-profile activities in managing and exploiting properties.

During the life of Company A, Mr Y set up a relationship with Bank EUR that provided for accounts and payment services. The property managed by Company A was used for activities by other companies owned by Mr X (for storage, for example).

Mr X. planned to buy office buildings for EUR 8,000,000 via Company A. The office buildings had to be renovated to be marketable.

Mr X. knew a licensed assessor (real estate agent), Mr Z. Mr X. and Mr Z found a way to set up a false but plausible assessments of the market value of the office buildings after renovation (EUR 13,000,000).

Mr X ordered Mr Y to negotiate a mortgage with Bank EUR to finance the purchase and renovation of the property. Based on the assessment, Bank EUR was willing to grant a mortgage of EUR 13,000,000.

Mr Y entered into the loan agreement on behalf of Company A as the buying party. After the disbursement of the loan, the real estate was paid for.

Mr X. then paid Mr Y EUR 500,000 and had the remaining EUR 4.5 million, together with the proceeds of other criminal activities, transferred into several bank accounts in countries with strict bank secrecy.

The mortgage of Bank EUR was presented to the foreign banks as the legitimate source of the funds that were being transferred to the accounts.

In this way, the money was layered and integrated. The renovation of the office buildings never took place. Meanwhile the activities of Company A rapidly decreased. Company A finally went into default. Bank EUR called the loan, but Mr Y was not in a position to reimburse it along with the interest payment. Mr Y stated that he was not aware of the persons behind Company A, their whereabouts and the background of the accounts to which the money was transferred.

Source: Netherlands

The risk-based approach: estate agents

Each country and its regulatory authorities should aim to establish a partnership with its real estate agents and other DNFBP sectors that will be mutually beneficial to combating money laundering and terrorist financing.

Note: FATF Recommendation 12 requires that the customer due diligence, record-keeping requirements, and transaction monitoring provisions set out in Recommendation 5, 6, and 8 to 11 apply to DNFBPs in certain circumstances. Specifically, Recommendations 12/16 applies to real estate agents when they are involved in transactions for their client concerning the buying and selling of real estate.

The worldwide real estate transaction business vastly differs. The residential, commercial, and agricultural real estate markets differ in terms of business practices, local regulations, cultural habits, and value and size of the market. Agents are no longer restricted to localised business. There is an increasing global market involving significant international investment, assisted by the development of technology, including international methods of communication, e.g. email.

It is also important to note that besides real estate agents, other professionals and organisations often undertake real estate transaction activity including real estate developers, builders, financial institutions, property managers, and corporate in-house real estate officers. Real estate agents are real estate professionals or companies who by representing the seller and/or the buyer act in a purchase and/or sale of a real property in a real estate transaction capacity and/or are exercising professional transactional activity, thus facilitating real property transfer.

Whilst the role of agents varies from country to country, the core functions may include:

- Traditional exclusive (and non-exclusive) seller representation.
- Traditional exclusive (and non-exclusive) buyer representation.
- Representation of both buyer and seller in the same transaction.
- A number of agents representing sellers or buyers.
- National and transnational referrals.
- Amalgamation or interaction of functions of other professionals, e.g. notaries, lawyers, lenders, valuers.
- Auctions.

In some markets real estate agents may assume additional functions relative to the transaction, such as mortgage loan assessment, valuation/appraisal and conveyance of property. The risk associated with these functions should be considered with reference to specific applicable regulations and/or guidance.

The risk-based approach: purpose, benefits and challenges

Purpose

The purpose of the risk-based approach effectively means that it is possible to ensure that measures to prevent or mitigate money laundering and terrorist financing are appropriate with the risks identified. This allows resources to be allocated in the most efficient way. The main principle is that resources should be directed in accordance with priorities so that the greatest risks receive the highest attention. The alternative approach is that resources are either applied evenly, or that resources are targeted, but on the basis of factors other than risk. This can, as previously mentioned, inadvertently lead to a 'tick box' approach with the focus on meeting regulatory requirements rather than on combating money laundering or terrorist financing efficiently and effectively.

A number of the DNFBP sectors, including real estate agents, are already subject to regulatory or professional requirements which complement AML/CFT measures. It is therefore beneficial for real estate agents to devise their AML/CFT policies and procedures in a way that coordinates with other regulatory or professional requirements. A risk-based AML/CFT regime should help ensure that the honest customers can access the services provided by real estate agents, but creates barriers to those who seek to misuse those services.

Real estate agents will need assistance from regulatory bodies to help them to identify higher risk customers, products and services, including delivery channels, and geographical locations. This intelligence will change over time, depending on how circumstances develop, and how threats evolve.

Proportionate procedures must be designed based on assessed risk. Higher risk areas should be subject to enhanced procedures; this would include measures such as enhanced customer due diligence checks. It also follows that in instances where risks are low, simplified or reduced controls can be applied.

An effective risk-based approach involves identifying and categorising money laundering and terrorist financing risks and establishing reasonable controls based on risks identified. This will allow real estate agents to exercise reasonable business and professional judgment with respect to customers. Application of a reasoned and well-articulated approach will justify the judgments made with regard to managing potential money laundering and terrorist financing risks.

It is, however, important that a risk-based approach should not be designed to prohibit real estate agents from continuing with legitimate business or from finding innovative ways to diversify their business.

Regardless of the strength and effectiveness of AML/CFT controls, criminals will continue to attempt to move illicit funds undetected and will, from time to time, succeed. They are more likely to target the DNFBP sectors if other routes become more difficult. For this reason, DNFBPs, including real estate agents, may be more or less vulnerable depending on the effectiveness of the AML/CFT procedures applied in other sectors. A risk-based approach allows DNFBPs, including real estate agents, to more efficiently and effectively adjust and adapt as new money laundering and terrorist financing techniques are identified.

An effectively designed and implemented risk-based approach will provide an appropriate and effective control structure to manage identifiable money laundering and terrorist financing risks. However, it must be recognised that any reasonably applied controls, including controls implemented as a result of a reasonably designed and effectively implemented risk-based approach, will not identify and detect all instances of money laundering or terrorist financing.

Benefits

The adoption of a risk-based approach to combating money laundering and terrorist financing can yield benefits for all parties including the public. Applied effectively, the approach should allow a more efficient and effective use of resources and minimise burdens on customers. Focusing on higher risk threats should mean that beneficial outcomes can be achieved more effectively.

For real estate agents, the risk-based approach allows the flexibility to approach AML/CFT obligations using specialist skills and responsibilities. This requires real estate agents to take a wide and objective view of their activities and customers.

Efforts to combat money laundering and terrorist financing should also be flexible in order to adapt as risks evolve. As such, real estate agents will use their judgment, knowledge and expertise to develop an appropriate risk-based approach for their particular organisation, structure and business activities.

The potential benefits can be summarised as follows:

- Better management of risks
- Efficient use and allocation of resources
- Focus on real and identified threats
- Flexibility to adapt to risks that change over time

Challenges

The potential challenges can be summarised as follows:

- Identifying appropriate information to conduct a sound risk analysis
- Addressing short term transitional costs
- Greater need for more expert staff capable of making sound judgments.
- Developing appropriate regulatory response to potential diversity of practice.

A risk-based approach is not necessarily an easy option, and there may be challenges to overcome when implementing the necessary measures. Some challenges may be inherent to the use of the risk-based approach. Others may stem from the difficulties in making the transition to a risk-based system. A number of challenges, however, can also be seen as offering opportunities to implement a more effective system.

There are both similarities and differences in the application of a risk-based approach to terrorist financing and money laundering. They both require a process for identifying and assessing risk. However, the characteristics of terrorist financing make its detection and the implementation of mitigation strategies challenging due to considerations such as the relatively low value of transactions involved in terrorist financing, or the fact that funds can be derived from legitimate as well as illicit sources, plus the nature of the funding sources may vary according to the type of terrorist organisation.

Where funds are derived from criminal activity, then traditional monitoring mechanisms that are used to identify money laundering may also be appropriate for terrorist financing, though it is possible that the activity, which may be indicative of suspicion, cannot be identified as, or connected with, terrorist financing. Investigations into terrorist attacks show that the financing of terrorism may be conducted in very small amounts, which, when applying a risk-based approach could be the very transactions that are frequently considered to be of minimal risk with regard to money laundering.

Where funds are from legal sources, it is even more difficult to determine if they could be used for terrorist purposes. In addition, the actions of terrorists may be overt and outwardly innocent in appearance, such as the purchase of materials and services to further their goals, with the only covert fact being the intended use of such materials and services purchased. Therefore, while terrorist funds may be derived from criminal activity as well as from legitimately sourced funds, transactions related to terrorist financing may not exhibit the same traits as conventional money laundering.

However, in all cases, **it is not the responsibility** of real estate agents to determine the type of underlying criminal activity, or intended terrorist purpose; the real estate agent's role is to identify and report the suspicious activity.

The ability of real estate agents to detect and identify potential terrorist financing transactions without guidance on terrorist financing methods or acting on specific intelligence provided by the authorities makes it significantly more challenging than is the case for potential money laundering and other suspicious activity. Detection efforts, absent specific national guidelines and intelligence, are likely to be based on monitoring that focuses on transactions with countries or geographic areas where terrorists are known to operate or on the other limited intelligence that may be available (many of which are indicative of the same techniques as are used for money laundering).

It goes without saying that particular individuals, organisations or countries may be the subject of terrorist financing sanctions, in a particular country. In such cases a listing of individuals, organisations or countries to which sanctions apply and the obligations on real estate agents to comply with those sanctions are decided by individual countries and are not a function of risk. Real estate agents may commit a criminal offence if they undertake business with a listed individual, organisation or country or its agent, in contravention of applicable sanctions.

To implement a risk-based approach requires the real estate agents having a sound understanding of the risks and are therefore able to exercise sound judgment. This requires the building of expertise including for example, through training, recruitment, taking professional advice and 'learning by doing'. This process will always benefit from information sharing by competent authorities and SROs. The provision of good practice guidance is also very important. Attempting to pursue a risk-based approach without sufficient expertise will lead to flawed judgments. Real estate agents may also over-estimate risk, which could lead to wasteful use of resources, or they may underestimate risk, thereby creating vulnerabilities.

As in other businesses Real estate agents may find that some staff members are uncomfortable making risk-based judgments. This may possibly lead to overly cautious decisions, or disproportionate time spent documenting the rationale behind a decision. This may also be true at various levels of management. However, in situations where management fails to recognise or underestimates the risks, a culture may develop that allows for inadequate resources to be devoted to compliance, leading to potentially significant compliance failures. It is also important to consider the size of the business as many estate agents are small operations with few staff.

In implementing the risk-based approach, real estate agents should preferably be given the opportunity to make reasonable judgments with respect to their particular situations. This may mean that no two real estate agents or no two businesses are likely to adopt the same detailed practice.

FATF Recommendation 25 requires that adequate feedback be provided to the financial sector and DNFBPs. Such feedback helps institutions and businesses accurately assess the money laundering and terrorist financing risks and adjust their risk programmes accordingly. Subsequently this makes the detection of suspicious activity more likely and improves the quality of suspicious transaction reports. As well as being an essential input to any assessment of country or sector wide risks, the promptness and content of such feedback is relevant to implementing an effective risk-based approach.

Levels of risk

Risk is referred to in several forms:

Higher risk – Under FATF Recommendation 5, a country must require its DNFBPs, including real estate agents, to perform enhanced due diligence for higher-risk customers, business relationships or transactions. FATF Recommendation 6 (politically exposed persons) is an example of this principle and is considered to be a higher risk scenario requiring enhanced CDD.

Lower risk – A country may also permit its DNFBPs, including real estate agents, to take lower risk into account in deciding the extent of the CDD measures they will take. Real estate agents may thus reduce or simplify (but not avoid completely) the required measures.

Risk arising from innovation – FATF Recommendation 8, recommends that a country must require its DNFBPs, including real estate agents, to give special attention to the risks arising from new or developing technologies that might favour anonymity.

Local jurisdiction responsibilities

Risk assessment mechanism – The FATF standards expect that there will be an adequate mechanism by which designated competent authorities or SROs assess or review the procedures adopted by the real estate agents to determine the degree of risk and how they manage that risk, as well as to review the actual determinations themselves. This expectation applies to all areas where the risk-based approach is applied. In addition, where the designated competent authorities or SROs have issued guidelines on a suitable approach to risk-based procedures, it will be important to establish that these have been followed. The Recommendations also recognise that country risk is a necessary component of any risk assessment mechanism).

Limitations to the risk-based approach

There are circumstances in which the application of a risk-based approach will not apply, or may be limited. There are also circumstances in which the application of a risk-based approach may not apply to the initial stages of a requirement or process, but then will apply to subsequent stages. The limitations to the risk-based approach are usually the result of legal or regulatory requirements that mandate certain actions to be taken.

Requirements to freeze assets of identified individuals or entities, in countries where such requirements exist, are independent of any risk assessment. The requirement to freeze is absolute and cannot be impacted by a risk-based process. Similarly, while the identification of potential suspicious transactions can be advanced by a risk-based approach, the reporting of suspicious transactions, once identified, is not risk-based.

There are several elements to customer due diligence (CDD) –

- identification and verification of the identity of customers and beneficial owners,
- obtaining information on the purposes and intended nature of the business relationships, and
- conducting ongoing due diligence.

Of these components, **the identification and verification of identity of customers** are requirements which must be completed regardless of the risk-based approach.

However, in relation to all other CDD components, a reasonably implemented risk-based approach may allow for a determination of the extent and quantity of information required, and the mechanisms to be used to meet these minimum standards. Once this determination is made, the obligation to keep records and documents that have been obtained for due diligence purposes, as well as transaction records, is not dependent on risk levels.

Countries may allow real estate agents to apply reduced or simplified measures where the risk of money laundering or terrorist financing is lower. However, these reduced or simplified measures do not necessarily apply to all aspects of customer due diligence. Moreover, where these exemptions are subject to certain conditions being met, it is necessary to verify that these conditions apply, and where the exemption applies under a certain threshold, measures should be in place to prevent transactions from being split artificially to avoid the threshold (smurfing). In addition, information beyond customer identity, such as customer location, may be needed to adequately assess risk (this may be a problem with middle eastern clients as many give PO Box numbers as their address). This will be an interactive process: the preliminary information obtained about a customer should be sufficient to determine whether to go further, and in many cases customer monitoring will provide additional information.

Some form of monitoring will be required in order to detect unusual and hence possibly suspicious transactions. Even in the case of lower risk customers, monitoring is needed to verify that transactions match the initial low risk profile and if not, trigger a process for revising the customer's risk rating. In other words act like a credit card provider by constantly evaluating whether the customer has become a risk or not

Equally, risks for some customers may only become evident once a relationship with a customer has begun. This makes appropriate and reasonable the monitoring of customer transactions as an essential component of a properly designed risk-based approach. It should be understood that not all transactions, accounts or customers will be monitored in exactly the same way and where there is an actual suspicion of money laundering or terrorist financing, this could be regarded as a higher risk scenario, and enhanced due diligence should be applied regardless of any threshold or exemption.

A risk-based approach: key elements

Real estate agents, designated competent authorities or SROs should have access to reliable and actionable information about the threats.

- There must be emphasis on cooperative arrangements among the policy makers, law enforcement, regulators, and the private sector.
- Authorities should publicly recognise that the risk-based approach will not eradicate all elements of risk.
- Authorities have a responsibility to establish an atmosphere in which real estate agents need not be afraid of regulatory sanctions where they have acted responsibly and implemented adequate internal systems and controls.
- Designated competent authorities' or SROs' supervisory staff must be well-trained in the risk-based approach, both as applied by designated competent authorities/SROs and by the real estate agents.

Real estate agents should be expected to have flexibility to adjust their internal systems and controls taking into consideration lower and high risks, so long as such systems and controls are reasonable. However, there are also minimum legal and regulatory requirements and elements that apply irrespective of the risk level, for example suspicious transaction reporting and minimum standards of customer due diligence.

Acknowledging that a real estate agent's ability to detect and deter money laundering and terrorist financing may sometimes be necessarily limited and that information on risk factors is not always robust or freely available. There can therefore be reasonable policy and monitoring expectations about what a real estate agent with good controls aimed at preventing money laundering and the financing of terrorism is able to achieve. A real estate agent may have acted in good faith to take reasonable and considered steps to prevent money laundering, and documented the rationale for its decisions, and yet still be abused by a criminal.

Acknowledging that not all high-risk situations are identical and as a result will not always require the application of precisely the same type of enhanced due diligence.

Designated competent authorities and SROs should not prohibit real estate agents from conducting business with high risk customers as long as appropriate policies, procedures and processes to manage the risks are in place. However, this does not exclude the need to implement basic minimum requirements. For instance, FATF Recommendation 5 (that applies to real estate agents through the incorporation of R.5 into R.12) states that 'where [the real estate agent] is unable to comply with (CDD requirements), it should not open the account, commence business relations or perform the transaction; or should terminate the business relationship; and should consider making a suspicious transaction report in relation to the customer.' So the level of risk should strike an appropriate balance between the extremes of not accepting customers, and conducting business with unacceptable or unmitigated risk.

Designated competent authorities and SROs expect real estate agents to put in place effective policies, programmes, procedures and systems to mitigate the risk and acknowledge that even with effective systems not every suspect transaction will necessarily be detected. Real estate agents rely on designated competent authorities and SROs to take appropriate measures once a report of suspicious activity has been filed and the risk-based approach no longer applies. Designated competent authorities and SROs should also ensure that those policies, programmes, procedures and systems are applied effectively to prevent real estate agents from becoming conduits for illegal proceeds and ensure that they keep records and make reports that are of use to national authorities in combating money laundering and terrorist financing.

Efficient policies and procedures will reduce the level of risks, but are unlikely to eliminate them completely. Assessing money laundering and terrorist financing risks requires judgment and it is not an exact science. Monitoring aims at detecting unusual or suspicious transactions among an extremely large number of legitimate transactions, furthermore the demarcation of what is unusual may not always be very straightforward since what is 'customary' may vary depending on the customers' business.

Customer profile

This is why developing an accurate customer profile is important in managing a risk-based system. Moreover, procedures and controls are frequently based on previous cases, but criminals will adapt their techniques to new controls/systems, which may quickly limit the utility of such typologies.

Additionally, not all high risk situations are identical, and therefore will not always require precisely the same level of enhanced due diligence. As a result, designated competent authorities/SROs will expect real estate agents to identify individual high risk categories and apply specific and appropriate mitigation measures.

Risk categories

In order to implement a reasonable risk-based approach, real estate agents should

- identify the criteria to assess potential money laundering and terrorist financing risks, and
- identify the money laundering and terrorist financing risks,

so that the extent that such financing risk can be identified by customer or categories of customers, and the transactions made will allow the real estate agents to determine and implement proportionate measures and controls to mitigate these risks.

Money laundering and terrorist financing risks may be measured using various categories. Application of risk categories provides strategy for managing potential risks by enabling real estate agents to subject customers to proportionate controls and oversight.

The most commonly used risk categories are:

- country or geographic risk,
- customer risk, and
- transaction risk.

The rating or measure given to each category (individually or in combination) in assessing the overall risk of potential money laundering and terrorist financing may vary from one real estate agent to another, depending upon their respective circumstances. Consequently, real estate agents will have to make their own determination regarding risk weighting. Regulations and compliance statutes set by law or regulation may limit a real estate agent's discretion.

While there is currently no agreed upon set of risk categories for real estate agents, the examples provided are the most commonly identified risk categories. There is no one single methodology to apply these risk categories, and the application of these risk categories is intended to provide a strategy for managing potential risks.

The following risk categories can indicate a higher risk of money laundering or terrorist financing, dependent upon all of the surrounding circumstances, taking into account the norms of the market at any given time.

Country/geographic risk

Potential elements contributing to risk include:

- Location of property(s) in relation to the buyer. Different countries pose different levels and types of risks pertaining to cross border, non-face to face transactions, e.g. some countries have higher or lower levels of criminality and/or regulation.
- Location of the buyer and seller.

There is no universally agreed definition by either competent authorities, SROs, or real estate agents that prescribes whether a particular country or geographic area represents a higher risk. Country risk, in conjunction with other risk factors, provides useful information as to potential money laundering and terrorist financing risks. Factors that may result in a determination that a country poses a higher risk include:

- Countries subject to sanctions, embargoes or similar measures issued by, for example, the United Nations (UN). In addition, in some circumstances, countries subject to sanctions or measures similar to those issued by bodies such as the UN, but which may not be universally recognised, may be given credence by a real estate agent because of the standing of the issuer and the nature of the measures.
- Countries identified by credible sources as lacking appropriate AML/CFT laws, regulations and other measures.
- Countries identified by credible sources as providing funding or support for terrorist activities that have designated terrorist organisations operating within them.

- Countries identified by credible sources (appendix 5) as having significant levels of corruption, or other criminal activity. (Personally, I think this statement is a bit vague as most countries appear to have a significant level of corruption at all levels especially politically.)
- Countries where there is no mandatory registration of real property.

Customer risk

The behaviour and motivations of customers can be a source of money laundering or terrorist financing risk. However, agents may also form concerns or suspicions about the other parties in a transaction, which may need to be reported to their own compliance office (often referred to as the Money Laundering Reporting Officer, depending on applicable laws and firms' procedures). Mitigation of customer risk primarily centres on CDD, including customer identification.

The main customer risk categories are:

- Significant and unexplained geographic distance between the agent and the location of the customer.
- Customers where the structure or nature of the entity or relationship makes it difficult to identify the true owner or controlling interest.
- Cash intensive businesses.
- Charities and other non-profit organisations that are not subject to monitoring or supervision.
- The use of intermediaries who are not subject to adequate AML/CFT laws and measures and who are not adequately supervised.
- Politically exposed persons (PEPs).

Transaction risk

This category of risk is associated with the factors related to the property, the financing of the transaction and the parties to the transaction. These risks are;

- Speed of the transaction (transactions that are unduly expedited without a reasonable explanation may be higher risk).
- Type of properties (residential or commercial, vacant land, investment, high-turnover properties, multi-unit properties for lettings/leases).
- Successive transactions, especially of same property in short period of time with unexplained changes in value.
- Conversion of properties into smaller units.
- Introduction of unknown parties at a late stage of transactions, e.g. arrangements made between purchasers.
- Third-party vehicles (i.e. trusts) used to obscure true ownership of buyer.

- Under- or over-valued transactions.
- Sale of properties immediately before restraint or insolvency.
- Property value not in the profile of the customer. (You know a Big Issue seller buying a penthouse in Knightsbridge.)

Financing risk

Financing risk is associated with the factors related to the funding and/or source of funding relative to a transaction. Potential elements contributing to financing risk include:

- Location of client's and/or customer's source of funds.
- Unusual sources, e.g. funds obtained from unknown individuals or unusual organisations.
- Purchase with large amounts of cash.
- Cash deposits or money orders from unusual sources or countries as identified under country/geographic risks.
- Use of complex loans, or other obscure means of finance, versus loans from regulated financial institutions.
- Unexplained changes in financing arrangements.

Financing practices obviously vary between countries, and cultural differences have to be recognised. While in some markets, large (or all cash) transactions may seem higher risk, this may be common in other markets, particularly where the currency may fluctuate a great deal or there is no well-functioning mortgage market.

Agents who are involved at any level in the obtaining, processing or closing of a loan, mortgage or other financial instrument must consider the specific risks that raises, and make reference to guidance for financial service providers. Real estate agents who handle purchase funds must also ensure that their policies and procedures are sufficiently robust to account for the additional risk this poses.

In some national systems it is a requirement or common practice that other professions or businesses with CDD requirements under the FATF Recommendations are involved with the transactions, predominantly lawyers, notaries, and financial institutions. This involvement of more than one profession or business might have implications regarding CDD and might reduce risk. However the most common excuse when a money laundering case is identified is 'I thought someone else was completing the appropriate control checks.'

Variables that impact upon risk

There are a number of variables that may impact upon these risk categories, dependent upon all of the surrounding circumstances:

- Involvement of other parties, e.g. financial institutions, lawyers or notaries, and whether they are subject to AML/CFT requirements.
- How the client was introduced to the agent.
- Method of communication between client and agent, e.g. email or personal contact.
- Whether the client is a PEP.
- Whether there is a beneficial owner that is different from the direct customer.
- The products/services used by the client or the purchaser.
- The person with whom the real estate agent has the relationship, for example legal persons or arrangements with no clear structure might pose a higher risk than a natural person.

Controls for higher risk situations

Real estate agents should implement appropriate measures and controls to mitigate the potential money laundering risks of those customers that are determined to be higher risk as the result of the agent's risk-based approach. These measures and controls may include:

- Increased awareness by the real estate agent of higher risk customers and transactions within business lines across the institution.
- Increased levels of know your customer (KYC) or enhanced due diligence.
- Escalation for approval of the establishment of an account or relationship.
- Increased monitoring of transactions.
- Increased levels of ongoing controls and frequency of reviews of relationships.

The same measures and controls may often address more than one of the risk criteria identified, and it is not necessarily expected that real estate agents establish specific controls targeting each and every risk criteria.

Application of risk-based approach

Real estate agents should conduct risk assessments of their business taking into account the following factors:

- The size of their business, e.g. the financial value of the transactions facilitated.
- Nature of business, overseas and/or domestic, residential and/or commercial.
- How instructions are obtained, e.g. through advertising, or through referrals.

Risk mitigation policies and procedures should be devised and implemented in the following areas. The effectiveness of these policies and procedures should be kept under constant review:

Customer due diligence

Customer Due Diligence/Know Your Customer is intended to enable a real estate agent to form a reasonable belief that it knows the true identity of each customer. In the normal course of acting for customers real estate agents may also learn surrounding information which may be helpful in terms of AML/CFT, e.g. the reason for the sale/purchase, and/or the source of funding.

The real estate agent's procedures should include procedures to:

- Identify and verify the identity of each customer/client.
- Identify the beneficial owner, and take reasonable risk-based measures to verify the identity of any beneficial owner. The measures that have to be taken to verify the identity of the beneficial owner will vary depending on the risk.
- Obtain appropriate additional information to understand the customer's circumstances and business, including the expected nature and level of transactions.

Failure to verify the identity of a beneficial owner to the real estate agent's satisfaction as a result of the lack of CDD information, could be the basis for an agent's reporting of the transaction as a suspicious transaction to the relevant authorities

Identification documents should be a secure form of document as recognised by the respective country (e.g. passport, driver's license). The extent of the verification will need to take into account the level of risk that the customer poses, and that the objective is to understand the overall ownership and control structure of the customer. These checks should be approached using a risk-based approach. This should ensure that the requirement does not become disproportionately onerous, but that greater checks are made in higher risk situations. Public sources of information may assist with checks on beneficial ownership.

When considering CDD, agents should bear in mind that there is unlikely to be different levels of risk between buyers and sellers in general as both sides are participating in a financial transaction, either by releasing finance from a property they already own, or by introducing purchase funds.

Monitoring of customers and transactions

The degree and nature of monitoring by a real estate agent will depend on:

- the size of the agent's business,

- the AML/CFT risks that it has,
- the monitoring method being utilised (manual, automated or some combination),
- and the type of activity under scrutiny.

The degree of monitoring should be based on the perceived risks associated with the customer, the transactions undertaken by the customer and the location of the customer and the real property. Monitoring methodologies and processes also need to take into account the resources of the real estate agent's firm.

Depending upon the size of the real estate agent's business, effective monitoring may include the following:

- the possibility of relationships between the sellers and buyers of a property who may be colluding to create a paper transaction for dishonest purposes.
- In transactions where either the vendor or purchaser is not a client/customer of a real estate agent, the agent acting in the transaction should apply reasonable risk-based CDD measures to the party that is not their client.
- Record keeping consistent with any relevant duty of care, and/or local domestic requirements or limitations.

The role of the compliance officer (e.g. Money Laundering Reporting Officer or MLRO) including their function in relation to:

- Monitoring transactions, e.g. routine or spot checking.
- Making external suspicious transaction reports to the national authorities.
- Regular reporting to senior management about AML/CFT performance.
- The role of the government in identifying cash elements of the transaction.

Suspicious transaction reporting

The reporting of suspicious transactions or activity is critical to a country's ability to utilise financial information to combat money laundering, terrorist financing and other financial crimes. Countries' reporting regimes are laid down in national law, requiring institutions to file reports when the threshold of suspicion is reached.

Where a legal or regulatory requirement mandates the reporting of suspicious activity once a suspicion has been formed, a report must be made and, therefore, a risk-based approach for the reporting of suspicious activity under these circumstances is not applicable.

A risk-based approach is, however, appropriate for the purpose of identifying suspicious activity, for example, by directing additional resources at those areas a real estate agent has identified as higher risk. As part of a risk-based approach, it is also likely that a real estate agent will utilise information provided by designated competent authorities or SROs to inform its approach for identifying suspicious activity. A real estate agent should also periodically assess the adequacy of its system for identifying and reporting suspicious transactions.

The requirement to make reports is supported by the following:

- Staff internal reporting line to the MLRO.
- Confidentiality of reports, i.e. how to deal with customers, and others involved in a transaction, after an internal or external report has been made.
- Counter financing of terrorism

Training and awareness

Real estate agents should consider the following:

- New staff, and update training for staff.
- Legal and other obligations.
- Good practice education which should include appropriate and proportional training with regard to money laundering and terrorist financing.

Registration of mortgages should aim to identify the cash elements of the transactions and to what may be suspicious.

FATF Recommendation 15 requires that real estate agents are provided with AML/CFT training, and it is important that agents receive appropriate and proportional training with regard to money laundering and terrorist financing.

Applying a risk-based approach to the various methods available for training, gives each real estate agent's firm additional flexibility regarding the frequency, delivery mechanisms and focus of such training.

A firm should review its own workforce and available resources and implement training programmes that provide appropriate AML/CFT information that is:

- Tailored to the appropriate staff responsibility (e.g. customer contact or operations).
- At the appropriate level of detail.
- At a frequency related to the risk level of the transactions involved.
- Testing to assess knowledge commensurate with the detail of information provided.

Internal control systems

In order for real estate agents to have effective risk-based approaches, the risk-based process must be imbedded within the internal controls of the firms. The success of internal policies and procedures will be dependent largely on internal control systems. Following are two key systems identified.

Culture of compliance amongst all

This should encompass:

- Developing, delivering, and maintaining a training program for all designated agents and employees.
- Monitoring of any government regulatory changes.
- Undertaking a regularly scheduled review of applicable compliance policies and procedures within the brokerage firms will help constitute a culture of compliance in the industry.

Senior management ownership

Strong senior management leadership and engagement in AML/CFT is an important aspect of the application of the risk-based approach. Senior management must create a culture of compliance, ensuring that staff adheres to the real estate agent firm's policies, procedures and processes designed to limit and

control risks. Within estate agencies, the front line of the transaction is with the individual agent. Therefore, policies and procedures are effective only at the point that firm/company owners and senior management support the guidance.

Having regard to the size of the real estate agent's firm, the framework of internal controls should:

- Provide increased focus on real estate agents' operations (products, services, customers and geographic locations) that are more vulnerable to abuse by money launderers and other criminals.
- Provide for regular review of the risk assessment and management processes, taking into account the environment within which the real estate agent operates and the activity in its market place.
- Designate an individual or individuals at management level responsible for managing AML/CFT compliance.
- Provide for an AML/CFT compliance function and review programme.
- Ensure that adequate controls are in place before new products are offered.
- Inform senior management of compliance initiatives, identified compliance deficiencies, corrective action taken, and suspicious activity reports filed.
- Provide for programme continuity despite changes in management or employee composition or structure.
- Focus on meeting all regulatory record keeping and reporting requirements, recommendations for AML/CFT compliance and provide for timely updates in response to changes in regulations.
- Implement risk-based customer due diligence policies, procedures and processes.

- Provide for adequate controls for higher risk customers, transactions and products, as necessary, such as transaction limits or management approvals.
- Enable the timely identification of reportable transactions and ensure accurate filing of required reports.
- Provide for adequate supervision of employees that handle currency transactions, complete reports, grant exemptions, monitor for suspicious activity, or engage in any other activity that forms part of the institution's AML/CFT programme.
- Incorporate AML/CFT compliance into job descriptions and performance evaluations of appropriate personnel.
- Provide for appropriate training to be given to all relevant staff.
- For groups, to the extent possible, there should be a common control framework.

9

The Risk-Based Approach: Trusts

There have been a number of articles and recommendations for the adoption of a risk-based approach to combating money laundering and terrorist financing which can yield benefits for all parties including the public. Applied effectively, the approach can allow a more efficient and effective use of resources and minimise burdens on customers. Focusing on higher risk threats should mean that beneficial outcomes can be achieved more effectively.

The potential benefits and potential challenges can be summarised as follows:

Potential benefits:
- Better management of risks
- Efficient use and allocation of resources
- Focus on real and identified threats
- Flexibility to adapt to risks that change over time

Potential challenges:
- Identifying appropriate information to conduct a sound risk analysis
- Addressing short term transitional costs
- Greater need for more expert staff capable of making sound judgements.
- Developing appropriate regulatory response to potential diversity of practice.

Applicability of the risk-based approach to terrorist financing

There are both similarities and differences in the application of a risk-based approach to terrorist financing and money laundering. They both require a process for identifying and assessing risk.

However, the characteristics of terrorist financing make its detection difficult and the implementation of mitigation strategies may be challenging due to considerations such as the relatively low value of transactions involved in terrorist financing (as mentioned previously), or the fact that funds can be derived from legitimate as well as illicit sources.

Funds that are used to finance terrorist activities may be derived either from criminal activity or may be, as discussed, from legal sources, and the nature of the funding sources may vary according to the type of terrorist organisation.

Criminal activity

Where funds are derived from criminal activity, then traditional monitoring mechanisms that are used to identify money laundering may also be appropriate for terrorist financing, though the activity, which may be indicative of suspicion, may not be identified as or connected to terrorist financing. As already discussed transactions associated with the financing of terrorism may be conducted in very small amounts, which in applying a risk-based approach could be the very transactions that are frequently considered to be of such minimal risk with regard to money laundering. One should not forget the old scheme of 'smurfing' where larger sums of dirty money were split into small packets below the reportable limits so as to avoid possible detection, the transactions only being discovered on the identification of many small deposits going into the same account on the same day.

Where funds are from legal sources, it is even more difficult to determine if they could be used for terrorist purposes. In addition, the actions of terrorists may be overt and outwardly innocent in appearance, such as the purchase of materials and services to further their goals, with the only covert fact being the intended use of such materials and services purchased. Therefore, while terrorist funds may be derived from criminal activity as well as from legitimate sources, transactions related to terrorist financing may not exhibit the same traits as conventional money laundering. However in all cases, it is not the responsibility of Trust and Company Service Providers (TCSPs) to determine the type of underlying criminal activity, or intended terrorist purpose; it is, the TCSP's role to identify and report the suspicious activity. The FIU and law enforcement authorities will then investigate the report further and determine if there is a link to terrorist financing.

The ability to detect and identify potential terrorist financing transactions without professional guidance on terrorist financing modus operandi or acting on specific intelligence provided by the authorities is significantly more challenging than is the case for potential money laundering and other suspicious activity. Detection efforts, absent specific national guidance and typologies, are likely to be based on monitoring that focuses on transactions with countries or geographic areas where terrorists are known to operate or on the other limited typologies available (many of which are indicative of the same techniques as are used for money laundering).

Particular individuals, organisations or countries may be the subject of terrorist financing sanctions, in a particular country. In such cases a listing of individuals, organisations or countries to which sanctions apply and the obligations on TCSPs to comply with those sanctions are decided by individual countries and are not a function of risk. TCSPs will commit a criminal offence if they undertake a business with a listed individual, organisation or country, or its agent, in contravention of applicable sanctions.

There are several components of customer due diligence ('CDD') identification and verification of the identity of customers and beneficial owners, obtaining information on the purposes and intended nature of the business relationships, and conducting ongoing due diligence. Of these components, the identification and verification of the identity of customers are requirements which must be completed regardless of the risk-based approach. However, in relation to all the other CDD components, a reasonably implemented risk-based approach may allow for a determination of the extent and quantity of information required, and the mechanisms to be used to meet these minimum standards. Once this determination is made, the obligation to keep records and documents that have been obtained for due diligence purposes, as well as transaction records, is not dependent on risk levels.

Various jurisdictions may allow reduced or simplified measures where the risk of money laundering or terrorist financing is lower. However, these reduced or simplified measures do not necessarily apply to all aspects of customer due diligence. Moreover, where these exemptions are subject to certain conditions being met, it is necessary to verify that these conditions apply, and where the exemption applies under a certain threshold, measures should be in place to prevent transactions from being split artificially (smurfing) to avoid the threshold. In addition, information beyond customer identity, such as customer location, may be needed to adequately assess risk. This will be an interactive process: the preliminary information obtained about a customer should be sufficient to determine whether to go further, and in many cases customer monitoring will provide additional information.

Some form of monitoring is required in order to detect unusual and hence possibly suspicious transactions. Even in the case of lower risk customers, monitoring is needed to verify that transactions match the initial low risk profile and if not, trigger a process for appropriately revising the customer's risk rating. Equally, risks for some customers may only become evident once a relationship with a customer has begun. This makes appropriate and reasonable monitoring of customer transactions an essential component of a properly designed risk-based approach; however, within this context it should be understood that not all transactions, accounts or customers will be monitored in exactly the same way. Moreover, where there is an actual suspicion of money laundering or terrorist financing, this could be regarded as a higher risk scenario, and enhanced due diligence should be applied regardless of any threshold or exemption.

Distinguishing between monitoring and policies/processes

Risk-based policies and processes should be distinguished from risk-based monitoring by designated competent authorities or SROs. There is a general recognition within supervisory/monitoring practice that resources should be allocated taking into account the risks posed by individual businesses. The methodology adopted by the designated competent authorities or SROs to determine allocation of monitoring resources should cover the business focus, the risk profile and the internal control environment, and should permit relevant comparisons between businesses. The methodology used for determining the allocation of resources will need updating on an ongoing basis so as to reflect the nature, importance and scope of the risks to which individual businesses are exposed. Consequently, this prioritisation should lead designated competent authorities or SROs to focus increased regulatory attention on businesses that engage in activities assessed to present a higher risk of money laundering or terrorist financing.

However, it should also be noted that the risk factors taken into account to prioritise the designated competent authorities' or SROs' work will depend not only on the risk associated with the activity undertaken, but also on the quality and effectiveness of the risk management systems implemented to address such risks.

Since designated competent authorities or SROs should have already assessed the quality of risk management controls applied throughout TCSPs, it is reasonable that their assessments of these controls be used, at least in part, to inform money laundering and terrorist financing risk assessments conducted by individual firms or businesses

A risk-based approach: key elements

TCSPs, designated competent authorities or SROs should have access to reliable and actionable information about the threats.

There must be emphasis on cooperative arrangements among the policy makers, law enforcement, regulators, and the private sector.

Authorities should publicly recognise that the risk-based approach will not eradicate all elements of risk.

Authorities have a responsibility to establish an atmosphere in which the various parties need not be afraid of regulatory sanctions where they have acted responsibly and implemented adequate internal systems and controls.

Designated competent authorities' or SROs' supervisory staff must be well-trained in the risk-based approach, both as applied by designated competent authorities/SRO and by regulated groups.

Effective systems for monitoring and ensuring AML/ CFT compliance

It is important to note that FATF Recommendation 24 **requires that TCSPs be subject to effective systems for monitoring and ensuring compliance with AML/CFT requirements.**

In determining an effective system, reference should be had to the risk of money laundering or terrorist financing in the sector. There should be a designated competent authority or SRO responsible for monitoring and ensuring compliance of TCSPs and the authority or SRO should have adequate powers to perform its functions, including powers to monitor and sanction.

It should be noted that the supervision of the various bodies varies from jurisdiction to jurisdiction. Some are supervised in the same way as banks and other financial institutions and others are subject to a separate monitoring/oversight regime.

Defining the acceptable level of risk

The level of AML/CFT risk will generally be affected by both internal and external risk factors. For example, risk levels may be increased by internal risk factors such as weak compliance resources, inadequate risk controls and insufficient senior management involvement. External level risks may rise due to factors such as the action of third parties and/or political and public developments.

All activity involves an element of risk. Designated competent authorities and SROs should not prohibit TCSPs from conducting business with high risk customers as long as appropriate policies, procedures and processes to manage the attendant risks are in place. Only in specific cases, for example when it is justified by the fight against terrorism, crime or the implementation of international obligations, are designated individuals, legal entities, organisations or countries denied categorically access to services.

However, this does not exclude the need to implement basic minimum requirements. For example FATF Recommendation 5 states that 'where [the TCSP] is unable to comply with (CDD requirements), it should not open the account, commence business relations or perform the transaction; or should terminate the business relationship; and should consider making a suspicious transaction report in relation to the customer.'

So the level of risk should strike an appropriate balance between;

- the extremes of not accepting customers, and
- conducting business with unacceptable or unmitigated risk.

Where TCSPs, are allowed to implement a risk-based approach, designated competent authorities and SROs should expect them to put in place effective policies, programmes, procedures and systems to mitigate the risk and acknowledge that even with effective systems not every suspect transaction will necessarily be detected.

They should also ensure that those policies, programmes, procedures and systems are applied effectively to prevent them from becoming conduits for illegal proceeds and ensure that they keep records and make reports that are of use to national authorities in combating money laundering and terrorist financing. Efficient policies and procedures will reduce the level of risks, but are unlikely to eliminate them completely. There is no doubt that assessing money laundering and terrorist financing risks requires judgment and is not an exact science. Monitoring aims at detecting unusual or suspicious transactions among an extremely large number of legitimate transactions; furthermore, the demarcation of what is unusual may not always be straightforward since what is 'customary' may vary depending on the customers' business. This is why developing an accurate customer profile is important in managing a risk-based system. Moreover, procedures and controls are frequently based on previous typologies cases, but criminals unfortunately change and adapt their techniques as conditions alter, which may quickly limit the utility of such typologies.

Additionally, not all high risk situations are identical with only passing similarities, (usually criminal activity differs from case to case) and therefore will not always require precisely the same level of enhanced due diligence. As a result, designated competent authorities/SROs will expect TCSPs to identify individual high risk categories and apply specific and appropriate mitigation measures.

Proportionate supervisory/monitoring actions

Designated competent authorities and SROs should seek to identify weaknesses through an effective programme of both on-site and off-site supervision, and through analysis of internal and other available information.

In the course of their examinations, designated competent authorities and SROs should review a TCSP's AML/CFT risk assessments as well as its policies, procedures and control systems to arrive at an overall assessment of the risk profile of TCSPs' business and the adequacy of its mitigation measures. Where available, assessments carried out by or for TCSPs may be a useful source of information. The designated competent authority/SRO assessment of management's ability and willingness to take necessary corrective action is also a critical determining factor. Designated competent authorities and SROs should use proportionate actions to ensure proper and timely correction of deficiencies, taking into account that identified weaknesses can have wider consequences. Generally, systemic breakdowns or inadequate controls will result in the most severe monitoring response.

Nevertheless, it may happen that the lack of detection of an isolated high risk transaction, or of transactions of an isolated high risk customer, will in itself be significant, for instance where the amounts are significant, or where the money laundering and terrorist financing modus operandi is well known, or where a scheme has remained undetected for a long time. Such a case might indicate an accumulation of weak risk management practices or regulatory breaches regarding the identification of high risks, monitoring, staff training and internal controls, and therefore, might alone justify action to ensure compliance with the AML/CFT requirements.

Designated competent authorities and SROs can and should use their knowledge of the risks associated with products, services, customers and geographic locations to help them evaluate TCSPs' money laundering and terrorist financing risk assessments, with the understanding, however, that they may possess information that has not been made available to them and, therefore, they would not have been able to take such information into account when developing and implementing a risk-based approach.

Designated competent authorities and SROs (and other relevant stakeholders) are encouraged to use that knowledge to issue guidelines to assist TCSPs in managing their risks. Where they are permitted to determine the extent of the CDD measures on a risk sensitive basis, this should be consistent with guidelines issued by their designated competent authorities and SROs. Guidance designed specifically for the various bodies is likely to be the most effective. An assessment of the risk-based approach will, for instance, help identify cases where they use excessively narrow risk categories that do not censure all existing risks, or adopt criteria that lead to the identification of a large number of higher risk relationships, but without providing for adequate additional due diligence measures..

In the context of the risk-based approach, the primary focus for designated competent authorities and SROs should be to determine whether or not the various bodies AML/CFT compliance and risk management programme is adequate to:

- meet the minimum regulatory requirements, and
- appropriately and effectively mitigate the risks.

The monitoring goal should not be to prohibit high risk activity, but rather to be confident that firms have adequately and effectively implemented appropriate risk mitigation strategies.

In considering the above factors it is clear that proportionate monitoring should be supported by two central features:

Regulatory transparency

In the implementation of proportionate actions, regulatory transparency will be of paramount importance. Designated competent authorities and SROs are aware that TCSPs, Accountants, while looking for operational freedom to make their own risk judgments, will also seek guidance on regulatory obligations. As such, the designated competent authority/SRO with AML/CFT supervisory/monitoring responsibilities should seek to be transparent in setting out what it expects, and will need to consider appropriate mechanisms of communicating these messages. For instance, this may be in the form of high-level requirements, based on desired outcomes, rather than detailed processes.

No matter what individual procedure is adopted, the guiding principle will be that there is an awareness of legal responsibilities and regulatory expectations. In the absence of this transparency there is the danger that monitoring actions may be perceived as either disproportionate or unpredictable which may undermine even the most effective application of the risk-based approach by TCSPs.

Training of competent authorities, SROs, and enforcement staff

In the context of the risk-based approach, it is not possible to specify precisely what a TCSP has to do, in all cases, to meet its regulatory obligations. Thus, a prevailing consideration will be how best to ensure the consistent implementation of predictable and proportionate monitoring actions. The effectiveness of monitoring training will therefore be important to the successful delivery of proportionate supervisory/monitoring actions.

Training should aim to allow designated competent authorities/SRO staff to form sound comparative judgments about AML/CFT systems and controls. It is important in conducting assessments that designated competent authorities and SROs have the ability to make judgments regarding management controls in light of the risks assumed by TCSPs and their firms and considering available industry practices. Designated competent authorities and SROs might also find it useful to undertake comparative assessments so as to form judgments as to the relative strengths and weaknesses of different firms or business arrangements.

The training should include instructing designated competent authorities and SROs about how to evaluate whether senior management has implemented adequate risk management measures, and determine if the necessary procedures and controls are in place. The training should also include reference to specific guidance, where available. Designated competent authorities and SROs also should be satisfied that sufficient resources are in place to ensure the implementation of effective risk management.

To fulfil these responsibilities, training should enable designated competent authorities' and SROs' monitoring staff to adequately assess:

- The quality of internal procedures, including ongoing employee training programmes and internal audit, compliance and risk management functions.
- Whether or not the risk management policies and processes are appropriate in light of the risk profile, and are periodically adjusted in light of changing risk profiles.
- The participation of senior management to confirm that they have undertaken adequate risk management, and that the necessary procedures and controls are in place.

Risk categories

In order to implement a reasonable risk-based approach, TCSPs should identify the criteria to assess potential money laundering and terrorist financing risks on a service-by-service basis. These risks will vary according to the activities undertaken by the TCSP.

Identification of the money laundering and terrorist financing risks, to the extent that such terrorist financing risk can be identified, of customers or categories of customers, and transactions will allow the various bodies to determine and implement proportionate measures and controls to mitigate these risks. While a risk assessment should always be performed at the inception of a customer relationship, for some customers, a comprehensive risk profile may only become evident through time, making monitoring of customer transactions and ongoing reviews a fundamental component of a reasonably designed risk-based approach. They may also have to adjust its risk assessment of a particular customer based upon information received from a designated competent authority or SRO.

Money laundering and terrorist financing risks may be measured using various categories. Application of risk categories provides a strategy for managing potential risks by enabling TCSPs to subject customers to proportionate controls and oversight.

The most commonly used risk criteria are:

- country or geographic risk;
- customer risk; and
- product/services risk.

The weight given to these risk categories (individually or in combination) in assessing the overall risk of potential money laundering may vary from one operation to another, depending upon their respective circumstances. Consequently, they will have to make their own determination as to the risk weights. Parameters set by law or regulation may limit their discretion.

While there is no agreed upon set of risk categories for these bodies, the examples provided herein are the most commonly identified risk categories. There is no one single methodology for applying these risk categories; however, the application of these risk categories is intended to assist in designing an effective strategy for managing the potential risks.

Countries/geographic risk

There is no universally agreed definition by either competent authorities or TCSPs that prescribes whether a particular country or geographic area (including the country within which the TCSP operates) represents a higher risk. Country risk, in conjunction with other risk factors, provides useful information as to potential money laundering and terrorist financing vulnerabilities. Factors that may result in the determination that a country poses a higher risk include:

- Countries subject to sanctions, embargoes or similar measures issued by, for example, the United Nations (UN). In addition, in some circumstances, countries subject to sanctions or measures similar to those issued by bodies such as the UN, but which may not be universally recognised, may be given credence by a TCSP because of the standing of the issuer and the nature of the measures.
- Countries identified by credible sources as lacking appropriate AML/CFT laws, regulations and other measures.
- Countries identified by credible sources as providing funding or support for terrorist activities that have designated terrorist organisations operating within them.
- Countries identified by credible sources as having significant levels of corruption, or other criminal activity.
- Note: the last two obviously include the UK with high criminal activity, terrorist cells, corruption in high places and lax anti-money laundering controls.

Customer risk

Determining the potential money laundering or terrorist financing risks, to the extent that such terrorist financing risks can be identified, posed by a customer, or category of customers, is critical to the development of an overall risk framework. Based on its own criteria, a TCSP will determine whether a particular customer poses a higher risk and the potential impact of any mitigating factors on that assessment. Application of risk variables may mitigate or exacerbate the risk assessment. Categories of customers whose activities may indicate a higher risk include:

Customers conducting their business relationship or transactions in unusual circumstances, such as:

- Significant and unexplained geographic distance between the TCSP and the location of the customer.

Customers where the structure or nature of the entity or relationship makes it difficult to identify and verify the true owner or controlling interests, such as:

- Unexplained use of corporate structures, express trusts and nominee shares, and use of bearer shares.
- Unexplained delegation of authority by the applicant or customer through the use of powers of attorney, mixed boards and representative offices.
- Unexplained relationship between an applicant's beneficial owners and controllers and account signatories.

In the case of express trusts, an unexplained relationship between a settlor and beneficiaries with a vested right, other beneficiaries and persons who are the object of a power.

- In the case of an express trust, an unexplained nature of classes of beneficiaries and classes within an expression of wishes.

Cash (and cash equivalent) intensive businesses

'Credible sources' refers to information that is produced by well-known bodies that generally are regarded as reputable and that make such information publicly and widely available. In addition to the Financial Action Task Force and FATF-style regional bodies, such sources may include, but are not limited to, supra-national or international bodies such as the International Monetary Fund, and the Egmont Group of Financial Intelligence Units, as well as relevant national government bodies and non-governmental organisations. The information provided by these credible sources does not have the effect of law or regulation and should not be viewed as an automatic determination that something is of higher risk.

TCSPs generally use the term 'client' instead of 'customer'. The definition of 'client' of the TCSP, may extend (for identification and verification purposes) to other relevant parties who might have some degree of control over the trust/company structure. This should include the settlor, the trustee or person exercising effective control over the trust and the beneficiaries. This may include protectors if they have any positive powers. Nevertheless it is generally accepted that not all beneficiaries are always beneficial owners. Different countries have adopted different approaches to deal with this issue.

Examples of cash intensive businesses include:

- Money services businesses (e.g. remittance houses, currency exchange houses, casas de cambio, bureau de change, money transfer agents and

bank note traders or other businesses offering money transfer facilities
- Casinos, betting and other gambling related activities.
- Businesses that while not normally cash intensive, generate substantial amounts of cash for certain transactions.
- Charities and other 'not for profit' organisations which are not subject to monitoring or supervision (especially those operating on a 'cross-border' basis).
- Other TCSPs, financial institutions, and other designated non-professional businesses and professions who are not subject to adequate AML/CFT laws and measures and who are not adequately supervised.
- Customers that are politically exposed persons (PEPs).
- Customers where there is no commercial rationale for a customer buying the products or services that he seeks, who request undue levels of secrecy, or where it appears that an 'audit trail' has been deliberately broken or unnecessarily layered.

Product/service risk

An overall risk assessment should also include determining the potential risk presented by products and services offered by a TCSP. TCSPs should be mindful of the risks associated with new or innovative products or services. A key element for TCSPs is establishing the existence of an apparent legitimate business, economic, tax or legal reasons for the structures the TCSP is asked to set up and manage. Determining the risks of products and services should include the consideration of such factors as:

- Shell companies, companies with ownership through nominee shareholding and control through nominee and corporate directors.
- Services where TCSPs, acting as financial intermediaries, actually handle the receipt and transmission of cash proceeds through accounts they actually control in the act of closing a business transaction.
- Other services to conceal improperly beneficial ownership from competent authorities.
- Situations where it is difficult to identify the beneficiaries of trusts. This might include situations where identification is hindered because the beneficiary of a trust is another trust or corporate vehicle, or where the trust deed does not include the names of the settlor, the beneficiaries or the class of beneficiaries.
- Commercial, private, or real property transactions or services with no apparent legitimate business, economic, tax, family governance, or legal reasons.
- Payments received from unassociated or unknown third parties where this would not be a typical method of payment.

- The offer by customers to pay extraordinary fees for services which would not ordinarily warrant such a premium.
- Services that inherently have provided more anonymity.
- Trusts which are pensions that may be considered lower risk.

Variables that may impact risk

A TCSP's risk-based approach methodology may take into account risk variables specific to a particular customer or transaction. These variables may increase or decrease perceived risks posed by a particular customer or transaction and may include:

- The purpose and intended nature of a relationship.
- The type, volume and value of activity expected.
- The source of funds and the source of wealth – the source of funds is the activity that generates the funds for a customer, while the source of wealth describes the activities which have generated the total net worth of a customer.
- Unusually high levels of assets or unusually large transactions compared to what might reasonably be expected of customers with a similar profile may indicate that a customer not otherwise seen as higher risk should be treated as such. Conversely, low levels of assets or low value transactions involving a customer that would otherwise appear to be higher risk might allow for a TCSP to treat the customer as lower risk.
- The level of regulation or other oversight of a government's regime to which a customer is subject. A customer that is a financial institution regulated in a country with a satisfactory AML regime poses less risk from a money laundering perspective than a customer that is unregulated or subject only to minimal AML regulation. Additionally, companies and their wholly owned subsidiaries that are publically owned and traded on a recognised exchange generally pose minimal money laundering risks. These companies are usually from countries with an adequate, recognised regulatory scheme, and, therefore, generally pose less risk due to the type of business that they conduct and the wider government's regime to which they are subject.
- The regularity or duration of the relationship. Long standing relationships involving frequent customer contact throughout the relationship may present less risk from the money laundering perspective.
- The familiarity with the country, including knowledge of local laws, regulations and rules, as well as the structure and extent of regulatory oversight, as a result of a TCSPs own operations within the country.
- The use of intermediate corporate vehicles or other structures that have no apparent commercial or other rationale or that will increase the complexity or

otherwise result in a lack of transparency. The use of such vehicles or structures, without an acceptable explanation, increases the risk.

Controls for higher risk situations

TCSPs should implement appropriate measures and controls to mitigate the potential money laundering risks of those customers that are determined to be higher risk as a result of their risk assessment. The same measures and controls may often address more than one of the risk criteria identified and it is not necessarily expected that a TCSP establish specific controls targeting each and every criteria. Appropriate measures and controls may include:

- General training on money laundering and terrorist financing methods and risks relevant to their operations.
- Targeted training for increased awareness of higher risk customers and transactions.
- Increased levels of customer due diligence or enhanced due diligence.
- Escalation of the approval of the establishment of a relationship.
- Increased monitoring of the services offered to determine whether the risk of money laundering occurring has increased.
- Increased levels of ongoing controls and frequency of reviews of relationships.

Application of a risk-based approach

Customer due diligence/know your customer

Customer Due Diligence/Know Your Customer is intended to enable a TCSP to form a reasonable belief that it knows the true identity of each customer and, with an appropriate degree of confidence, knows the types of business and transactions the customer is likely to undertake. Their procedures should include procedures to:

- Identify and verify the identity of each customer on a timely basis.
- Identify the beneficial owner, and take reasonable measures to verify the identity of any beneficial owner. The measures that have to be taken to verify the identity of the beneficial owner will vary depending on the risk.
- Obtain appropriate additional information to understand the customer's circumstances and business, including the expected nature and level of transactions. Relevant customer due diligence information should be periodically updated together with its risk assessment. In the event of any change in beneficial ownership or control of the applicant, or third parties on

whose behalf the applicant acts, reasonable measures should be taken to verify identity.

The starting point is for them to assess the risks that a customer may pose taking into consideration any appropriate risk variables before making a final determination. They will determine the due diligence requirements appropriate to each customer. This may include:

- A standard level of due diligence, to be applied to all customers.
- The standard level being reduced in recognised lower risk scenarios, such as:
  - Publicly listed companies subject to regulatory disclosure requirements.
  - Financial institutions (domestic or foreign) subject to an AML/CFT regime consistent with the FATF Recommendations.

An increased level of due diligence in respect of those customers that are determined to be of higher risk. This may be the result of a customer's business activity, ownership structure, anticipated or actual volume or types of transactions, including those transactions involving higher risk countries or defined by applicable law or regulation as posing a higher risk, such as:

- PEPs.
- Sanctioned countries.

Monitoring of customers and transactions

The degree and nature of monitoring by a TCSP will depend on the size of their operation, the AML/CFT risks that the institution has identified, the monitoring method being used (manual, automated or some combination), and the type of activity under scrutiny. In applying a risk-based approach to monitoring, they, and where appropriate their regulatory supervisors must recognise that not all transactions or customers will be monitored in the same way. The degree of monitoring will be based on the perceived risks associated with the customer, the products or services being used by the customer, the location of the customer, and the particular transaction. Monitoring methodologies and processes also need to take into account the resources of the various operations..

Monitoring under a risk-based approach allows them to determine which activity need not be reviewed or reviewed less frequently. Defined situations used for this purpose should be reviewed on a regular basis to determine the adequacy for the risk levels established. They should also assess the adequacy of any systems and processes on a periodic basis. The results of such monitoring should always be documented.

Suspicious transaction reporting

The reporting of suspicious transactions or activities is critical to a country's ability to utilise financial information to combat money laundering, terrorist financing, and other financial crimes. Countries' reporting regimes are laid down in national law, requiring institutions to file reports when the threshold of suspicion is reached. The requirement to report a suspicious transaction will arise when they engage in a transaction for a client, or on behalf of a client,

Where a legal or regulatory requirement mandates the reporting of a suspicious activity once the suspicion has been formed, a report must be made and, therefore, a risk-based approach for the reporting of a suspicious activity under these circumstances is not applicable.

A risk-based approach is, however, appropriate for the purpose of identifying a suspicious activity, for example, by directing additional resources at those areas where they have identified as higher risk. As part of a risk-based approach, it is also likely that they will utilise information provided by designated competent authorities or SROs to inform its approach to identifying suspicious activity. They should also periodically assess the adequacy of their systems for identifying and reporting suspicious transactions.

Training and awareness

The FATF and financial regulatory bodies in various jurisdictions recommend that TCSPs provide their employees with AML/CFT training, and it is important that their employees receive appropriate and proportionate training with regard to money laundering and terrorist financing. Their commitment to having successful controls relies on both training and awareness. This requires an enterprise-wide effort to provide all relevant employees with at least general information on AML/CFT laws, regulations and internal policies.

Applying a risk-based approach to the various methods available for training, however, gives each organisation additional flexibility regarding the frequency, delivery and focus of such training. They should review their own workforce and available resources and implement training programmes that provide appropriate AML/CFT information that is:

- Tailored to the appropriate staff responsibility (e.g. customer contact or operations).
- At the appropriate level of detail (e.g. frontline personnel, complicated products or customer managed products).
- At a frequency related to the risk level of the business involved.
- Tested to assess staff knowledge commensurate with the detail of information provided.

Internal controls

Many DNFBPs differ significantly from financial institutions in terms of size. By contrast to most financial institutions, a significant number of DNFBPs have only a few staff. This limits the resources that small businesses and professions can dedicate to the fight against money laundering and terrorist financing. For a number of DNFBPs, a single person may be responsible for the functions of front office, back office, money laundering reporting, and senior management. This particularity of DNFBPs, including TCSPs, should be taken into account in designing a risk-based framework for internal controls systems.

In order for TCSPs to have effective risk-based approaches, the risk-based process must be imbedded within the internal controls of the institutions. Senior management is ultimately responsible for ensuring that they maintain an effective internal control structure, including suspicious activity monitoring and reporting. Strong senior management leadership and engagement in AML is an important aspect of the application of the risk-based approach. Senior management must create a culture of compliance, ensuring that staff adheres to the organisations policies, procedures and processes designed to limit and control risks.

In addition to other compliance internal controls, the nature and extent of AML/CFT controls will depend upon a number of factors including:

- The nature, scale and complexity of the business.
- The diversity of the operations, including geographical diversity.
- The customer, product and activity profile.
- The volume and size of the transactions.
- The degree of risk associated with each area of the operation.
- The extent to which they are dealing directly with the customer or is dealing through intermediaries, third parties, correspondents, or non face-to-face access.
- The frequency of customer contact (either in person or by other means of communication).

Having regard to the size of the operation, the framework of internal controls should generally:

- Provide increased focus on the operations (products, services, customers and geographic locations) that are more vulnerable to abuse by money launderers and other criminals.
- Provide for a regular review of the risk assessment and management processes, taking into account the environment within which the organisation operates and the activity in its market place.
- Designate an individual or individuals at management level responsible for

managing AML/CFT compliance.

- Provide for an AML/CFT compliance function and review programme.
- Ensure that adequate controls are in place before new products or services are offered.
- Inform senior management of compliance initiatives, identified compliance deficiencies, corrective action taken and suspicious activity reports filed.
- Provide for programme continuity despite changes in management or employee composition or structure.
- Focus on meeting where appropriate, all regulatory record keeping and reporting requirements, recommendations for AML/CFT compliance and provide for timely updates in response to changes in regulations.
- Implement risk-based customer due diligence policies, procedures and processes.
- Provide for adequate controls for higher risk customers, transactions and products/services, as necessary, such as transaction limits or management approvals.
- Enable the timely identification of reportable transactions and ensure accurate filing of required reports.
- Provide for adequate supervision of employees that handle transactions, complete reports, grant exemptions, monitor for suspicious activity, or engage in any other activity that forms part of the institution's AML/CFT programme.
- Incorporate AML/CFT compliance into job descriptions and performance evaluations of appropriate personnel.
- Provide for appropriate training to be given to all relevant staff.

For groups, to the extent possible, there should be a common control framework.

Senior management will need to have a means of independently validating the development and operation of the risk assessment and management processes and related internal controls, and obtaining appropriate comfort that the adopted risk-based methodology reflects the risk profile of the operation. This independent testing and reporting should be conducted by, for example, the internal audit department, external auditors, specialist consultants or other qualified parties who are not involved in the implementation or operation of the AML/CFT compliance programme. The testing should be risk-based (focusing attention on higher risk customers, products and services) and including comprehensive procedures and testing that cover all activities. It should also evaluate the adequacy of the overall AML/CFT programme and the quality of its operational risk management programme.

10

The Risk-Based Approach: Accountants

As with other professions where money is involved there are anti-money laundering regulations and legislation in most jurisdictions in respect of accountants.

The FATF Recommendations for accountants when they prepare for or carry out transactions on behalf of their clients concerning the following activities:

- Buying and selling of real estate;
- Management of client money, securities or other assets;
- Management of bank, savings or securities accounts.
- Organisation of contributions for the creation, operation or management of companies.

These recommendations refer to sole practitioners, partners or employed professionals within professional firms. They do not apply to 'internal' professionals that are employees of other types of businesses (automobile manufacturers, oil companies etc), nor to professionals working for government agencies, who may already be subject to measures that would combat money laundering.

Where accountants are subject to obligations of professional secrecy or legal professional privilege (similar in nature to that of legal professionals), they are not required to report their suspicions if the relevant information was obtained in circumstances where they are subject to professional secrecy or legal professional privilege under the laws of that country. **Professional secrecy/legal professional privilege are not the same as client confidentiality.**

Various jurisdictions have determined the matters that would fall under legal professional privilege or professional secrecy. (However in many countries these recommendations have not been implemented and even in those countries where they have money laundering cases involving accountants constantly come out of the proverbial woodwork).This normally covers information lawyers, notaries or other independent legal professionals receive from or obtain through one of their clients:

- in the course of ascertaining the legal position of their client, or
- in performing their task of defending or representing that client in, or concerning judicial, administrative, arbitration or mediation proceedings.

Where accountants are subject to the same obligations of secrecy or privilege, they are also not required to report suspicious transactions.

Activities carried out by accountants

This chapter is addressed to accountants in public practice, on applying a risk-based approach to compliance with local legislation and FATF's Recommendations that may apply to them. It refers to sole practitioners, partners or employed professionals within professional firms. It is not meant to refer to 'internal' professionals that are employees of other types of businesses, nor to professionals working for government agencies, who may already be subject to measures that would combat money laundering.

Accountants within business should refer to professional or other alternative sources of guidance on the appropriate action to take in relation to suspected illegal activity by their employer or a third party.

Accountants in practice may provide a very wide range of services, to a very diverse range of clients. For example, services may include (but are not restricted to):

- Audit and assurance services.
- Book-keeping and the preparation of annual and periodic accounts.
- Tax compliance work, and advice on the legitimate minimisation of tax burdens.
- Internal audit, and advice on internal control and risk minimisation.
- Regulatory and compliance services, including outsourced regulatory examinations and remediation services.
- Insolvency/receiver-managers/bankruptcy related services.
- Advice on the structuring of transactions, and succession advice.
- Advice on investments and custody of client money.
- Forensic accountancy.

In many countries, accountants are the first professional consulted by many small businesses and individuals when seeking general business advice and a wide range of regulatory and compliance advice. Where services are not within their competence, accountants usually advise on an appropriate source of further assistance.

Accountants typically refer to those benefiting from their services as 'clients' rather than 'customers

Some of the functions performed by accountants that are the most useful to the potential launderer include:

- **Financial and tax advice.** Criminals with a large amount of money to invest may pose as individuals hoping to minimise their tax liabilities or desiring to place assets out of reach in order to avoid future liabilities.
- **Creation of corporate vehicles or other complex legal arrangements** (trusts, for example). Such structures may serve to confuse or disguise the links between the proceeds of a crime and the perpetrator.
- **Buying or selling of property.** Property transfers serve as either the cover for transfers of illegal funds (layering stage) or else they represent the final investment of these proceeds after their having passed through the laundering process (integration stage).
- **Performing financial transactions.** Sometimes accountants may carry out various financial operations on behalf of the client (for example, cash deposits or withdrawals on accounts, retail foreign exchange operations, issuing and cashing cheques, purchase and sale of stock, sending and receiving international funds transfers, etc.).
- **Gaining introductions to financial institutions.**

The risk-based approach: purpose, benefits and challenges

As mentioned in the chapter on Real Estate (see page 199),, adopting a risk-based approach allows resources to be allocated in the most efficient ways. The principle is that resources should be directed in accordance with priorities so that the greatest risks receive the highest attention.

The alternative approaches are that resources are either applied evenly, or that resources are targeted, but on the basis of factors other than risk. This can inadvertently lead to a 'tick box' approach with the focus on meeting regulatory requirements rather than on combating money laundering or terrorist financing efficiently and effectively.

A number of the DNFBP sectors, including accountants in countries where accountancy is a regulated profession, are already subject to regulatory or professional requirements which complement AML/CFT measures. There is no doubt that it is beneficial for accountants to devise their AML/CFT policies and procedures in a way that harmonises with other regulatory or professional requirements. A risk-based AML/CFT regime can help ensure that honest clients can access the services provided by accountants, but should also create barriers to those who seek to misuse those services.

A risk analysis must be performed to determine where the money laundering and terrorist financing risks are the greatest. Accountants will need the assistance of the regulatory bodies in their jurisdiction to identify the main vulnerabilities so as to help them to identify higher risk customers, products and services, delivery channels, and geographical locations. These assessments are constantly changing as the war on terrorism and organised crime continues to develop. One must always remember that Meyer Lansky was a financial wizard who set up complex money laundering schemes to keep ahead of the FBI, IRS and other nosy people. The current organised crime and terrorist syndicates will also use 'experts' to fight their battles against the identification of their funds.

The strategies to manage and mitigate the identified money laundering and terrorist financing activities are typically aimed at preventing the activity from occurring through a combination of:

- deterrence (e.g. appropriate Customer Due Diligence 'CDD' measures),
- detection (e.g. monitoring and suspicious transaction reporting), and
- record-keeping (e.g. to facilitate investigations).

Proportionate procedures should be designed based on assessed risk. Higher risk areas should be subject to enhanced procedures; this would include measures such as enhanced CDD checks and enhanced transaction monitoring. However in instances where risks are low, simplified or reduced controls could be applied.

An effective risk-based approach involves:

- identifying and categorising money laundering and terrorist financing risks, and establishing reasonable controls based on risks identified.
- will allow accountants to exercise reasonable business and professional judgment with respect to clients.

A reasoned and well-articulated risk-based approach will justify the judgements made with regard to managing potential money laundering and terrorist financing risks. A risk-based approach **should not be designed to prohibit** accountants from continuing with legitimate business or from finding innovative ways to diversify their business.

The history of white collar crime confirms that, regardless of the strength and effectiveness of AML/CFT controls, the dedicated professional criminal will continue to attempt to move illicit funds undetected and will, from time to time, succeed. They will frequently target DNFBP sectors if other routes become more difficult to manipulate. For this reason, DNFBPs, including accountants, will be more vulnerable depending on the effectiveness of the AML/CFT procedures applied in other sectors of the financial market place.

A risk-based approach allows DNFBPs, including accountants, to more efficiently and effectively adjust and adapt as new money laundering and terrorist financing methods are identified.

However, it should always be recognised that any reasonably applied controls, including controls implemented as a result of a reasonably designed and effectively implemented risk-based approach will not identify and detect all instances of money laundering or terrorist financing.

Potential benefits and challenges

Benefits

As mentioned previously the adoption of a risk-based approach to combating money laundering and terrorist financing can yield benefits for all parties including the public. Applied effectively, the approach should allow a more efficient and effective use of resources and minimise burdens on clients. Focusing on higher risk threats should mean that beneficial outcomes can be achieved more effectively.

For accountants, the risk-based approach allows the flexibility to approach AML/CFT obligations using specialist skills and responsibilities. This approach requires accountants to take a wide and objective view of their activities and clients.

Efforts to combat money laundering and terrorist financing should also be flexible in order to adapt as risks evolve. As such, accountants should use their judgment, knowledge and expertise to develop an appropriate risk-based approach for their particular organisation, structure and business activities.

Challenges

A risk-based approach is not necessarily an easy option, and there may be challenges when implementing the necessary measures. Some challenges may be inherent to the use of the risk-based approach. Others may stem from the difficulties in making the transition to a risk-based system, A number of challenges, however, can also be seen as offering opportunities to implement a more effective system.

The risk-based approach is challenging to both public and private sector entities. Such an approach requires resources and expertise to gather and interpret information on risks, both at the country and institutional levels, to develop procedures and systems and to train personnel.

It further requires that sound and well-trained judgment be exercised in the design and implementation of procedures and systems. It will certainly lead to a greater diversity in practice which should lead to innovations and improved compliance. However, it may also cause uncertainty regarding expectations, difficulty in applying uniform regulatory treatment, and an increased lack of understanding by clients regarding information required.

Implementing a risk-based approach requires that accountants have a sound understanding of the risks and are able to exercise sound judgment. This requires the building of expertise including for example, through training, recruitment, taking professional advice and 'learning by doing'. The process will always benefit from information sharing by designated competent authorities and SROs. The provision of good practice guidance is also valuable. Attempting to pursue a risk-based approach without sufficient expertise may lead to flawed judgments. Accountants may over-estimate risk, which could lead to wasteful use of resources, or they may under-estimate risk, thereby creating vulnerabilities.

Accountants may find that some staff members are uncomfortable making risk-based judgments. This may lead to overly cautious decisions, or disproportionate time spent documenting the rationale behind a decision. This may also be true at various levels of management of accounting firms. However, in situations where management fails to recognise or underestimates the risks, a culture may develop that allows for inadequate resources to be devoted to compliance, leading to potentially significant compliance failures.

A risk-based approach requires an accountant to exercise professional judgment. This will probably result in diversity of practice and detail between firms, although both may meet legislative requirements.

The FATF has recommended that adequate feedback/intelligence should be provided to the financial sector and DNFBPs. Such feedback obviously helps institutions and businesses to more accurately assess the money laundering and terrorist financing risks and to adjust their risk programmes accordingly.

This in turn makes the detection of suspicious activity more likely and improves the quality of suspicious transaction reports. As well as being an essential input to any assessment of country or sector wide risks, the promptness and content of such feedback is relevant to implementing an effective risk-based approach.

The potential benefits and potential challenges can be summarised as follows:

- Better management of risks
- Efficient use and allocation of resources
- Focus on real and identified threats
- Flexibility to adapt to risks that change over time
- Identifying appropriate information to conduct a sound risk analysis
- Addressing short term transitional costs
- Greater need for more expert staff capable of making sound judgements.
- Developing appropriate regulatory response to potential diversity of practice.

Internal control systems

Following advice from the FATF and introduction of anti-money laundering legislation the development of 'appropriate' internal policies, training and audit systems should include a specific, and ongoing, consideration of the potential money laundering and terrorist financing risks associated with clients, products and services, geographic areas of operation and so forth. It is also recommended that countries should ensure that accountants are subject to effective systems for monitoring and ensuring compliance with AML/CFT requirements.

In determining whether the system for monitoring and ensuring compliance is appropriate, regard should be had to the risk of money laundering or terrorist financing in a given business, i.e. if there is a proven low risk then lesser monitoring measures may be taken.

Applicability of the risk-based approach

There are both similarities and differences in the application of a risk-based approach to terrorist financing and money laundering. They both require a process for identifying and assessing risk. However, the typical characteristics of terrorist financing makes its detection more difficult and the implementation of mitigation strategies challenging, due to considerations such as the relatively low value of transactions involved in terrorist financing, or the fact that funds can be derived from legitimate as well as illicit sources.

As mentioned previously funds that are used to finance terrorism may be derived either from criminal activity or may be from legal sources, and the nature of the funding sources may vary according to the type of terrorist organisation.

Funds from criminal activity

Where funds are derived from criminal activity, then traditional monitoring mechanisms that are used to identify money laundering may also be appropriate for terrorist financing, though the activity, which may be indicative of suspicion, may not be identified as or connected to terrorist financing.

It should be noted that transactions associated with the financing of terrorism can be in very small amounts,(as shown in the funding of recent attacks) which in applying a risk-based approach could be the very transactions that are frequently considered to be of minimal risk with regard to money laundering.

Funds from legal sources

Where funds are from legal sources, it is even more difficult to determine if they could be used for terrorist purposes. In addition, the actions of terrorists may be innocent in appearance, such as the purchase of materials and services to further their aims, with the only secret being the intended use of any materials and services purchased. Thus whereas terrorist funds may be derived from criminal activity as well as from legitimate sources, transactions related to terrorist financing may not show the same signs as conventional money laundering.

However in all cases, it is not the responsibility of the accountants to determine the type of underlying criminal activity, or intended terrorist purpose. The accountant's role is to identify and report the suspicious activity. The FIU and law enforcement authorities will investigate the activity further and determine if there is a link to terrorist financing.

It is important to note that the ability of accountants to detect and identify potential terrorist financing transactions, without appropriate guidance on terrorist financing methods or acting on specific intelligence provided by the authorities, is considerably more challenging than other cases of potential money laundering and other suspicious activity.

Detection efforts with non-existent specific national guidance are more likely to be based on monitoring which focuses on transactions with countries or geographic areas where terrorists are known to operate).

Certainly the accountant should examine the various databases that list particular individuals, organisations or countries who be the subject of terrorist financing sanctions, in a particular country. In such cases a listing of individuals, organisations or countries to which sanctions apply and the obligations on accountants to comply with those sanctions are decided by individual jurisdictions and are not a function of risk. Accountants may commit a criminal offence if they undertake business with a listed individual, organisation or country, or its agent, in contravention of applicable sanctions.

Whereas it is clearly preferable that a risk-based approach be applied where reasonably practicable, further consultation with key stakeholders is required to identify a more comprehensive set of indicators of the methods and techniques used for terrorist financing.

These can then be used as a basis for strategies to assess terrorist financing risks and devise measures to mitigate them. DNFBPs, including the accountants, would then have an additional basis upon which to more fully develop and implement a risk-based process for terrorist financing.

Limitations to the risk-based approach

There are some circumstances in which the application of a risk-based approach will not apply, or may be limited. There are also some circumstances in which the application of a risk-based approach may not apply to the initial stages of a requirement or process, but then will apply to subsequent stages. Any limitations to the risk-based approach are usually the result of legal or regulatory requirements that mandate certain actions to be taken.

Statutory requirements to freeze assets of identified individuals or entities, in jurisdictions where such requirements exist, are by their nature independent of any risk assessment. These requirements to freeze are absolute and cannot be impacted by a risk-based process.

Similarly, while the identification of potential suspicious transactions can be advanced by a risk-based approach, the reporting of suspicious transactions, once identified, is not risk-based.

As mentioned in most 'know your client' guides, there are several components to customer due diligence ('CDD'):

- Identification and verification of identity of customers and beneficial owners,
- obtaining information on the purposes and intended nature of the business relationships, and
- conducting ongoing due diligence.

Of these components, the identification and verification of identity of customers are requirements which must be completed regardless of the risk-based approach.

However, in relation to all the other CDD components, a reasonably implemented risk-based approach may allow for a determination of the extent and quantity of information required, and the mechanisms to be used to meet these minimum standards. Once this determination is made, the obligation to keep records and documents that have been obtained for due diligence purposes, as well as transaction records, is not dependent on risk levels.

Jurisdictions may allow accountants to apply reduced or simplified measures where the risk of money laundering or terrorist financing is lower. However, these reduced or simplified measures do not necessarily apply to all aspects of CDD.

However, where these exemptions are subject to certain conditions being met, it is necessary to verify that these conditions apply, and where the exemption applies under a certain threshold, measures should be in place to prevent transactions from being split artificially to avoid the threshold. **In other words, no smurfing**.

Additional information as well as client identity, such as client location, may be needed to adequately assess risk. This additional data will probably be already available having been obtained within the preliminary information about a client and this should be sufficient to determine whether to go further. In many cases client monitoring will provide additional information.

Some form of client monitoring is required in order to detect unusual and hence possibly suspicious transactions. Even in the case of lower risk clients, monitoring is needed to verify that transactions match the initial low risk profile and if not, initiate a process for revising the client's risk rating. Equally, risks for some clients may only become evident once a relationship with a client has begun. These facts make appropriate and reasonable monitoring of client transactions an essential component of a properly designed risk-based approach.

However it should be understood that not all transactions, accounts or clients will be monitored in exactly the same way. More importantly, where there is an actual suspicion of money laundering or terrorist financing, this must be regarded as a higher risk scenario, and enhanced due diligence should be applied regardless of any threshold or exemption.

Distinguishing between monitoring and policies/ processes

Accountants, designated competent authorities and SROs should have access to sufficiently detailed, reliable and actionable information about the threats, and how to implement a risk-based approach.

There must be emphasis on cooperative arrangements among the policy makers, law enforcement, regulators, and the private sector.

Authorities should publicly recognise that the risk-based approach will not eradicate all elements of risk.

Authorities have a responsibility to establish an atmosphere in which accountants need not be afraid of regulatory sanctions where they have acted responsibly and implemented adequate internal systems and controls.(in other words no jobsworths or box tickers but regulators who are prepared to work with the private sector to reach the same targets)

Regulators' and SROs' supervisory staff must be well-trained in the risk-based approach, both as applied by supervisors/SRO and by the accountants.

Risk categories

It is frequently the function of accountants in public practice to assist their clients in managing their affairs in a complex world, providing an individually tailored service. In many circumstances, they will encounter (or recommend) unusual or complex structures as a means of gaining commercial advantage or of dealing in the most appropriate way with complex situations or risks, with no criminal or other ulterior motives. Many factors that to outsiders might be considered indicators of money laundering/terrorist financing (ML/TF) risk, on further examination have an appropriate commercial rationale and the ML/TF risk is in fact normal, rather than high. Nevertheless, accountants will experience higher AML/CFT risk situations, which they need to take into account in their work. In theory, ML/TF risks can be organised into three categories: geographic risk, client risk and service risk. However, in practice these risks may fall into more than one category and should be viewed not as separate and distinct but as inter-related.

In the 'Client risk' section below, key factors associated with the main client risk category are:

- Factors indicating that the client is attempting to obscure understanding of its business, ownership or the nature of its transactions.

- Factors indicating certain transactions, structures, geographical location, international activities or other factors which are not in keeping with the accountant's understanding of the client's business or economic situation.
- Client industries, sectors or categories where opportunities for money laundering or terrorist financing are particularly prevalent.
- Clients falling within this category may be high risk clients although, after adequate review, the accountant may determine that they are pursuing a legitimate purpose. Provided that the economic rationale for the structure and transactions of a client can be made clear, the accountant may be able to demonstrate that the client is carrying out legitimate operations for which there is a rational and non-criminal purpose.

There are also some categories of service provided by practising accountants which may be used by money launderers for their own purposes, and which are therefore subject to a higher degree of risk. These are listed below under 'Service Risk'.

There is no universally accepted set of risk categories as each 'expert' will have their own opinion, but the following examples identify those that may apply in the circumstances of individual firms or client relationships. There is no one single methodology to apply to these risk categories, and the application of these risk categories is merely intended to provide a suggested framework for approaching the management of potential risks.

Country/geographic risk

Whether a country/jurisdiction represents a particular level of risk changes as the war on terror develops and the improvement of anti-money laundering legislation improves the situation. There is no universally agreed definition that prescribes whether a particular country or geographic area represents a higher risk. Geographic risk, in conjunction with other risk factors, can provide useful information as to whether potential money laundering and terrorist financing destination of funds, are located in a country that is, although it should be considered that lower risk and legitimate commercial enterprises may be located in high risk countries.

Nevertheless, clients may be judged to pose a higher than normal risk where they, or their source are;

- Subject to sanctions, embargoes or similar measures issued by, for example, the United Nations ('UN'). In some circumstances, this would include countries subject to sanctions or measures similar to those issued by bodies such as the UN.
- Identified by credible sources as lacking appropriate AML/CFT laws, regulations and other measures.

- Identified by credible sources as providing funding or support for terrorist activities that have designated terrorist organisations operating within them.
- Identified by credible sources as having significant levels of corruption, or other criminal activity.

Client risk

Factors that may indicate a higher than normal ML/TF risk include:

- Lack of face-to-face introduction of client.
- Subsequent lack of contact, when this would normally be expected.
- Beneficial ownership is unclear.
- Position of intermediaries is unclear.
- Inexplicable changes in ownership.
- Company activities are unclear.
- Legal structure of client has been altered numerous times (name changes, transfer of ownership, change of corporate seat).
- Management appear to be acting according to instructions of unknown or inappropriate person(s).
- Unnecessarily complex client structure.
- Reason for client choosing the firm is unclear, given the firm's size, location or specialisation.
- Frequent or unexplained change of professional adviser(s) or members of management.
- The client is reluctant to provide all the relevant information or the accountant has reasonable doubt that the provided information is correct or sufficient.
- Transactions or Structures out of line with Business Profile

Factors that may indicate a higher than normal ML/TF risk include the following:

- Client instructions or funds outside of their personal or business sector profile.
- Individual or classes of transactions that take place outside the established business profile, and expected activities/transaction unclear.
- Employee numbers or structure out of keeping with size or nature of the business (for instance the turnover of a company is unreasonably high considering the number of employees and assets used).
- Sudden activity from a previously dormant client.
- Client starts or develops an enterprise with unexpected profile or early results.
- Indicators that client does not wish to obtain necessary governmental approvals/filings, etc.

- Clients offer to pay extraordinary fees for services which would not ordinarily warrant such a premium.
- Payments received from un-associated or unknown third parties and payments for fees in cash where this would not be a typical method of payment.

Higher risk sectors and operational structures

Some client sectors and operational structures present a higher than normal ML/TF risk. Such risk factors may include:

- Entities with a high level of transactions in cash or readily transferable assets, among which illegitimate funds could be obscured.
- Politically exposed persons.
- Investment in real estate at a higher/lower price than expected.
- Large international payments with no business rationale.
- Unusual financial transactions with unknown source.
- Clients with multijurisdictional operations that do not have adequate centralised corporate oversight.
- Clients incorporated in countries that permit bearer shares.

In addition, the existence of fraudulent transactions, or ones which are improperly accounted for, should always be considered high risk. These might include:

- Over and under invoicing of goods/services.
- Multiple invoicing of the same goods/services.
- Falsely described goods/services – Over and under shipments (e.g. false entries on bills of lading).
- Multiple trading of goods/services.

Service risk

Services which may be provided by accountants and which (in some circumstances) risk being used to assist money launderers may include:

- Misuse of pooled client accounts or safe custody of client money or assets.
- Advice on the setting up of legal arrangements, which may be used to obscure ownership or real economic purpose (including setting up of trusts, companies or change of name/corporate seat or other complex group structures).
- Misuse of introductory services, e.g. to financial institution.

Variables that may impact on risk

Some factors that may increase or decrease risk in relation to particular clients, client engagements or practising environments include the following:

- Involvement of financial institutions or other DNFBPs.
- Unexplained urgency of assistance required.
- Sophistication of client, including complexity of control environment.
- Sophistication of transaction/scheme.
- Country location of accountant.
- Working environment/structure of accountant, e.g. sole practitioner, large firm.
- Role or oversight of another regulator.
- The regularity or duration of the relationship. Long-standing relationships involving frequent client contact throughout the relationship may present less risk.
- The purpose of the relationship and the need for the accountant to provide services.
- Clients who have a reputation for probity in the local communities.
- Private companies that are transparent and well know in the public domain.
- The familiarity of the accountant with a country, including knowledge of local laws and regulations as well as the structure and extent of regulatory oversight.

Controls for higher risk situations

Accountants and accounting firms should implement appropriate measures and controls to mitigate the potential money laundering risks of those clients that are determined to be higher risk as the result of the institution's risk-based approach. These measures and controls may include:

- Increased awareness of higher risk clients and transactions, across all departments with a business relationship with the client, including the possibility of enhanced briefing of client teams.
- Increased levels of know your customer (KYC) or enhanced due diligence.
- Escalation for approval of the establishment of a business engagement, or involvement in the client service.

Application of a risk-based approach

Customer due diligence/Know your customer

As with other sectors of the financial community the standards of Customer Due Diligence/Know Your Customer are intended to enable an accountant to form a reasonable belief that he knows the true identity of each client and, with an appropriate degree of confidence, knows the types of business and transactions the client is likely to undertake.

An accountant's procedures should include procedures to:

- Identify and verify the identity of each client on a timely basis.
- Identify the beneficial owner, and take reasonable measures to verify the identity of any beneficial owner. The measures which have to be taken to verify the identity of the beneficial owner will vary depending on the risk.
- Obtain appropriate additional information to understand the client's circumstances and business, including the expected nature and level of transactions. Relevant customer due diligence information should be periodically updated together with its risk assessment. In the event of any change in beneficial ownership or control of the client, or third parties on whose behalf the client acts, reasonable measures should be taken to verify identity.

Practising accountants should thus identify, and verify the identity of their clients, in sufficient detail to provide them with reasonable assurance that the information they have is an appropriate and sufficient indication of the true identity.

A standard level of due diligence should be applied to all clients with the possibility to carry out reduced or simplified customer identification in recognised lower risk scenarios. By contrast, an increased level of due diligence will apply in respect to clients that are determined to be of higher risk. These activities can be carried out in conjunction with firms' normal client acceptance procedures, and should take into account any specific jurisdictional requirements for client due diligence. In the normal course of their work, accountants are likely to learn more about some aspects of their client, such as their client's business or occupation and/or their level and source of income, than other advisors. This information is likely to assist in AML/CFT terms.

The beneficial owners of the client should be identified, including forming an understanding of the ownership and control structure, and taking reasonable measures to verify the identity of such persons. Public information sources may assist with this requirement. The procedures that need to be carried out can vary, in accordance with the nature and purpose for which the entity exists, and the extent to which the underlying ownership differs from apparent ownership by the use of nominees and complex structures.

The types of measures that normally would be needed to satisfactorily perform this function would require identifying:

- The natural persons with a controlling interest.
- The natural persons who comprise the mind and management of the legal person or arrangement.
- Physical location.

A risk-based approach varies according to the risk level. For example, where the client or the owner of the controlling interest is a public company that is subject to regulatory disclosure requirements, and that information is publicly available, fewer checks may be appropriate.

In the case of trusts, foundations or similar legal entities where the beneficiaries are distinct from the legal owners of the entity, it will be necessary to form a reasonable level of knowledge and understanding of the classes and nature of the beneficiaries; the identities of the settlor, trustees or managers; and an indication of the purpose of the trust. Assurance will be needed that the declared purpose of the trust is in fact its true purpose.

Identification of clients should be reviewed (on an appropriate risk related basis) to ensure that changes in ownership or other factors have not resulted in an effective change in the nature of the client, with a consequent need to review or repeat client identification and verification of identity procedures. This may be carried out in conjunction with any professional requirements for client continuation processes.

Monitoring of client business and transactions for suspicious activity

It is impossible for Accountants to scrutinise every transaction that goes through their clients' books and some accounting services are provided only on a once-off basis, without a continuing relationship with the client. However, many of the professional services provided by accountants put them in a relatively good position to encounter and recognise suspicious activities carried out by their clients or by their clients' business associates. These activities, which would not necessarily be recognised by other service providers, an accountant can recognize them through inside knowledge of, and access to, the client's records and management processes, as well as through close working relationships with senior managers and owners.

Practising accountants need to be continually alert for events or situations which are indicative of a reason to be suspicious of money laundering or terrorist financing, employing their professional experience and judgment in the forming of suspicions where appropriate. An advantage in carrying out this function is the professional scepticism which is a defining characteristic of many professional accountancy functions and relationships. One can also compare this logic with the fact that most fraud investigators are cynics.

Ongoing monitoring of the business relationship should be carried out on a risk related basis, to ensure that the client retains the same identity and risk profile established initially. This requires an appropriate level of scrutiny of activity during the relationship, including

- enquiry into source of funds where necessary, and
- to judge consistency with expected behaviour based on accumulated CDD information.

As mentioned in the following, ongoing monitoring may also give rise to filing a suspicious transaction report.

Investigations into suspected money laundering should not be conducted unless these are within the scope of the engagement, and information is limited to that to which the accountant normally would be entitled in the course of business. Within the scope of engagement, an accountant should be mindful of the criminal offence of 'tipping off' the client where a suspicion has been formulated. Carrying out additional investigations, which are not within the scope of the engagement, are unnecessary and could risk alerting a money launderer.

Normal business activities should be maintained and such information or other matters which flow from this will form the proper basis of suspicious transaction reports. To decide whether or not a matter is suspicious, accountants may need to make additional enquiries (within the normal scope of the assignment or business relationship) of the client or their records. Normal commercial enquiries, being made to fulfil duties to clients, may assist in understanding a matter to determine whether or not it is suspicious. Certainly if in doubt about whether such enquiries can be completed discreetly, the accountant should consider the services of expert accredited professionals.

Suspicious activity reporting

The requirement to file a suspicious transaction report is not subject to a risk-based approach, but must be made whenever required in the country concerned. This would include both suspicious situations, such as business structures or management profiles which have no legitimate economic rationale and suspicious transactions, such as the misappropriation of funds, false invoicing or company purchase of goods unrelated to the company's business.

However, it should be noted that a risk-based approach is appropriate for the purpose of identifying a suspicious activity, by directing additional resources at those areas an accountant has identified as higher risk. The designated competent authorities or SROs may provide information to accountants, which will be useful to them to inform their approach for identifying suspicious activity, as part of a risk-based approach. An accountant should also periodically assess the adequacy of its system for identifying and reporting suspicious transactions.

In making a decision on whether to make a report, the accountant needs to consider the following factors and take them into account.

- Whether or not the activities in question consist of instances of reportable (suspected) money laundering or terrorist financing in the country concerned.
- Whether the information was obtained in circumstances where they are subject to professional secrecy or legal professional privilege.
- In the absence of a requirement to report a suspicion, in the country concerned, whether it would be permitted to report a suspicion, and whether it would be consistent with the accountants' professional ethical obligations, including the requirement to consider the public interest in carrying out their professional activities.

Accountants should also consider any other specific legal or professional requirements which apply in the country within which the accountant is acting.

In many (or most) circumstances, accountants will have no flexibility in judging whether or not a suspicion report should be made, but will find that they are either required to make such a report (by the operation of legal requirements in their country) or forbidden to do so (by the operation of legal or professional requirements). However, where there is any element of flexibility, accountants should take into account the fact that the reporting of suspicious transactions or activities is critical to a country's ability to utilize financial information to combat money laundering, terrorist financing and other financial crimes.

Training and awareness

Accountants are within the scope of FATF Recommendation 15, which requires firms to provide their employees with appropriate AML/CFT training. In ensuring compliance with this requirement, accountants may take account of AML/CFT training included in entry requirements and continuing professional development requirements for their professional staff. They must also ensure appropriate training for any relevant staff without a professional qualification, at a level appropriate to the functions being undertaken by those staff, and the likelihood of their encountering suspicious activities.

Internal Controls

Many DNFBPs differ significantly from financial institutions in terms of size. By contrast to most financial institutions, a significant number of DNFBPs have only a few staff. This obviously limits the resources that small businesses and professions can dedicate to the fight against ML and FT. in many cases a single person may be responsible for the functions of front office, back office, money laundering reporting, and senior management. This situation should be taken into account in designing a risk-based framework for internal controls systems. The FATF's Interpretative Note to Recommendation 15, (dealing with internal controls), specifies that the type and extent of measures to be taken for each of its requirements should be appropriate having regard to the size of the business.

In order for accountants to have effective risk-based approaches, the risk-based process must be imbedded within the internal controls of the firm. The success of internal policies and procedures will be dependent largely on internal control systems. Two key systems that will assist in achieving this objective follow.

Culture of compliance

This should encompass:

- Developing, delivering, and maintaining a training program for all accountants.
- Monitoring for any government regulatory changes.
- Undertaking a regularly scheduled review of applicable compliance policies and procedures within accountancy practices, which will help constitute a culture of compliance in the industry
- Senior management ownership and support

Strong senior management leadership and engagement in AML/CFT is an important aspect of the application of the risk-based approach. They must create a culture of compliance, ensuring that staff adheres to the firm's policies, procedures and processes designed to limit and control risks. Policies and procedures can only be effective at the point that firm/company owners and senior management support the policies.

Having regard to the size of accounting firm, the framework of internal controls should:

- Provide increased focus on accountants' operations (products, services, clients and geographic locations) that are more vulnerable to abuse by money launderers and other criminals.
- Provide for regular review of the risk assessment and management

processes, taking into account the environment within which the accountant and the accounting firm operates and the activity in its market place.

- Designate an individual or individuals at management level responsible for managing AML/CFT compliance.
- Provide for an AML/CFT compliance function and review programme.
- Ensure that adequate controls are in place before new products are offered.
- Inform senior management of compliance initiatives, and identify compliance deficiencies, corrective action taken, and suspicious activity reports filed.
- Provide for programme continuity despite changes in management or employee composition or structure.
- Focus on meeting all regulatory record keeping and reporting requirements, recommendations for AML/CFT compliance and provide for timely updates in response to changes in regulations.
- Implement appropriate risk-based CDD policies, procedures and processes.
- Provide for adequate controls for higher risk customers, transactions and products, as necessary, such as transaction limits or management approvals.
- Enable the timely identification of reportable transactions and ensure accurate filing of required reports.
- Provide for adequate supervision of employees that handle currency transactions, complete reports, grant exemptions, monitor for suspicious activity, or engage in any other activity that forms part of the firm's AML/CFT programme.
- Incorporate AML/CFT compliance into job descriptions and performance evaluations of appropriate personnel.
- Provide for appropriate training to be given to all relevant staff.
- For groups, to the extent possible, there should be a common control framework.

A risk assessment for the firm as a whole, taking into account the size and nature of the practice; the existence of high risk clients (if any); and the provision of high risk services (if any) will be of assistance in setting the required procedures within the firm.

Depending on the assessed ML/TF risks, and the size of the firm, it may be possible to simplify both risk assessments and internal procedures. For example, for sole practitioners, client acceptance may be reserved to the sole owner/proprietor taking into account their business and client knowledge and experience (which may be highly specialised). The involvement of the sole owner/proprietor may also be required in detecting and assessing possible suspicious activities. For larger firms, more sophisticated procedures and risk assessments are likely to be necessary.

Other sources of information

In determining the levels of risks associated with particular country or cross border activity accountants and governments can draw on a range of publicly available information sources, these may include reports that detail observance of international standards and codes, specific risk ratings associated with illicit activity, corruption surveys and levels of international cooperation.

11

The Risk-Based Approach: Dealers in Precious Metal and Stones

This chapter recognizes the differing practices of dealers in precious metals and dealers in precious stones ('dealers') in different countries, and the different levels and forms of monitoring that may apply. Each country and its national authorities should aim to establish a partnership with its dealers that will be mutually beneficial to combating money laundering and terrorist financing. Obviously this is an important financial marketplace as gold has historically been the currency of many, especially criminals, and the illegal diamond trade has financially supported recent wars (Sierra Leone/Liberia)

Dealers conduct activities which fall within the ambit of the FATF Recommendations, as described below. The term 'dealer' encompasses a wide range of persons engaged in these businesses, from those who produce precious metals or precious stones at mining operations, to intermediate buyers and brokers, to precious stone cutters and polishers and precious metal refiners, to jewellery manufacturers who use precious metals and precious stones, to retail sellers to the public, to buyers and sellers in the secondary and scrap markets.

FATF Recommendation 12 states that the requirements for customer due diligence, record-keeping, and paying attention to all complex, unusual large transactions set out in their Recommendations 5, 6, and 8 to 11 apply to dealers in precious metals and stones when they engage in any cash transaction with a customer equal to or above USD/EUR 15,000.

Also FATF Recommendation 16 requires that FATF Recommendations 13 to 15 regarding reporting of suspicious transactions and internal AML/CFT controls, and FATF Recommendation 21 regarding measures to be taken with respect to countries that do not or insufficiently comply with the FATF Recommendations, apply to dealers in precious metals and dealers in precious stones when they engage in any cash transaction with a customer equal to or above the applicable designated threshold (USD/EUR 15,000)..

Diamonds, jewels and precious metals have unique physical and commercial properties which carry value in small, easily transportable and frequently hidden/smuggled quantities. The worldwide trade varies from modern international transactions conducted through the financial system, to localized informal markets. Dealers range from very poor individuals in some of the most remote and troubled places on the planet notably Africa, to the wealthiest individuals, to large multinational companies working in major financial centres. Transaction methods also range from anonymous exchanges of handfuls of stones or nuggets for cash, to exchange-based government-regulated deals.

A risk assessment is obviously familiar to dealers in diamonds, jewels and precious metals because of the risks of theft and fraud.(see Brinks – Matt bullion robbery in Classic Cases) Risks of money laundering and terrorist financing should be added to those traditional industry concerns as precious metals and stones are ideal for laundering the proceeds of crime and funding terrorism. Diamond dealers in particular will be familiar with such a programme as the worldwide Kimberley Process (appendix 6)which was designed to ameliorate risks of conflict finance in rough diamonds (Sierra Leone/Liberia).

The risk-based approach – purpose, benefits and challenges

Purpose

The purpose, benefits and challenges of the risk-based approach is similar to that as already detailed in respect of Estate agents, Accountants and other DNFBPs in previous chapters of this book and apply to Dealers. The following only details any peculiarities in respect of the precious metals/stones marketplace.

In some countries dealers will be licensed and some of their activities will be overseen by government agencies. Where possible, it is beneficial for dealers to devise their AML/CFT policies and procedures in a way that links in with other regulatory or professional requirements. A risk-based AML/CFT regime will help to ensure that honest customers and counterparties can access the services provided by dealers, but create barriers to those who seek to misuse these services.

Regardless of the strength and effectiveness of AML/CFT controls, criminals will always continue to attempt to move illicit diamonds, gold, and precious stones etc. undetected and will, frequently succeed. They are more likely to target dealers in precious metals and stones who may be more or less vulnerable depending on the effectiveness of the AML/CFT procedures applied in other sectors. A risk-based approach allows dealers, to more efficiently and effectively adjust and adapt as new money laundering and terrorist financing methods are identified.

For dealers, the risk-based approach allows the flexibility to approach AML/CFT obligations using specialist skills and responsibilities. This requires dealers to take a wide and objective view of their activities and customers and counterparties.

Efforts to combat money laundering and terrorist financing should also be flexible in order to adapt as risks evolve. As such, dealers can use their judgment, knowledge and expertise to develop an appropriate risk-based approach for their particular organisation, structure and business activities.

Dealers may find that some staff members are uncomfortable making risk-based judgments. This may lead to overly cautious decisions, or disproportionate time spent documenting the rationale behind a decision. This may also be true at various levels of management.

In implementing the risk-based approach, dealers should be given the opportunity to make reasonable judgments with respect to their particular situations. This may mean that no two dealers in precious metals or dealers in precious stones or no two businesses within the same sector are likely to

Jurisdictions should ensure that their dealers are subject to effective systems for monitoring and ensuring compliance with AML/CFT requirements. In determining whether the system for monitoring and ensuring compliance is appropriate, regard may be had to the risk of money laundering or terrorist financing in a given business, i.e. if there is a proven low risk then lesser monitoring measures may be taken.

The ability of dealers to detect and identify potential terrorist financing transactions without guidance on terrorist financing methods or without acting on specific intelligence provided by the authorities is considerably more challenging than is the case for the identification of potential money laundering and other suspicious activity.

Particular individuals, organisations or countries who are the subject of terrorist financing sanctions require identification. In such cases a listing of individuals, organisations or countries to which sanctions apply and the obligations on dealers to comply with those sanctions are decided by individual countries and are not a function of risk. Dealers will commit a criminal offence if they undertake business with a listed individual, organisation or country, or its agent, in contravention of applicable sanctions.

Countries may allow dealers to apply reduced or simplified measures where the risk of money laundering or terrorist financing is lower. However, these reduced or simplified measures do not necessarily apply to all aspects of customer and counterparty due diligence. Where these exemptions are subject to certain conditions being met, it is necessary to verify that these conditions apply, and where the exemption applies under a certain threshold, measures should be in place to prevent transactions from being split artificially to avoid the threshold.

FATF Recommendation 24 requires that dealers in precious metals/dealers in precious stones be subject to effective systems for monitoring and ensuring compliance with AML/CFT requirements. In determining the design of an effective system, regard should be had to the risk of money laundering or terrorist financing in the sector. There should be a designated competent authority or SRO responsible for monitoring and ensuring its functions, including powers to monitor and sanction. It should be noted that in some countries, dealers in precious metals/dealers in precious stones are supervised in the same way as financial institutions. Other countries apply a separate monitoring/oversight regime.

Designated competent authorities and SROs expect dealers to put in place effective policies, programmes, procedures and systems to mitigate risks, while acknowledging that even with effective systems not every suspect transaction will necessarily be detected. They should also ensure that those policies, programmes, procedures and systems are applied effectively to the purpose of preventing dealers from becoming conduits for illegal proceeds and ensure that they keep records and make reports that are of use to national authorities in combating money laundering and terrorist financing.

Efficient policies and procedures will reduce the level of risks, but are unlikely to eliminate them completely. Assessing money laundering and terrorist financing risks requires judgment and is not an exact science. Monitoring aims at detecting unusual or suspicious transactions among an extremely large number of legitimate transactions, furthermore the demarcation of what is unusual may not always be straightforward since what is 'customary' may vary depending on the customers' or counterparty's business. This is why developing an accurate customer/counterparty profile is vital in managing a risk-based system. Moreover, procedures and controls are frequently based on previous identified cases, but criminals usually adapt their techniques quickly to keep ahead of the 'game ' thus limiting the benefit of reference to previous methods.

In the context of the risk-based approach, it is not possible to specify precisely what a dealer in precious metals or a dealer in precious stones has to do, in all cases, to meet its regulatory obligations. Thus, a prevailing consideration will be how best to ensure the consistent implementation of predictable and proportionate monitoring actions. The effectiveness of monitoring training will therefore be important to the successful delivery of proportionate monitoring actions.

Peculiar risks

Geographic risk – where a product is mined

Some of the most prolific mining for precious products is in Africa and over the past few decades much of the trade has been controlled by insurgents, rebel armies and in some cases terrorist organisations, the product being treated as a source of revenue for funding needs. Mining can be particularly vulnerable to terrorist financing if it occurs in remote locations with minimal governmental presence or infrastructure. In some areas, for example, gold mining can be dominated by armed non-governmental groups.

Mining for jewels is similarly geographically widespread, and frequently occurs in areas of significant unrest and turmoil. Unlike diamond mining, mining for jewels is largely small and informal, carried on by local prospectors and owners in alluvial sources, very few of which, if any, are publicly traded companies.

Some jewel mines are government owned, and some mines have licenses issued by government agencies involved with natural resources, but frequently such mines are often remote from strong governmental oversight, and often in areas of substantial conflict and crime, including terrorism. Buyers travel to the mines or to nearby communities and buy jewels, sometimes in a manner controlled by government, sometimes either directly from miners or from local intermediaries. Because many of these areas do not have reliable financial systems, payments are often in cash and informal, or are made through third party accounts, again increasing risk and resulting in the loss of any audit trail to establish any route of dirty money.

Factors that should always be considered in a determination that a country may or may not pose a higher risk with regard to a proposed transaction in diamonds, jewels or precious metals include:

- For rough diamonds, whether a producing or trading country participates in the Kimberley Process.
- Whether there is known mining or substantial trading of the transaction product – diamonds, jewels or precious metals – in a transaction source country.
- Whether a country would be an anticipated source of large stocks of existing diamonds, jewels or precious metals, based upon national wealth, trading practices and culture (centres of stone or jewel trading, such as Antwerp, Belgium) or unanticipated (large amounts of old gold jewellery in poor developing countries). *It should be recognized, however, that gold and silver have cultural and economic significance in a number of developing countries, and very poor people may have, buy and sell these metals.*
- The level of government oversight of business and labour in mining and/or trading areas.
- The extent to which cash is used in a country.
- The level of regulation of the activity.
- Whether informal banking systems operate in a country, e.g. Hawallas operate in many developing countries.
- Whether designated terrorist organisations or criminal organisations operate within a country, especially in small and artisan mining areas.

- Whether there is ready access from a country to nearby competitive markets or processing operations, e.g. gold mined in Africa is more frequently refined in South Africa, the Middle East or Europe rather than in the United States, and a proposal to refine African gold in the United States would be unusual and higher risk.
- Whether, based on credible sources (see Appendix 4), appropriate AML/CFT laws, regulations and other measures are applied and enforced in a country.
- The level of enforcement of laws addressing corruption or other significant organised criminal activity.
- Whether sanctions, embargoes or similar measures have been directed against a country.

Retail customer risk

A retail customer of precious metals or precious stones will, in general, not have a business purpose for a purchase of an article of jewellery, a precious stone of a precious metal. A purchase is likely to be made for purely personal and emotional reasons that cannot be factored into an AML/CFT risk assessment. Higher risk can be seen, however, in certain retail customer transaction methods:

- Use of cash. It should be recognized, however, that many persons desire anonymity in jewellery purchases for purely personal reasons, or at least the absence of paper records, with no connection to money laundering or terrorist financing.
- Payment by or delivery to third parties. However, not all third party payments are indicative of AML/CFT. It is relatively common in jewellery purchases that a woman will select an article of jewellery, and a man will later make payment and direct delivery to the woman.
- Structuring.

Business counterparty risk

There are many different stages and transactions and counterparties involved in the precious stones and precious metals businesses. As previously detailed, miners range from international companies to individuals. Intermediaries may be well established local buyers from miners, or itinerant foreign buyers, or Hawallas. Retail jewellers may buy articles of used jewellery, as may direct buyers and pawnshops. Each of these businesses may present a money laundering risk. Dealers may buy from or sell to other counterparties who also work in their precious metals or precious stones businesses, or sell to the public through retail sales (which may often be anonymous). Dealers will need to consider the risks associated with each stage at which they participate. A risk-based approach should account for higher risk customers and counterparties at every stage.

Apart from the retail sector, trade in diamonds, jewels and precious metals is traditionally private, as a matter of commercial protection or security. Dealers have traditionally protected their counterparties, their materials, and their business practices from public knowledge, in the interest of protecting themselves from criminal activity, and from potential independent interaction by competitors with their customers and counterparties or suppliers. However, it is necessary for dealers themselves to know that they are dealing with legitimate counterparties.

In some sectors within precious metals and precious stones businesses, trust based on personal contact is an essential element of conducting business, and such trust and personal contact assist in lowering counterparty risk. In addition, each industry has trade resources, such as trade associations and directories, with which to establish some background and credit information and these should always be consulted. Checks must be made upon any new counterparty that is unknown to a dealer, and particularly if also unknown within the dealer's industry. A counterparty, who proposes a transaction in diamonds, jewels or precious metals should have the knowledge, experience and capacity, financial and technical, to engage in that transaction.

These credible sources does not have the effect of law or regulation and should not be viewed as an automatic determination that something is of higher risk.

Higher risk counterparties include a person who:

- Does not understand the industry in which he proposes to deal, or does not have a place of business or equipment or finances necessary and appropriate for such engagement, or does not seem to know usual financial terms and conditions.
- Proposes a transaction that makes no sense, or that is excessive, given the circumstances, in amount, or quality, or potential profit.
- Has significant and unexplained geographic distance from the dealer in precious metals or dealer in precious stones.
- Uses banks that are not specialised in or do not regularly provide services in such areas, and are not associated in any way with the location of the counterparty and the products.
- Makes frequent and unexplained changes in bank accounts, especially among banks in other countries.
- Involves third parties in transactions, either as payers or recipients of payment or product, without apparent legitimate business purpose.
- Will not identify beneficial owners or controlling interests, where this would be commercially expected.
- Seeks anonymity by conducting ordinary business through accountants,

lawyers, or other intermediaries, see the paragraph above.
- Uses cash in its transactions with the dealer in precious metals or dealer in precious stones, or with his own counterparties in a nonstandard manner.
- Uses money services businesses or other non-bank financial institutions for no apparent legitimate business purpose.
- Is a politically exposed person (PEP).

Product/service risk

An overall risk assessment should also include a determination of the potential risks presented by products and services offered by a dealer in precious metals or a dealer in precious stones. The determination of risks of products and services should include a consideration of the following factors:

Products offered

All diamonds, jewels, and precious metals can potentially be used for money laundering and terrorist financing, but the utility and consequent level of risk are likely to vary depending on the value of the product. Unless transactions involve very large quantities, lower value products are likely to carry less risk than higher value products. However, dealers must be aware that values can be volatile dependent upon supply and demand. Relative values of some materials can vary dramatically between different countries, and over time.

Dependent upon the nature of the transaction, counterparties, and quantities, gold can be higher risk. Pure gold, or relatively pure gold, is the same substance worldwide, with a worldwide price standard published daily, and it can also be used as currency itself, e.g. by Hawallas. Gold is available in a variety of forms, e.g. bars, coins, jewellery, or scrap, and trades internationally in all of these forms.

Although scrap gold alloys or other gold-bearing scrap may require substantial processing and refining to reach an end market, the costs will be discounted in advance, and the scrap may still trade for high value in multi-billion dollar worldwide markets. One of the main aspects of the BRINKS-MATT robbery and subsequent money laundering was the write-off of the difference between the value of the pure gold as stolen and the scrap gold alloy stolen (some of this difference was negated by the VAT fraud).Values of many scrap materials are uncertain and not precisely knowable until they have been processed and assayed, which can present an AML risk if the parties undervalue or overvalue international shipments.

Alluvial gold and gold dust can be indicative of informal mining by individuals and small groups, often in areas that are characterized by informal banking and absence of regulation, and so may be higher risk.

The physical characteristics of the products offered are also a factor to consider. Products that are easily portable and which are unlikely to draw the attention of law enforcement are at greater risk of being used in cross border money laundering. For example, diamonds are small, light in weight, not detected by metal detectors, and a very large value can be easily concealed.

Finally, the risk of dealing in stolen or fraudulent products must be taken into account. As with all valuable objects, diamonds, jewels and precious metals are attractive to thieves, and dealers must be aware of the risks of trading in stolen products. For example, jewellery dealers, pawn shops and buyers of used gold jewellery should remain alert to the possibility of being offered stolen jewellery. In addition to stolen goods, dealers should be aware of the risks associated with fraudulent goods, such as synthetic diamonds represented as natural diamonds, or 14 karat gold represented as 18 karat. One must not forget that traditionally criminals have always been drawn to the dealing in stolen goods, especially gold (see La Mina, Chapter 3).

Services offered

Major gold dealers create metal accounts for their customers, for temporary secure storage or for investment, and they transfer counterparties' gold credits in these accounts among themselves, and among repositories and delivery destinations worldwide, with services comparable to those provided by banks with money and financial credits. Such services, by banks as well as by major gold dealers, are useful to money launderers and terrorist financiers to move high values through international commerce, under the guise of legitimate business, although unlikely to be anonymous and irregular, it is well known that criminal organisations and terrorists often use front companies an mix crime/dirty money with genuine business.

Market characteristics

It is helpful to bear in mind the following broad principles which may lower the risk levels of particular transactions:

- Limited resale opportunities – limited resale opportunities are likely to be unattractive to money launderers.
- Size of market – a small market is likely to make it more difficult for a money launderer to structure transactions, to layer multiple transactions (to create distance between the seller and the ultimate purchaser), and to conduct anonymous transactions, and will thus be less attractive to money launderers.
- Degree of expertise required – if specialized expertise is required for transactions, risk of use of such transactions by money launderers may be lower. For example, diamonds are unique.

For example, spent industrial catalysts that contain platinum group metals generally have resale opportunities limited to platinum refiners, and thus are of lower risk in money laundering.

Silver used in imaging and electronics, which are specialized applications from which value is not easily removed, is similarly of lower risk. Platinum and silver jewellery and coins could, of course, be used by money launderers. Silver has been used for centuries as money, as has special prominence in some geographical areas and cultures, e.g. India.

Objects, some with extremely high value, some with much less, all dependent upon size and physical characteristics, usually as judged by persons with expertise in diamond evaluation. As transaction values increase, either because of higher numbers of diamonds involved or higher quality of individual diamonds, so does the need for expertise and specialized markets increase. Money launderers may not have such expertise. Such expertise exists, however, in many places, and money launderers may be able to obtain it, or to employ it.

- Degree of market regulation – if a market is regulated, depending upon the degree of regulation, transactions in that market may be lower risk (see below the other variables to take into account for the determination of risks).

Transaction costs

Money laundering and terrorist financing can involve multiple transactions, with criminals first placing illegal assets within a legitimate product, as anonymously as possible, then layering those assets through intermediate transactions, and then removing them at a different time and place. Money launderers want to get as much as possible of their illegal assets out of these transactions. They may be prepared to accept losses in these layering transactions, but may prefer to keep them to a minimum. Therefore transactions involving high value product and low transaction costs may be particularly attractive to money launderers and terrorist financiers. For example, a purchase of pure gold coins, and subsequent sale of those coins at another location, will quickly return most of the original purchase price. On the other hand a purchase of a specialty gold alloy may have a resale value of only the gold content, losing any value added in manufacturing, and losing gold refining charges as well. Such a transaction will cause a money launderer to pay substantial transaction costs and may therefore be lower risk.

Financing methods

The method of payment used affects the risk of money laundering and terrorist financing taking place. The risks are likely to be reduced if transactions take place through the mainstream banking system. Conversely, the risk may increase in the following situations:

Cash, especially in large amounts, can be a warning sign, especially if the use of cash is anonymous or intentionally hides an identity, e.g. the true purchaser funds the transaction by giving cash to a third party, who then becomes the nominal and identified purchaser.

- Payments or delivery of product to or from third party accounts, e.g. accounts in the names of persons other than approved counterparties.
- Payments to or from accounts at financial institutions that are unrelated to a transaction or approved counterparties, such as banks located in countries other than the location of the counterparty or transaction.
- Non-bank financial mechanisms such as currency exchange businesses or money remitters.

Variables that may change risk determination

The level of effective AML/CFT regulation or other oversight or governance regime to which a counterparty is subject varies widely. A counterparty that is a dealer in precious metals or a dealer in precious stones operating in a country under a robust AML/CFT regime, or a system such as the Kimberley Process, poses less risk from a money laundering perspective than a counterparty that is unregulated or subject only to minimal AML regulation. To be given such a lower risk consideration, a counterparty should have a compliance program and certify to compliance with its applicable regulatory system.

The type and level of regulation varies greatly among the different types of precious metals and precious stones. For example, in some countries, dealers are required to have a government issued license for their particular businesses, in others they are not. There may be no or limited regulation when a product is mined and sold for the first time, but the level of regulation may increase as the product continues to be traded.

Some governments are also involved in transactions through export and import regulatory systems, often for the purpose of collecting taxes or duties, which require traders to describe their materials and declare values and counterparties of export or import. Such government involvements may lower risk, but may vary from country to country, and impacts upon risk must be evaluated directly by a dealer in precious metals or a dealer in precious stones.

There is some government regulation of precious metals trading, but most transactions are not conducted in regulated markets. Gold is traded worldwide in very large amounts in direct physical transactions and through financial derivatives, i.e. forwards and futures, which can be used to acquire and sell rights in physical gold stocks. Such paper gold transactions, of any size, are highly unlikely to be anonymous or conducted in cash, certainly in regulated markets and probably in unregulated markets, but should not be ignored for anti money laundering purposes.

A large proportion of rough diamond sales are made through Belgium, which strictly regulates dealers and transactions (including the physical inspection and value assessment of all imported and exported diamonds, hence for instance excluding valuation and synthetic diamonds related risks), and through bourses with stringent membership rules of practice. Some countries participate in the Kimberley Process. The Kimberley Process applies to dealers in rough diamonds, including importers and exporters of rough diamonds, when they operate in participant countries. When it applies the Kimberly Process significantly lessens the ML/TF risk level. Systems of dealer warranties and transactions through bourses further reduce risk in the trade of polished diamonds and jewellery containing diamonds, as do dealings with only bank transfer payments among regulated and government supervised dealers.

Risk assessments

- The size of the transaction, with larger transactions presenting higher risk, always bearing in mind the possibility of deliberate structuring of smaller transactions.
- The level of government regulation of counterparty's business and accounting practices. Companies and their wholly owned subsidiaries that are publicly owned and traded on a regulated exchange, or that have publicly issued financial instruments, generally pose minimal money laundering risks. Note however that this is not always so, and publicly traded companies may be established by money launderers
- Government trade flow inspection mechanisms that involve physical inspections, trade flow follow up and/or valuation verifications. In general, if a government has developed a gate keeper role that monitors incoming and/or outgoing trade flows, including physical inspection of goods and value assessments, the money laundering risk may be considerably reduced, as well as risks related to the use of synthetic diamonds.
- The nature and extent of banking involvement. In general, a lower risk level is present where a transaction is entirely financially settled, both at the side of the dealer and the counterparty, through a banking institution that is situated in an FATF member country and that is known to be actively involved in payment flows and financing arrangements in the particular trade, provided the transaction is generally routine (including payment that

closely follows routine trade flows) and that the documentation contains adequate identification of all parties concerned
- The regularity or duration of the business relationship, or of general knowledge of the counterparty's role in the industry. Longstanding relationships involving frequent contact provide an understanding of a counterparty's legitimacy within the dealer's industry, and information by which a proposed transaction can be evaluated for consistency with industry norms.
- The familiarity of a dealer in precious metals or a dealer in precious stones with a counterparty's country, including knowledge of applicable local laws, regulations and rules, as well as the structure and extent of regulatory oversight.

Controls for higher risk situations

Dealers should implement appropriate measures and controls to mitigate the potential money laundering and terrorist financing risk of those customers that are assessed to be a higher risk. The same measures and controls may often address more than one of the risk criteria identified. Appropriate measures and controls may include:

- General training for appropriate personnel on money laundering and terrorist financing methods and risks relevant to dealers.
- Targeted training for appropriate personnel to increase awareness of higher risk customers or transactions.
- Increased levels of know your customer/counterparty (KYC) or enhanced due diligence.
- Escalation within dealer management required for approval.
- Increased monitoring of transactions.
- Increased controls and frequency of review of relationships.

Application of a risk-based approach

A risk-based approach should be applied across the full breadth of an enterprise, including a multinational enterprise. Policies, standards and procedures should be similar, if not identical across an enterprise or business, and separate parts of an enterprise or a business should communicate with each other regarding the implementation of their AML/CFT program. If a person or transaction is classified in a high risk category in one part of an enterprise, the other parts of that enterprise that might encounter such person or transaction need to be advised at the same time.

Legal standards and enforcement cultures vary, and persons engaged in business in a country must be aware of and respond to that country's laws and competent authorities. There should be similarity along the following common implementation steps:

CDD/KYC

The CDD/KYC within a dealer's AML/CFT program should enable the dealer in precious metals or the dealer in precious stones to form a reasonable belief that it knows the true identity of each counterparty/customer and the types of transactions the counterparty proposes. A dealer's program should include procedures to:

- Identify and verify counterparties/customers before establishing a business relationship, such as entering into contractual commitments. This identified natural or legal person or authorized and fully identified agents should then be the only person or persons to whom payment is authorized to be made, or product delivered, unless legitimate and documented business reasons exist, and any third party is appropriately identified and its identity verified.
- Identify beneficial owners and take reasonable measures to verify the identities, such that the dealer is reasonably satisfied that it knows who the beneficial owners are. The measures which have to be taken to verify the identity of the beneficial owner will vary depending on the risk. For legal persons and arrangements this should include taking reasonable measures to understand the ownership and control structure of the counterparty/customer.
- Obtain information to understand the counterparty's/customer's circumstances and business, including the expected nature and level of proposed transactions.

Where the FATF Recommendations are applicable (i.e. for transactions involving cash equal to or above USD/EUR 15,000), counterparties/customers must be subject to the full range of CDD measures. In addition Identify Your Counterparty/Customer activity and procedures should be applied to higher risk determinations (such as PEPs or transactions involving higher risk countries). In these cases, for instance, a dealer in precious metals or a dealer in precious stones should implement additional measures and controls to mitigate that risk. Such measures could include increased levels of know your counterparty or enhanced due diligence and greater direct contact with a counterparty (for example, observing its operations, personnel and equipment, would provide additional verification of its legitimacy). It will also require increased monitoring of transactions.

These actions should be recorded and maintained in a file regarding each counterparty/customer. In circumstances defined by the public authorities where there are lower money laundering or terrorist financing risks, dealers may be allowed to apply reduced or simplified CDD measures when identifying and verifying the identity of the counterparty/customer and the beneficial owner having regard to the type of counterparty/customer, product or transaction.

In other circumstances (i.e. for transactions not involving cash equal to or above USD/EUR 15,000) and where national law does not require otherwise, counterparty/customer identification can, however, be accomplished through broader industry practices and associations that already maintain comparable data to which the authorities have ready access, or by reference to government held databases (registered dealer database, VAT related database, etc.). This will reduce transaction burdens, particularly upon small and mid-size dealers who already rely upon such industry resources to maintain security and high standards in their business practices.

For example, in the diamond industry, transactions for rough diamonds are conducted within the scope of the Kimberley Process. Trading in rough diamonds and polished diamonds can occur through bourses that are members of the World Federation of Diamond Exchanges. Dealers might transparently reference these sources of counterparty/customer identification rather than recreate all identification data in multiple dealer and transaction files.

In similar circumstances, other regulatory programs and/or industry associations may provide similar counterparty information and assurances. Transactions with well-known, longstanding counterparties might also be identified by transparent reference to existing information of a dealer, rather than be recreated. Such streamlined counterparty identification practices should, of course, be limited to transactions with standard trading and bank payment practices that do not give rise to suspicion and concern, and do not in any case fully eliminate the need to apply risk-based analysis to transactions, customers, or counterparties.

Monitoring of counterparties/customers and transactions

The degree and nature of monitoring by a dealer in precious metals or a dealer in precious stones will depend upon the size of the business and the risk assessment that the dealer has made. Based on such risk assessment and in accordance with any legislative or regulatory requirements, not all transactions or counterparties/customers will be monitored in the same way and to the same degree. A risk may only become evident once a counterparty has begun transactions, particularly if such transactions differ from those originally anticipated, and changes in transactions should be noted and evaluated. A monitoring program and results of monitoring should always be documented, and a dealer in precious metals or a dealer in precious stones should periodically assess its monitoring program for adequacy.

Suspicious transaction reporting

The circumstances that will trigger a requirement to report a suspicious transaction or activity to a dealer's competent authority are usually rules-based and set forth in national law, and a risk-based approach for such reports is not applicable.

An AML/CFT program that is founded on the risk-based approach will, however, direct attention and resources toward higher risk activities, will more readily identify suspicious activity, and should encourage reporting of suspicious activity.

The capabilities of a dealer's AML/CFT program to identify and properly report suspicious activity should be periodically reviewed.

Training and awareness

The success of a dealer's AML/CFT programme will depend upon its application throughout the full range of the dealer's business activities, and thus upon appropriate training of employees. A dealer should inform all employees that it has an AML/CFT program designed and intended to detect and deter money laundering and terrorist finance, and that their awareness and participation are important. All employees should be encouraged and trained to contact management regarding suspicious activity that they observe or of which they become aware.

Training of specific employees will vary according to their roles, e.g. counterparty/customer contact, receiving and inspection, trading, banking, accounting, IT, and according to the levels of risk associated with counterparties/customers and transactions with which they have a business association. This training should be periodically reviewed for effectiveness and repeated as appropriate. Each AML/CFT incident or inquiry arising in the course of business should also be used as an opportunity to reinforce the awareness and understanding of employees regarding a dealer's AML/CFT program and their roles in implementation of that program. If circumstances of suspicion, concern or higher risk are revealed in monitoring, additional training should be specifically directed to those circumstances with appropriate employees.

Internal controls

Many Dealers differ significantly from financial institutions in terms of size. By contrast to most financial institutions, a significant number of Dealers have only a few staff. This limits the resources that small businesses and professions can dedicate to the fight against money laundering and terrorist financing. For a number of Dealers, a single person may be responsible for the functions of front office, back office, money laundering reporting, and senior management. This should be taken into account in designing a risk-based framework for internal controls systems. The Interpretative Note to FATF Recommendation 15, (dealing with internal controls), specifies that the type and extent of measures to be taken for each of its requirements should be appropriate having regard to the size of the business.

In order for dealers to have effective risk-based approaches, the risk-based process must be imbedded within the internal controls of the firm. The success of internal policies and procedures will be dependent largely on internal control systems. Two key elements that will assist in achieving this objective follow.

1. Culture of compliance
This should encompass:

- Developing, delivering, and maintaining a training program for all dealers.
- Monitoring for any government regulatory changes.
- Undertaking a regularly scheduled review of applicable compliance policies and procedures within industry practices, which will help constitute a culture of compliance in the industry.

2. Senior management ownership and support
A risk-based AML/CFT program requires commitment, participation and authority of owners and controlling persons. It should be part of a culture of legal and ethical compliance that these senior management officials should inculcate to all employees, and to counterparties, and to other persons associated with the business.

The nature and extent of AML/CFT controls will depend upon a number of factors including:

- The nature, scale and complexity of a dealer's business.
- The diversity of a dealer's operations, including geographical diversity.
- The dealer's customer, product and services profile.
- The volume and size of the transactions.
- The degree of risk associated with each area of the dealer's operation.
- The extent to which the dealer is involved directly with the customer or through third parties or non face-to-face access.
- The frequency of customer contact (either in person or by other means of communication).

A risk-based AML/CFT program should be established and implemented in coordination with other business compliance and security programs. Verification of employees, for example, through background and security screening can be cross-checked with AML/CFT verification of customers and counterparties. Daily checks of inventories by independent groups within a company to dissuade and minimize theft losses can also inform an AML/CFT program of suspicious activity.

A risk-based AML/CFT program in respect of the precious metals/stones industry requires specialized expertise about a dealer's particular business within that industry, and about particular counterparties. It also requires knowledge of money laundering techniques, and how such techniques might be used within particular industry transactions and areas of operation.

Within many small, privately held and family businesses in these industries, all of these skills and authorities are available primarily, or only, at the level of ownership/senior management. Within larger enterprises, a person with these skills will need to be designated and authorized as a Compliance Officer.

A designated Compliance Officer should have a reputation within the dealer's enterprise for integrity and sound judgment, should be authorized and willing to contradict persons with more limited interests in proposed transactions and counterparties, including the owners, and should be known within a dealer's enterprise as such a person.

When considering the ML/TF risks and the size of the dealer, a dealer's AML/CFT internal control programme should include procedures that:

- Ensure that regulatory record keeping and reporting requirements are met, and that changes in regulatory requirements are incorporated6.
- Implement risk-based counterparty due diligence procedures.
- Provide for adequate controls for higher risk counterparties, transactions and products.
- Enable the timely identification of reportable transactions and ensure accurate filing of required reports.
- Provide for adequate monitoring.
- Provide for adequate supervision of employees.
- Provide for appropriate and updated training.

An AML/CFT programme should always be current and active, changing as new circumstances arise, adapting to increased understanding of its elements, such as information derived from periodic review, monitoring and suspicious activity, and responding to recommendations. Dealers should also take account of relevant material published by designated competent authorities and SROs.

Senior management and its designated Compliance Officer should also arrange for regular periodic review of the AML/CFT program and its operation, for implementation of recommendations arising from such review, and for ongoing improvement of the program. Such review need not be by persons outside of a dealer's business, but should be by a qualified person who, if practicable, is independent of the Compliance Officer. A person who is not directly involved in the day-to-day operation of the AML/CFT program will bring a fresh view to program activities.

In small and mid size companies where ownership/senior management is directly involved in the AML/CFT program, periodic review need not be as formal an undertaking. If a dealer reports transactions to designated competent authorities or SROs, and receives appropriate feedback from such authorities, written reports of this regulatory activity may serve as such review or as a database for it.

Senior management not directly associated with the AML/CFT program should be briefed upon its operations and lessons learned from experience, and should be asked for questions and comments. This dialogue will both strengthen the programme, and ensure that its principles are integrated within the enterprise or business.

The application of an AML/CFT Program will not be complete without documentation of such application. Documentation requires systematic analysis, which is the foundation of a risk-based approach. It also provides an institutional memory of that analysis, and its determinations and actions. It facilitates information sharing within a dealer's business, and, when appropriate, with competent authorities. It also provides a basis upon which an AML/CFT program and practices can be measured and improved.

12

Commercial Websites and Internet Payment Systems

All criminals, since the involvement of 'financial experts ' such as Meyer Lansky, have shown adaptability and opportunism in finding new schemes to launder the proceeds of their illegal activities and to finance terrorism. As the internet grows larger every minute, commercial websites and Internet payment systems are potentially subject to a wide range of risks and vulnerabilities that can be exploited by criminal organisations and terrorist groups.

Research shows that mediated customer-to-customer websites as the most vulnerable to abuse because of their popularity, accessibility (to the public), and high volume of cross border trade transactions.

The following are the known vulnerabilities of commercial websites and Internet payment systems:

- non face-to-face registration,
- possible anonymity of the users,
- speed of transactions,
- limited human intervention,
- high number of transactions,
- international presence,
- limited jurisdictional competences,
- difficulties for traditional financial institutions to monitor and detect suspicious financial transactions with the consequence that their abilities in the detection of suspicious financial transactions, when an Internet payment service provider is used, could be affected.

The financial transactions that are initiated from a bank account or a credit card (which is the majority of online payments) already involve a customer identification process as well as transaction record keeping and reporting obligations. While low value transactions do not necessarily equate to low risk, these transactions are subject to the regulatory controls already applicable to the financial sector and may be consequently less risky.

However the risks associated with the non-face-to-face registration and the possible anonymity of the users, there is an obvious need for online identity verification solutions (the electronic identity card used in certain countries for instance) to help commercial websites and Internet payment service providers reduce the risk of criminal activity. However it is apparent that if Internet payment service providers adequately monitor the financial transactions of their customers, monitoring for and acting on deviations from the customer transaction profile, the lack of face-to-face contact at the beginning of the relationship with the commercial website and Internet payment service provider may not be a problem. It is preferable that online and offline retail merchants and payment services should have comparable anti-money laundering and terrorist funding obligations.

The international fight against potential money laundering by commercial websites and Internet payment service providers in different countries should not be hampered by divergent privacy legislation, potentially interfering with the amount of customer information that service providers could exchange

Although the challenges to identifying terrorist financing apply equally to Internet payment systems (the suspicions being mostly based on name matching with the names provided by the competent authorities and commercial database providers), it is not always necessary for Internet payment service providers to identify terrorist funding in their suspicious transactions reports. Any suspicious activity is important to report regardless of the type of activity.

Some Internet payment service providers have initiated systems to detect, monitor and analyse suspicious transactions – even for small amounts.

The risk of fraud and the sale of illegal goods are among the concerns of commercial websites and Internet payment systems. These concerns are among the motives for commercial websites and Internet payment systems to secure their communications, websites and payment systems. In some jurisdictions, online commercial websites are not as such required to detect or fight against money laundering/terrorist funding, but have a market incentive to detect fraud. In other words ensure that the website is nothing more than a retailer of stolen goods.

Currently many websites are under investigation for the sale of non-existent tickets, goods that differ from the advertised detail and product piracy. Replica watches being a favourite, the watches being made in China, using sweat shop labour, and the profits being used to fund drugs and other criminal activity.

Research of some commercial websites and Internet payment service providers, (aware of the risk of being used for illegal activity),shows that they have set up departments to screen and monitor the transactions of their customers, using a risk-based approach.

In addition to monitoring for fraud, some Internet payment service providers have also set up anti-money laundering mechanisms.

Best practices in the sector, include;

- customer due diligence,
- monitoring transactions,
- not accepting anonymous forms of payment (cash for instance)
- imposing transactions limits,
- maintaining transactions records,
- and reporting large or suspicious transactions to the competent authorities.

As mentioned previously criminals use a wide variety of mechanisms to launder the proceeds of their criminal activities and to finance terrorism, including using the formal financial system, the physical movement of cash by couriers and the movement of value through trade.

Commercial websites can be divided into five categories:

- Mediated customer-to-customer, sites that allow private individuals to sell to one another via an online marketplace (e.bay).
- Mediated business-to-customer, sites that allow multiple merchants to sell to consumers via an online marketplace.(Amazon etc)
- Non-mediated customer-to-customer (i.e. Bulletin board services and online classifieds), sites that only allow customers to advertise goods they want to sell.
- Direct business-to-customer, merchants that sell goods to consumers via their own websites.
- Direct business-to-business websites, merchants selling to merchants.

Mediated customer-to-customer sites are popular, easy to access, open to the public, and facilitate a high volume of cross border trade transactions. As such these sites are easily susceptible to criminal misuse. This type of commercial website facilitates transactions between private parties as opposed to simply providing seller contact information with any transactions occurring off-line.

Online classified-advertising sites, bulletin boards and social networking sites often allow sellers to post items for sale with the transaction taking place offline. While these businesses facilitate the introduction and communication of buyers and sellers, they do not play a significant role in the final sale nor financial settlement. This type of 'non-mediated' person-to-person website is therefore not often in a position to see any aspect of the transaction process after the introduction of buyer and seller.

'Mediated' websites, on the other hand, play an active role in the completion of underlying transactions, such as by setting the selling price through an online auction, providing some form of verification process for buyers and sellers (including aggregating feedback from other customers), or facilitating financial settlement of transactions (such as providing escrow, or similar intermediary, services)..

Mediated business-to-customer websites are also subject to money laundering/terrorist funding risks. A website can sell what appears to be normal goods much of the day, and will appear legitimate to its Internet payment service provider, but the website address (URL) may in fact be used to sell child pornography material for several hours each night. In some cases, businesses have allowed third party merchants to sell their own goods and services through the business's online portal.

It is worth mentioning that certain commercial websites belong to more than one category.

Commercial websites and Internet payment service providers can be used for illegal transactions, including

- the sale of illegal drugs,
- weapons, firearms,
- counterfeit products
- and child pornography.

They can also be used to facilitate fraud. Internet payment service providers can be used afterwards to launder the proceeds of these illegal activities.

Consumers are attracted to Internet payment systems because such systems often are convenient, and serve as an alternative to making payments via a bank account or credit card which may not be available to everyone.

Commercial websites

Commercial websites usually have some if not all of the following characteristics:

- A simple Internet connection is sufficient to open an Internet account with a commercial website and to buy and sell items on the Internet.
- Websites can potentially be accessed from any location in the world.
- A customer can gain access from his own Internet connection or from the Internet connection of a third party (e.g. cyber cafes or phone shops that provide Internet access) or another access point that is not registered to the customer.
- A customer can register in one country and connect from another country.
- Registration is very easy and very rapid (only a few minutes are necessary to register).
- Registration is non face-to-face.
- A limited amount of information is required to register.

- No procedure to verify customer identification in certain cases.
- Anonymous e-mail addresses may be used as customer contact information.(hotmail)
- Commercial transactions are performed very rapidly. E-mail messages are used to inform the seller that the item he put on sale has been sold.
- Customers have access to a wide range of items (from small value items to high value items) on sale on a wide range of commercial websites located all over the world.
- Goods can be sold for either a fixed or variable price. For example, on auction sites, the price may be set by the seller or by different buyers, creating uncertainty over the true market value of the goods being sold.

Some of these characteristics are characteristics of the Internet and also apply to Internet payment service providers

- Commercial websites may provide facilities for sale and financial settlement but leave delivery arrangement to buyers and sellers. Usually, the only indication of non-delivery of goods will be if the buyer complains.
- Some commercial websites and Internet payment service providers apply a risk-based approach when identifying customers. If the risk profile of the customer and transaction are high, additional verification methods are applied (simplified Customer Due Diligence vs. enhanced Customer Due Diligence).

The mechanisms of verification can be adapted to the country of registration and changed as necessary to adapt to criminal techniques where they attempt to bypass identification and verification processes. There are indications that criminals do attempt to circumvent these processes and although none of the methods had a zero-failure rate, they were effective on a risk-weighted basis.

In certain countries, online customer identification mechanisms using an electronic identity card are used and reduce the risk of identity theft. However one has to consider the massive increase in identity theft and forgeries over the past few years.

Internet payment systems

The structure and operations of a given Internet payment system vary drastically. However, usually such systems usually require a consumer, or user, to register with the Internet payment system before any transactions can be effected by the system. This registration process typically involves the collection and verification of some identification and/or contact information. An Internet payment system may require a user to:

- input his or her email address,
- telephone number,
- street address, and information needed to create a password and user identification (User ID) that will be required for the user to log into the Internet payment system.

Other information may be required based upon the business practices of the Internet payment system largely depending upon the type of services provided and the risk management processes required by regulatory authorities. The information collected is then verified using a variety of methods, ranging from the examination of paper copies of identity documentation to the use of online identity verification solutions provided by third parties.

Before a user of an Internet payment system can effect a transfer of funds through the system he generally must first fund the transfer. Funding a transfer through an Internet payment system may involve funding an 'account' from which funds will be drawn for subsequent transactions or transfers, or providing the Internet payment system with the equivalent amount of funds the user wishes to transfer. Depending upon the operations of a given Internet payment system, the user may have several options for funding a transaction, and may not be limited to the use of the user's credit card or personal bank account. To avoid fraud or any form of criminal misuse, the Internet payment service provider may attempt to verify that the customer has control over and is authorised to use certain funding methods, such as a credit card or bank account. Once the user has successfully been verified, the user is free to conduct transactions through the Internet payment system.

It is important to note that in order for an Internet payment system to provide transaction services for their users, they must interact with traditional banking and settlement systems. For example, an Internet payment system that accepts major credit cards as a funding source from its users usually is required to maintain a merchant account at a financial institution. Through this merchant account the Internet payment system can receive funds from its users, via major credit card networks. Such funds can then be applied to a transaction instruction that has been initiated by a user within the Internet payment system. A similar type of relationship typically exists with an Internet payment system that accepts funds from its users via the user's personal bank account. Once again, the Internet payment system is typically required to maintain an operating account at a bank where the transfer of funds from a user's personal banking account can be received. Typically these types of transfers are effected through clearing systems.

At the time of registration an Internet payment system may not require a user to input their personal identification number (e.g. social security number, passport number, etc.) or date of birth. Based upon the best practices of a given Internet payment system such information may not ever be collected from a user

Internet payment systems may support various types of payment methods for consumers purchasing goods and/or services online from a business website (commonly referred to as Consumer-to-Business transaction or C2B transaction) and businesses purchasing goods and/or services online from another business (a Business-to-Business or B2B transaction). However, the type of transaction that is of concern for potential ML and TF vulnerability is a person-to-person (P2P) transaction, involving a transaction between two consumers, as when buyers and sellers interact via a mediated website.

Other types of funding could be provided directly by certain commercial websites (transactions not powered by an Internet payment provider) or requested by consumers selling items on P2P commercial websites:

- Credit cards.
- Prepaid scheme-branded cards (anonymous in certain countries).
- Wire transfers (in favour of the bank account of the commercial website for further transfer to the seller).
- Wire transfers to the seller bank account (with a message accompanying the transfer and referring to a sale on the Internet).
- Gift cards or gift cheques (anonymous and transferable).
- Cheques (sent to the commercial website in certain countries, to the customers in other countries).
- Bank cheques.
- Postal orders/money orders in favour of the seller.
- Money transfers in favour of the seller.
- Cash is accepted on certain commercial websites.

Payment in cash can be made directly between buyer and seller, but this mechanism is not believed to be regularly used.

With Internet payment systems, the transaction takes place electronically very rapidly.

For global stakeholders (commercial websites and Internet payment systems available in different countries), the policies, practices, facilities (commercial and payments) made available to customers, may be different depending on the location of the parent company, local branch, or local website.

Some commercial websites and Internet payment service providers offer their customers the opportunity to use a more secured method of payment called the 'third party of confidence'. Using this facility (against the payment of a commission), the buyer knows that the funds for his purchases on Internet will be made available to the seller only if the goods purchased have been delivered and if he is satisfied that the goods correspond to the description on the commercial website.

Banks, newspapers and retail outlets in certain countries offer prepaid scheme-branded cards (preloaded cards) to customers for whom banks do not want to open a credit limit (unemployed or persons without a regular income).I mentioned this in my previous book when it became apparent that it was proposed that machines would be installed in public houses and night clubs where individuals could pay money into the machine to load a pre-pay credit card with cash. Although that scheme never got off the ground it is still possible to obtain a pre-loaded card and send that card to anyone who has not been vetted for them to use.

Some commercial websites advise their users to be cautious when accepting money orders as payment facilities when purchasing items on the Internet, as experience has shown that money orders are often used by criminals who commit fraud (selling items they do not deliver for instance).

As mentioned commercial websites and Internet payment systems are used to sell/purchase illegal products, like drugs or counterfeit goods. In some cases the sold/purchased dual use or precursor products are not illegal but correspond to dual use goods such as products used to make explosives, weapons or other controlled goods. Postal and express freight are frequently used to distribute these goods.

Commercial websites and Internet payment systems can be used for committing illegal transactions, fraudulent transactions or illegal activities. The commercial websites and Internet payment systems are used to collect the proceeds of these illegal activities, and to facilitate money laundering and terrorist funding transactions (by making the funds disappear: transferring the funds on a bank account in the country of the criminals or abroad, using them for other purchases on commercial websites).

The use of commercial websites and Internet payment systems to sell drugs

The bank account of an individual in Belgium was credited by wire transfers from an Internet payment service provider (small amounts for a total of EUR 4,700). The subject was under investigation in another European country for the sale of drug starters. Information from law enforcement confirmed that the subject was selling drug starters via a commercial website.

In this case, the Internet payment service provider was used to collect the proceeds of the illegal activities and may afterwards be used to perpetrate the illegal activities and operations. The criminal could use the proceeds of his illegal activities to buy new drug starters and continue to carry out his illegal activities via the commercial website.

The use of commercial websites and Internet payment systems to sell counterfeit goods

A bank reported the suspicious transactions of a young girl who from January 2005 to August 2005 (eight months), the bank account of the young girl, a student, was credited by wire transfers and cheques written out by individuals located all over France. The amount of each cheque was rather small (EUR 20 to 40). Regarding the debiting operations, the girl made cash withdrawals and wire transfers bearing the mention 'Internet payment provider bills'. The purchases amounted to a total of EUR 6,340 split into 43 operations.

In September 2005, she began to use a credit card so that it became more difficult for the bank to understand and analyse her transactions. Only a global amount of payments is registered monthly on her bank account.

Investigations showed that, from September 2005 to March 2006 (eight months), she made 63 purchases online for a total amount of EUR 39,282.24.

The young lady was selling counterfeit pearls of a famous brand at half price. She was using a provider in another European country which sold her parcels used to send the goods she had sold online.

Over 16 months, she earned more than EUR 43,000, roughly more than EUR 2,800 a month.

The use of commercial websites and Internet payment systems to sell explosive precursor products

A foreign Financial Intelligence Unit (FIU) informed the Belgian FIU that they received a suspicious transaction report (STR) from an Internet payment service provider concerning a national from a European country selling the following items on an associated commercial website:

- *potassium,*
- *chlorate,*
- *barium nitrate,*
- *strontium nitrate,*
- *ammonium nitrate.*

These items are considered as dual use goods, because, put together, they can be used to make explosives. The goods were sold to customers in Eastern Europe.

The criminals involved planned to collect the proceeds of their 'illegal' sales on the Internet through the Internet payment service provider and consequently to launder these proceeds, also using the Internet payment service provider.

The use of commercial websites and Internet payment systems related to weapons trafficking

A case reported by a French bank involved a lawyer who received and initiated a large number of Internet payments on and from his three personal bank accounts, ordering international wire transfers to individuals, receiving cheques and making cash deposits with no apparent economic sense.

From the messages on his bank account accompanying the financial transactions with the Internet payment service provider and the analysis of the wire transfers, it was possible to identify his online activity as related to weapons and elements of weapons sales transactions.(references being made to guns/pistols)

The French (FIU's) investigations revealed that:

- *over four years he made more than 1,600 selling operations, and the frequency of this online activity revealing a potential illegal business activity related to the use of weapons commercial websites;*
- *he regularly travelled to countries from Central and Eastern Europe which are vulnerable to weapons trafficking and often stayed more than one week there, so it was probable that he might have smuggled weapons.*

This case was reported to the judicial authorities for weapons trafficking.

Internet payment service provider and personal bank account transfers (I wire transfers to individuals) and the number of transactions (nearly one a day) made his online activity suspicious, going beyond what may have been a simple hobby, and appeared to be a real business.

The use of commercial websites and Internet payment systems to sell goods illegally (avoiding tax obligations)

Commercial websites and Internet payment systems can also be used for commercial activities performed without VAT registration and without paying taxes.

> The persons on this particular investigation were directors of an Australian company involved in purchasing large quantities of duty free cigarettes and alcohol to sell on the domestic market contrary to their export-duty free status, thus avoiding tax obligations.
>
> Due to not paying any tax on the goods the company was able to markedly increase profits. The syndicate also generated false receipts that purported to come from an export company detailing their alleged cigarette exports. Investigations with the purported company confirmed that no such exports had ever been made. On arrival of the cigarettes, payment was made to the delivery driver on a cash-on-delivery basis.
>
> A large number of the company's sales occurred over the Internet from customers paying via credit card. A majority of the sales on the Internet were illegitimate and came from three different email addresses. Payments for these orders were made from one of two credit cards linked to Belize bank accounts. One of these cards was held in the company's name.
>
> The money in the Belize bank account was sent there by one of the directors using several false names from not only Australia but Belize, Hong Kong, and Vietnam. The director conducted structured wire transfers under false names and front company accounts. The funds were purchased at well known banks with multiple transactions occurring on the same day at different bank locations and all of the cash transfers conducted in amounts of just under AUD 10,000 to avoid the reporting threshold.

Criminals can also develop their own commercial website to sell illegal products or perform illegal activities and use Internet payment service providers to collect the proceeds of these crimes.

In various reports of new payment methods precious metals are a new online payment system that involves the exchange of options or the right to purchase an amount of precious metals at a specific price. These derivatives can be exchanged, like traditional commodity or securities derivatives, between account holders in a digital precious metal service. Consumers purchase a quantity of virtual precious metal holdings based on the current price of the metal on the world commodity exchanges. Once a purchaser has acquired a quantity of the virtual precious metal, those holdings or a portion of them can be transferred either to another individual or a merchant in exchange for goods and services, also online. As a result, digital precious metal exchanges allow for the transfer of fixed 'value' between unrelated third parties, functioning as a money and value transmission business.

The use of e-gold as payment method – E-Gold Ltd/Gold & Silver Reserve Inc

On 27 April 2007, a federal grand jury in Washington, D.C., indicted two companies operating a digital currency business and their owners. The indictment charged E-Gold Ltd., Gold and Silver Reserve, Inc., and their owners with;

- *one count each of conspiracy to launder monetary instruments,*
- *conspiracy to operate an unlicensed money transmitting business,*
- *operating an unlicensed money transmitting business under federal law,*
- *and one count of money transmission without a license under D.C. law.*

According to the indictment, persons seeking to use the alternative payment system E-Gold were only required to provide a valid e-mail address to open an E-Gold account – no other contact information was verified.

The indictment was the result of a 2½-year investigation by the US Secret Service with cooperation among investigators, including the Internal Revenue Service (IRS), the Federal Bureau of Investigation (FBI), and other state and local law enforcement agencies. According to Jeffrey A. Taylor, US Attorney for the District of Columbia, 'The defendants operated a sophisticated and widespread international money remitting business, unsupervised and unregulated by any entity in the world, which allowed for anonymous transfers of value at a click of a mouse. Not surprisingly, criminals of every stripe gravitated to E-Gold as a place to move their money with impunity.'

Commercial websites and Internet payment systems can also be used by criminals to commit fraud. One of the many mechanisms used is the sale of fictitious items which the seller will not deliver to the buyer after receiving the payment.

Where commercial websites are used to attract buyers (in this case the victims of the fraud), Internet payment systems are not necessarily used to collect the funds (the crime proceeds of these activities). Criminals frequently use bank accounts in traditional financial institutions or money transfers and postal orders to be paid for the goods they do not deliver. The same financial channels are thereafter used to launder the proceeds of these illegal activities by making the funds disappear.

Transfers related to fraudulent sales on commercial websites (items never delivered)

The Belgian FIU received several STRs from banks in Belgium concerning bank accounts credited by wire transfers, apparently related to/justified by sales on commercial websites, and followed by cash withdrawals.

The majority of the wire transfers were of small amounts (maximum EUR 800), originating from various senders and, following the message accompanying the payment, related to sales on a commercial website, frequently the sales of luxury goods. Payments were not made through an Internet payment service provider but originated from the bank account of the buyer and were credited on the bank account of the seller. The wire transfers were followed by instant withdrawals in cash.

The goods were never delivered to the buyer (victim of a non-delivery fraud).

In some of these STR reports the wire transfers were not followed by cash withdrawals but by transfers in a country known for producing counterfeit products (in cases related to the sale of counterfeit goods).

The fraudulent bank account was used only during a short period (because of buyer's complaints).

Investigation showed that false names were used on the commercial website (the name used by the seller on the commercial website (certainly a fictitious name) and the name of the bank account holder where the payment is made was different).

In one case file, information received from law enforcement indicated that the subject was known for using different names on the commercial website. In another case file, the subject was using two different passports and different names.

Sale of fictitious goods on commercial websites and the use of Western Union (Finland) to collect the proceeds of these fictitious sales

This is a very interesting case where the two main suspects in Finland were acting as Western Union agents.

The offices of the agents were closed on 27 March 2007, and the two suspects were taken into custody.

People from other countries outside of Finland were fooled into buying fictitious goods (in this case; cars or other vehicles) on a commercial websites and sending the payment to fictitious persons in Finland via Western Union.

> The two Western Union agents in Finland picked up the money with the identities of the fictitious persons. Subsequently, the agents forwarded, again with more fictitious identities, the money as Western Union transactions outside of Finland.
>
> The two suspects in Finland received text messages from two persons (money flow managers) using mobile phone numbers including:
>
> - information about the victims abroad (their name, the expected receiver of the money, the amount sent as well as
> - instructions for forwarding the money abroad (the name of the receiver, the amount and the country to which send the money).
>
> The money flow managers are/were living in European countries.
>
> The total number of victims was over 300 and the total loss for the victims is estimated as EUR 1.07 million. The main source countries for the assets were the USA and the UK, but there were also a number of other source countries (about 25 countries).
>
> The two Western Union agents in Finland claimed, after interviews, that they received 10 per cent of the money picked up by them. They also claimed that both the money flow managers visited Finland during the activity and took with them a significant amount in cash.
>
> Based on the subsequent investigations into this case at least one of the money flow managers appeared to have similar arrangements with local Western Union agents in a number of other European countries.
>
> Further searches at various Western Union offices and the homes of the agents resulted in further arrests on 27 March 2007.
>
> The forensic investigation of the phones, SIM cards and PCs provided good evidence. Hundreds of text messages as well as a few e-mail messages were found in which instructions were given to the Western Union agents concerning the fraud cases and the money transactions.
>
> To support the Police investigation and the case in court, information has been requested in respect of possible offences being committed abroad. Therefore, requests to various agencies (FIU, Interpol or MLA) have been sent to 24 countries.
>
> At this current time information has been received about some 200 + fraud cases from 19 different countries.

Some commercial websites have proposed security mechanisms to their customers to avoid their site being used to commit such type of fraudulent activities. These include:

- organising rating systems to evaluate users' (buyers and sellers) reliability based on their previous transactions with the commercial website,
- advising their customers not to use money orders,
- encouraging the use of an Internet payment service provider associated with the commercial website because this is more secure,
- tracking and banning fraudsters.

Potential vulnerabilities

Criminals may use fictitious commercial transactions on commercial websites to justify movements of funds using traditional financial institutions or Internet payment systems. This typology shares many similarities with trade-based money laundering, where the transfer of funds for a transaction is disproportionate to the value of the goods delivered.

Fictitious sales on commercial websites followed by real payments

Buyer and seller know each other and may live in different countries or continents. No goods are delivered. Certain commercial websites between private individuals only put buyers and sellers in touch. They are not liable for the delivery, for checking the quality and/or the reality/existence of the goods offered for sale. The buyer will never complain for the non-delivery because seller and buyer are in league with each other. The buyer will pay the seller who will receive the funds on his bank account abroad. The beneficiary will have no difficulties justifying the origin of the funds received because the funds apparently come from sales on the Internet.

The buyer can also easily explain that he uses his credit card to buy something on the Internet. Commercial websites between private individuals allow the sale of goods of relatively high value, which will allow criminals to launder considerable amounts.

The use of a commercial website to launder the proceeds of drug trafficking

A drug trafficker can use commercial websites to receive the payment of his illicit sales. Instead of raising his bank's suspicion with unjustified cash deposits, he publishes an announcement for whatever fictitious products. His drug clients then proceeds with an online immediate purchase. Once the drug trafficker receives the payment, he can deliver the drugs as well as justifying the credit operations on his bank account with 'online sales operations'. This implies that there is coordination between 'seller' and 'buyer'.

The sale of goods at an overrated price

The mechanism is the same as in the above-mentioned example, except that the goods sold do exist and are sold at an overrated price through several fictive buyers. The net difference between the nominal sale price and the actual value of the goods delivered equals the value of money laundered. This type of transaction provides additional security for the launderers by creating a record trail of actual delivered goods, requiring law enforcement to prove that the value of the sale is grossly out of proportion with the actual market value of the goods.

Alternatively, value can be laundered in the reverse direction by having the buyer buy significantly less than the market value of the goods and then reselling the goods for a profit. The buyer would then be able to claim the difference in value was a profitable arbitrage deal while the seller would be to write off the difference as a market loss.

Many online businesses, particularly auction sites, sell goods that do not have a readily available market price. Also, overbidding is not unusual and could reflect legitimate transactions. In addition, since the items being sold remain in the possession of the seller throughout the auction process, the online auction company has little ability to ascertain the true market value of the item.

As already mentioned above counterfeit products or stolen products could be sold on commercial websites, aka a 'virtual fence'. Internet Payment systems could be used to move and launder the proceeds of these sales.

The sale of counterfeit or stolen products using multiple identities and user names

A criminal sells via a Customer to Customer website stolen and counterfeit goods. By multiplying identities and user names, he reduces the risk of being identified by the monitoring unit of the shopping website. He can either use the proceeds generated by his illegal sales to buy other goods or services online or transfer it to his personal bank account, the crediting operations being justified by 'online sales operations'.

Not only counterfeit luxury goods could be sold on commercial websites, but also real luxury goods purchased with cash by smurfs recruited by criminals to launder the proceeds of their illegal activities.(I thought we had got away from the dreaded smurf but obviously they are alive and well)

The use of commercial websites to sell at a reduced price, of goods (not counterfeit) purchased by smurfs in luxury goods shops with cash

Criminals send smurfs to luxury goods shops to buy articles of relatively high value (handbags...) that they pay in cash. This first stage of the money laundering process allows criminals to inject cash, possibly in small denominations into the financial system. This stage takes place in luxury good shops, which are less aware of money laundering.

Yes I realize there are directives to ensure that businesses apply certain controls on cash purchases above a certain amount (EUR 15,000) but smurfs will purchase for cash good of a lesser value (and with the current state of the world's economy how many blind eyes will be turned should that customer come through the shop door with a wad of cash – sorry Woollies you never sold luxury goods)

The luxury goods are subsequently sold on commercial websites, at a lower price. Criminals accept to lose a lot of money to launder the proceeds of their illegal activities. The proceeds of the sale arrive on the bank account of the seller abroad.

Money Laundering (ML) transactions not only take place in the first stage of the money laundering process (placement), but happen also during the two other ML stages (layering and integration).

Criminals usually try to make the financial transactions more sophisticated for law enforcement authorities and investigators, using a combination of the different ML stages. Commercial websites and Internet payment services providers could be used at various stages of the ML process. Traditional financial institutions could be used during the placement stage and commercial websites and Internet payment services providers at later stages such as during the layering stage (the above mentioned potential case study) and the integration (the purchase of goods or items with illegal funds already injected in the financial systems). The two following case studies provide examples of the use of the ML process at the integration stage.

The use of an electronic purse in conjunction with other ML methods

An individual residing at the country border regularly imports tobacco and alcohol products exceeding the duty-free quantities from the neighbouring country.

He sells them to individuals. The cash collected is used to credit a savings account opened in the name of one of his underage children. The justification given can be cash donations from the family to the child.

The funds crediting the savings account of the child are regularly transferred to the bank account of the individual held in another bank. The origin of the funds appears to be legal – it comes from the savings account of one of his children; the justification for the transfers can be temporary financial difficulties, expenses made for the child like buying a scooter or paying driving lessons, etc.

The funds transferred on the bank account of the individual can then credit an electronic purse to buy goods and services online.

Commercial websites and Internet payment systems can potentially be used to finance terrorism, taking into consideration the fact that terrorism financing may involve small amounts of money.

As already mentioned, commercial websites and Internet payment service providers depend on information they obtain from law enforcement and other authorities to facilitate the detection of suspicious transactions related to terrorist financing and it is not always necessary for Internet payment service providers to identify Terrorist Funding in their Suspicious Transaction Reports in order to help counter terrorist financing

---

The use of a commercial website and Internet payment service provider to finance terrorist activities also in conjunction with other Money Laundering methods

'Y', a well-known terrorist, under close surveillance of the German intelligence services, wants to send funds to Z, residing in France so that Z can buy cell phones or other items necessary to make explosive devices.

Afraid of being detected if he uses funds transfer systems like Western Union or MoneyGram, he decides to use an alternative way to make his funds available.

He asks a student to register on a Customer to Customer website and to open an Internet payment provider account. Y gives the student a prepaid card of EUR 799 to credit his Internet account.

- *The student can then order a transfer from his Internet account to the Internet account of another student located in France.*
- *The student located in France can then credit his bank account with the funds received on his Internet account and buy prepaid cards to be handed over to Z.*
- *Z can use the prepaid cards directly or credit his bank account with them.*

Front individuals or intermediaries such as the 'students' in the example above are even recruited on the Internet, lured by the payment of a commission amounting from 5% to 10% of the funds to be transferred. Massive spams are sent, proposing to become the associate of a 'financial company', the job consisting of receiving and transferring funds. These mules are used for Money Laundering/Terrorist Financing.

Potential money laundering indicators are;

- The customer opens his individual Internet account with the payment service provider in one country but logs in regularly on the website from a single or multiple third countries.

- The account opened by the customer is loaded with funds transferred from a third country, which could indicate that the customer does not live in the country from which he registered but in another country where he cannot register (not accepted by the website for security reasons) or that he registered in one country but commits illegal activities in a third country, or that he concealed the results of his illegal activities in a third country.
- The customer starts to purchase items on the Internet for amounts not in line with his previous transactions profile.
- The customer loads his Internet account with cash,(if the Internet payment services provider allows loading with cash)
- The customer account with payment service provider is loaded with funds transferred by a third party apparently not related to the customer.
- The transactions of the customer suddenly deviate from its previous transactions profile after his customer account had been loaded with money from a third party.
- The customer purchases items of high value or purchases middle high value items on a regular basis with a prepaid debit card, an anonymous prepaid credit card or a gift card where the origin of the funds is difficult to retrace.

It is probably worth mentioning that the loading of an account or a card with cash is not sufficient in itself to give rise to a suspicion of Money laundering. Cash could have a legal origin. Confronted with cash, the Internet payment service provider needs to apply higher standards of control or due diligence (monitoring of transactions, limits and restrictions, etc.).

It is also worth mentioning that systems which do not accept cash may be less risky.

Because the average value of a commercial transaction and the subsequent payment on commercial websites are very low. Money launderers wanting to use commercial websites and Internet payment service providers for their criminal activities and the Money laundering may need to carry out several consecutive small transactions if they want to avoid being detected. It is sometimes difficult for Internet payment service providers to distinguish between a normal credit card and a prepaid credit card as credit card companies use similar credit card numbers for both credit cards.

It is worth mentioning that Gift cards have generally low face values. Criminals need to purchase several gift cards to make their ML transactions economically viable.

- Some customers apparently resell goods purchased beforehand, without any economic reasons, or with a significant discount or increase on the price. The buyer requests that the goods be delivered to a post office box or to a different address from the one registered to the account (facilities depending on the country of destination).

- A customer uses an account with an Internet payment service provider not to purchase items on Internet but to hide a sum of money obtained illegally. A customer opens an account with an Internet payment service provider, loads the account with important amounts of money, leaves the funds on the account during a certain period of time and requests the redemption of the funds later on.
- A customer requesting the balance from his Internet account to be transferred to a third party without apparent relation with him.
- The use of credit cards, particularly prepaid, issued in a foreign country.
- A customer sells illegal items or the goods appear on a list of forbidden items.
- Abnormality with the proposed price on an auction site or during an auction sale indicating a possible complicity between buyer and seller (a customer offers to purchase an item at a price largely higher than the requested price). Additional factors could include multiple transactions between the same buyers and sellers.
- The purchased goods are regularly shipped to a foreign country.
- The customer uses a credit card issued by a bank in an offshore centre or in a FAFT non-cooperative country.
- The funds originate from a non-cooperative country.
- The country of origin of the customer is known by the FATF as a non-cooperative country in the fight against money laundering or terrorism financing.
- An unexpected turnover for a recently established commercial website or an unexpected increase in the value of the commercial website after a few sales.

Suspicious behaviour or transaction may result from one indicator or a set of indicators.

Money laundering and terrorist financing risks

The AML/CFT risks of trade-based money laundering and non face-to-face transactions apply also to commercial websites and Internet payment systems. The AML/CFT regulations of commercial websites could be comparable to the ones existing for traditional commerce (those regulations only apply to merchants accepting cash over a predefined threshold) and the ones of Internet payment systems to the common payments systems, even if the relationship is non face-to-face, because risk-based CDD and monitoring measures are taken to reduce and mitigate the ML/TF risks.

These risks can be classified according to the ML phases:

Placement

- Anonymity of customers on certain commercial websites and Internet payment services providers. Both the registration and transactions could in certain circumstances be performed anonymously (on certain websites an anonymous e-mail address is enough for registration).
- The relationship with customers is a non face-to-face relationship. Transactions are non face-to-face transactions, which makes it more difficult for the commercial websites and Internet payment services providers to be sure that they are working with the customer who has been identified at registration.
- The possibility to use multiple registrations. The use of multiple (anonymous) registrations to purchase and sell items could create problems when screening, monitoring and reconstructing transactions and flow of funds.
- Remote access to commercial websites and Internet payment systems. Connection to commercial websites and Internet payment systems is available everywhere in world. A criminal can connect himself to the Internet from web terminals not affiliated or registered to his or her identity, which makes more difficult for law enforcement to locate and to pursue criminals and money launderers.
- Relative 'anonymity' associated with certain methods of payment. With prepaid credit cards, gift cards/gift cheques and when cash is used, the origin of the funds cannot be (easily) retraced.

Layering: (the speed of movement)

- Transactions via commercial websites and Internet payment systems can be done very rapidly as transactions between sellers and buyers are performed electronically.
- A good identification is a vital for detecting a suspicion related to an individual/company but also for a serious and effective investigation of a suspicious operation.
- Even if anonymous gift cards are generally issued for relatively small amounts, this can quickly add up to a considerable total.
- Even if measures of internal control exist to monitor and to supervise the sale of gift cards at local shops or supermarkets, it is unlikely that a survey of sudden increases in the number of gift cards issued and amounts loaded (analysis of purchase details, pattern of purchases and spending locations, IP addresses, physical monitoring of premises) will be able to *completely* avoid anonymity.

- The international character and the jurisdictional issue of where the transaction takes place make these transactions difficult to investigate quickly. Transactions on commercial websites and Internet payment systems can be performed across international borders and the jurisdiction where the Internet payment service provider is located may not be competent to investigate and prosecute Money Laundering or Terrorist Financing. Likewise, no single jurisdiction currently has clear responsibility for regulating and monitoring activity.
- The speed of movement, the international character of the transaction and the jurisdictional issue related to the use of the commercial websites and Internet payment systems will without doubt impact on Financial Investigation Units and law enforcement agencies who investigate cases of money laundering or terrorism financing.
- Volume of movement (number of transactions and amounts per transaction). The high number of transactions and consequently amounts per transactions make it more difficult for Internet Payment services providers to define criteria to monitor and screen transactions (which types of transactions should be regarded as suspicious?)
- As less human intervention is associated with transactions via commercial websites and Internet payment systems, traditional first level detection mechanisms which rely heavily on the face-to-face relationship with the customer, are no longer available and must be replaced by sophisticated second level detection.
- The absence or inadequacy of audit trails, record keeping or suspicious transactions reporting by certain Internet payment services providers.

Integration – the possibility to buy high value items

- Buying (high value) goods, precious metals, real estate or securities on commercial websites using an Internet payment system.
- By limiting the use of an account, the Internet payment service provider should be able to limit the potential risk.
- It is worth mentioning that it is also difficult for traditional financial institutions to define criteria to monitor the transactions of their customers using computer software.
- If Internet payment service providers adequately monitor the financial transactions of their customers by detecting deviations from their customer's known profile of transactions, the face-to-face contact at the beginning of the relationship with the commercial website and Internet payment service provider may not constitute a problem.
- In general regulations are imposed to commercial websites mainly in the

field of the protection of the consumer (better inform their users on their rights and duties, general terms of use and the use of electronic contracts, identification of the commercial website, advertising...), the prohibition to sell certain goods and the possibility to cancel a purchase made online.

- In most cases, there is no identification or Suspicious Transaction Report obligations in place for commercial websites. In the UK there is no specific regulatory regime for electronic commerce, although the Financial Services Authority does regulate electronic money in the UK, as well as the sale of financial services by electronic means by firms in the UK.

- E-money is defined in UK law as monetary value as represented by a claim on the issuer which is stored on an electronic device, issued on receipt of funds and accepted as a means of payment by persons other than the issuer. E-money is considered as an electronic surrogate for coins and banknotes, intended to effect payments of limited amounts.

- The FSA's approach to regulating e-money is based on requirements of the EU's E-money Directive. E-money issuers also have obligations under the Money Laundering Regulations 2007 to, for example, apply customer due diligence measures and to undertake ongoing monitoring of their business relationships. In the event that potentially suspicious activity is detected, the firm has a legal obligation to report this to the authorities. The FSA would expect e-money issuers to be able to demonstrate that they deploy an adequate range of controls for the type of risks that they encounter. Discussion of steps that can be taken by e-money issuers to meet their legal obligations is provided by Guidance issued by the Joint Money Laundering Steering Group (JMLSG).

Rest of Europe

Most other countries in Europe have similar controls and guidance as recommended by the EEC.

United States

Banking organisations that provide payment methods used for electronic commerce in the United States are subject to a full range of AML/CFT requirements, including among other things, requirements to: detect and report suspicious transactions; maintain records of funds transfers, and to implement AML compliance and customer identification programs. The cornerstone to this strong AML compliance program is the adoption and implementation of comprehensive customer due diligence policies, procedures, and processes for all customers. These processes assist US banking organisations in determining when transactions are potentially suspicious.

When a banking organisation within the United States determines a transaction is suspicious, it is required to file a Suspicious Activity Report (SAR) with the US financial intelligence unit, known as the Financial Crimes Enforcement Network (FinCEN). Banking organisations within the United States are required to report transactions involving or aggregating to at least USD 5,000 that are attempted or conducted by, at, or through the institution in which the organisation 'knows, suspects, or has reason to suspect' the transaction:

- involves funds derived from illegal activities or is conducted to disguise funds derived from illegal activities,
- is designed to evade the reporting or record keeping requirements of the Bank Secrecy Act (BSA) (e.g. structuring transactions to avoid currency transaction reporting), or
- 'has no business or apparent lawful purpose or is not the sort in which the particular customer would normally be expected to engage, and the banking organisation knows of no reasonable explanation for the transaction after examining the available facts, including the background and possible purpose of the transaction.'

The Federal banking agencies and the US Department of the Treasury's Financial Crimes Enforcement Network (FinCEN) are the primary government agencies responsible for enforcing compliance with the relevant AML/CFT regulations.

The US Federal banking agencies have been charged (under US Federal banking laws 12 USC 1818(s) and 12 USC 1786(q) for banks and saving banks) with ensuring that banking organisations, subject to their respective jurisdictions, maintain effective Bank Secrecy Act/Anti Money Laundering compliance programs.

Several other regulations apply to electronic funds transfer activities. They concern the rights, liabilities, and responsibilities of parties in electronic fund transfers (EFT) and protect consumers using EFT systems, such as ATMs and debit cards.

Singapore

E-money is broadly referred as Stored Value Facility (SVF) in Singapore. Under Singapore law, a SVF is a form of prepaid electronic cash or card that can be used within the system of the SVF issuer. The SVF issuer is also known as the holder of the SVF.

The issuance and management of SVFs are governed by the Payment Systems (Oversight) Act 2006 (PS(O)A) and its related regulations. Any entity can issue a

SVF and hold the stored value. However, SVF with total outstanding stored value exceeding SGS 30 million will require approval from the Monetary Authority of Singapore (MAS) and a bank licensed by the MAS to be fully liable for the stored value. SVFs whose aggregated stored value falls below the prescribed SGD 30 million do not require MAS's approval to operate but are required to provide disclosure to advise potential users that such SVFs are not subject to MAS' approval.

In addition to the PS(O)A regulatory requirements, any holder SVF which issues a SVF that has a load limit of more than SGD 1,000 has to adhere to and apply the MAS AML/CFT Notice to holders of SVF on the prevention of money laundering and countering the financing of terrorism.

The Notice imposes preventive measures to holders to limit the risk of SVFs being used for illegitimate purposes. The Notice sets out obligations which require holders to take measures to mitigate money laundering and financing of terrorism risk in the following fields; i.e. due diligence measures (simplified, enhanced), identification of users (customers), verification of identification of users, identification and verification of identities of Beneficial Owners, non face-to-face verification, review of relevant transactions, record keeping, suspicious transactions reporting, internal policies, audit and training.

Any holder of SVF which fails or refuses to comply with the requirements under the Notice shall be liable on conviction to a fine not exceeding SGD 1,000,000 and, in case of a continuing offence, to a further fine of SGD 100,000 for every day during which the offence continues after conviction (under section 27B of the MAS Act).

The MAS has also issued SVF Guidelines which recommend sound principles and risk mitigating factors for all holders of SVFs. These principle-based recommendations address issues such as transparency, disclosure, public confidence, stored value protection, prevention of money laundering and countering the financing of terrorism.

China

There are no regulations in place addressing Electronic Commerce or Internet payment systems in China. Nevertheless, on 13.12.2007, the Chinese Ministry of Commerce issued an opinion on Enhancing the regularised Development of Electronic Commerce. The objectives of the guidance are to help the third-party electronic payment service providers to improve the reputation of the industry, operate in a prudent and stable manner, prevent blind business expansion and out-of-order competition, and ensure the safety of users' funds. The guidance encourages measures like standardised operation and management, overseeing business flow, secure electronic payment, keeping transaction data, and prevents online illegal financial transactions ...

Hong Kong, China

Hong Kong, China does not have licensing systems for e-money and Internet payment service providers. In Hong Kong, China, 'e-money' is very much represented by Multi-purpose stored value cards. Institutions in Hong Kong China issuing or facilitating the issuance of Multi-purpose stored value cards must be authorised by the Hong Kong Monetary Authority (HKMA) under the Banking Ordinance, Cap. 155 (BO). These institutions are called authorised institutions (AIs) and are subject to supervision of the HKMA.

Internet payment service providers, in Hong Kong, China, only provide a platform for the users to settle various types of payment through transferring money from their designated bank accounts to that of the vendor of goods or services. Nevertheless, when such service providers carry on a business of taking deposits and cash, they have to get a licence from HKMA to conduct business as an AI.

The HKMA has set out various supervisory policies and requirements to be observed by AIs in the form of supervisory guidelines. The supervisory guidelines issued by the HKMA with respect to AML/CFT are the 'Guideline on Prevention of Money Laundering' and the 'Supplement to the Guideline on Prevention of Money Laundering'. These guidelines are issued in the form of a statutory guideline pursuant to section 7(3) of the BO. These guidelines impose obligations on AIs to put in place effective systems and procedures for combating money laundering and terrorist financing and are developed based on the latest international standards including the current 40 Recommendations on anti-money laundering and 9 Special Recommendations on countering the financing of terrorism of the FATF. The requirements in these guidelines apply to AIs which issue Multi-purpose stored value cards.

Under the AML/CFT guidelines, AIs are required to i) conduct the customer due diligence process to identify and verify the identity of their customers and the beneficial owners of their customers using reliable, independent source information, ii) obtain information on the purpose and intended nature of the business relationship, and iii) conduct on-going due diligence and scrutiny of transactions throughout the business relationship. AIs are required to adopt a risk-based approach in their CDD process. AIs should develop customer acceptance policies and procedures that aim to identify the types of customers that are likely to pose a higher money laundering/terrorist financing risk. For those customers identified with higher ML/TF risk, AIs should adopt a more extensive customer due diligence process and subject them to close monitoring. In undertaking the CDD

A Multi-purpose stored value card is defined in the BO as a card on which data may be stored in electronic, magnetic or optical form and for or in relation to which a person pays a sum of money to the issuer of the card (directly or indirectly) in exchange for i) the storage of the value of that money, in whole or in part on the card; and ii) an undertaking by the issuer (express or implied) that the issuer or a third party will, on production of the card, supply goods and services (which may include money). There is currently only one issuer of Multipurpose stored value cards (i.e. Octopus Cards Limited) in Hong Kong, China. The Octopus Cards Limited is authorised as a deposit-taking company under the BO. Octopus cards are designated for small amount retail payments and there is a maximum storage limit of HKD1,000 per card.

AIs should, whenever possible, conduct a face-to-face interview with a new customer to ascertain the customer's identity and background. In cases where a face-to-face interview is not conducted, they should apply equally effective customer identification procedures and on-going monitoring standards to mitigate the risk. The AML/CFT guidelines also require AIs to keep proper account and transaction records.

Section 25A of the Organised and Serious Crimes Ordinance, CAP 455, (and similar provisions under Hong Kong's anti-terrorist financing legislation) provides requirements for reporting of suspicious transactions by all persons in Hong Kong to Hong Kong's Joint Financial Intelligence Unit, (JFIU). Failure to report a suspicious transaction is a criminal offence. All parties engaged in financial transactions of any kind must have systems in place to detect suspicious transactions to comply with this law, but the exact methods used are the responsibility of each company. Moreover, under the HKMA's AML/CFT guidelines, AIs should put in place effective management information systems to enable them to identify and report suspicious transactions. The Organised and Serious Crime Ordinance and Drug Trafficking (Recovery of Proceeds) Ordinance, (and similar provisions under Hong Kong's anti-terrorist financing legislation) makes provision for reporting of STRs to the JFIU. The reporting obligations apply to any person who knows or suspects that any property represents any person's proceeds of an indictable offence, or the property was used in connection with or is intended to be used in connection with an indictable offence, he shall disclose that knowledge or suspicion to an authorised officer (i.e. JFIU officer) as soon as practicable.

The HKMA ensures compliance of AIs with its AML/CFT guidelines through its on-going supervisory process. If an AI fails to comply with a requirement under the AML/CFT guidelines, the HKMA will require the AI to take appropriate remedial actions to rectify the situation. The HKMA will follow up with the AI to ensure that the deficiency has been satisfactorily addressed. Where the non-compliance is considered to be serious, the HKMA will impose supervisory measures against the AI.

Australia

Payment methods are regulated largely by a combination of the Payments System (Regulation) Act 1998, the Payment Systems and Netting Act 1998, and the Electronic Funds Transfer (EFT) Code. The Reserve Bank of Australia (RBA) administers the Payments System (Regulation) Act 1998, and the Payment Systems and Netting Act 1998 with the goal of achieving efficiency, competition and stability. The Australian Securities and Investments Commission administers the EFT Code with the goal of providing consumer protection.

Australia's primary anti-money laundering and counter-terrorism financing (AML/CTF) legislative package includes the Anti-Money Laundering and Counter-Terrorism Financing Act 2006 (AML/CTF Act) and Anti-Money Laundering and Counter Terrorism Financing Rules. The AML/CTF Act sets out general AML/CTF principles and obligations. With the details of how these obligations are to be carried out being set out in subordinate legislative instruments known as the AML/CTF Rules.

The AML/CTF Act covers the financial sector, gambling sector and bullion dealing and any other professionals or businesses that provide particular designated services. Being activities-based,

There is a broad range of supervisory measures available to the HKMA. They include for example issuing a statement of warning to the senior management of the AI, imposing restriction on the AI's business, downgrading the supervisory ratings of the AI and commissioning an external auditor to review the AML/CFT system of the AI. In the event that the AI fails to take appropriate remedial actions, the HKMA will consider exercising its formal powers under the BO, which include withdrawing the consent given to the responsible directors and chief executives, attaching conditions to the AI's authorisation, requiring the AI to seek advice from an Advisor appointed by the HKMA and suspending or revoking the authorisation of the AI. The supervisory measures to be taken in each case will depend on the seriousness of the deficiencies identified in the AI and are considered to be effective, proportionate and dissuasive. under the AML/CTF, it does not matter how designated services are provided (i.e. electronic, paper or face to face).

The AML/CTF Act imposes a number of obligations on businesses (called reporting entities) when they provide these designated services. These obligations include: customer due diligence (identification, verification of identity and ongoing monitoring of transactions); reporting (suspicious matters, threshold transactions and international funds transfer instructions); record keeping, and establishing and maintaining AML/CTF program.

The AML/CTF Act implements a risk-based approach to regulation. Businesses are able to determine the way in which they meet their obligations based on their assessment of the risk of whether providing a designated service to a customer may facilitate money laundering or terrorism financing. The AML/CTF Rules specify how the obligations may be complied with by a reporting entity putting in place appropriate risk-based systems and controls. When determining and putting in place appropriate risk-based systems and controls, the reporting entity must have regard to the nature, size and complexity of its business and the type of ML/TF risk that it might reasonably face. In identifying its ML/TF risk a reporting entity must also consider the risk posed by the following factors: its customer types, including any politically exposed persons, the types of designated services it provides, the methods by which it delivers designated services; and the foreign jurisdictions with which it deals.

The Australian Prudential Regulation Authority (APRA) authorises certain e-commerce payment mechanisms to be a Purchased Payment Facility (PPF). PPFs, such as smart cards and electronic cash, are facilities which consumers pay for in advance and use to make various types of payments. Consumers rely on the holder of the stored value redeeming that value on demand.

APRA's prudential standard regarding PPF's seeks to ensure that those who provide PPF facilities are subject to prudential requirements commensurate with their risk profile. A PPF provider is not authorised to conduct general banking business. Under the prudential standard, a PPF provider is required to comply with AML/CTF requirements as administered by AUSTRAC (under the Anti-Money Laundering and Counter-Terrorist Financing Act 2006).

APRA also authorises those who carry on a credit card issuing and/or acquiring business in Australia as a 'specialist credit card institution' (SCCI). SCCIs are a special class of authorised deposit-taking institutions (ADIs) that are authorised to perform a limited range of banking activities. SCCIs may only perform credit card issuing and/or acquiring business and any other services related to credit card issuing and/or acquiring. SCCIs are not permitted to accept deposits (other than incidental credit balances on credit card accounts).

Risk management measures taken by the sector

As with any type of business, commercial websites and Internet payment systems are confronted with various types of risks ranging from the technical safeguards of their websites from computer hackers and viruses to the outright criminal misuse of their systems by criminals for purposes of facilitating fraud, and Internet payment systems for money laundering and other financial crimes.

Risk management is therefore an ongoing process that may be developed by commercial websites and Internet payment systems to minimise their exposure to various risks. This may include the establishment of customer user agreements and policies by a company that set strict rules and policies for the use of their respective system by a user. In addition, commercial websites and Internet payment systems may also establish 'best practices' designed to set internal standards for how a company may safely operate while at the same time providing effective services to their users.

Risk management may also encompass Anti-Fraud and Anti-Money Laundering/Terrorist Financing (AML/TF) programs that may have been implemented by commercial websites and Internet payment systems. Finally, a risk-based approach may also integrate other initiatives that are undertaken by a commercial websites and Internet payment systems that are required under the regulatory regime of a specific country or jurisdiction where a commercial websites and Internet payment systems may provide services, e.g. reporting requirements (for Internet payment systems), etc. Other stakeholders (such as the tax authorities and authorities supervising payments) are or must be involved in the fight against ML or TF and the mitigation of ML or TF risks. If commercial websites have no reporting obligations they are controlled by these stakeholders.

AML/CFT mechanisms used to mitigate risks

Internet Payment service providers, subject to regulations from a supervision authority, mitigate the above mentioned ML/TF risks by applying different mechanisms. During the study the project team obtained confirmation on the use of such mechanisms by consulting, as mentioned in the introduction, one of the most important mediated customer-to-customer commercial websites and Internet payment service provider as well as a smaller electronic money issuer and the Electronic Money Association representing a range of e-money issuers and payment service providers. The project team also obtained confirmation that AML/CFT regulations imposing similar mechanisms apply to Internet payment service providers in the most industrialised countries.

A non-exhaustive list of these mechanisms is provided in this section:

- Implementing important worldwide security teams patrolling sites to detect fraud and misuse.
- Applying risk-based Customer Due Diligence (simplified CDD vs. enhanced CDD).
- Scoring customer risk at opening of account.
- Risk-based verification of information entered by customers (e-mail address/IP address, identity of credit card holder, stolen credit cards ...).
- Automated call, random charges to verify identities of customers.
- Sending a letter to verify customers address.
- Credit cards address verification.
- Consulting commercial databases to confirm information received from customers;

- Phone calls by staff to obtain additional information from customers.
- Activity limits, sending and withdrawals limits.
- Verification of funding source.
- Real time screening of customers, their activities and items sold.
- Monitor, using risk models built to detect bad activities, information:
- obtained from customers (identity, address, e-mail and IP addresses used, About Me page, ...)
- collected from customers (phone call to sellers, ...)
- obtained internally (previous transactions, item country location, customer location, shipping methods used, behaviour of customers during auction processes, accepted payments, ...)
- obtained from external sources (countries at risk for certain forms of criminalities, check listings of presumed terrorists or terrorist groups, ...)
- Risk models to detect abnormal (with regards to previous transactions) or high volume activity.
- Models/software to detect suspicious activities (based on various red flags and indicators).
- Manual review of abnormal transactions and of higher use accounts.
- Detect abnormal and suspicious activities in withdrawals.
- Refuse transactions on prohibited items (drugs, firearms, counterfeit products...).
- Remove offending items from the website.
- Cooperate with commercial company to detect counterfeit products and remove them from sales.
- Analyse the physical and electronic evidence left by criminals on the net.
- Delay a transaction.
- Display message to customers on regulation applying to certain countries and transactions.
- Encourages the reporting of suspicious items on sale, suspicious auctions or suspicious behaviour of customers (sellers or buyers) – scoring of customers (buyers and sellers by each other).
- Does not accept or distribute cash.
- Maintain full audit trails of commercial transactions and payments.

The most organised Internet payment service providers collect a range of data and information about movements of funds between buyers and sellers, located in different countries all over the world but customers of the same Internet payment service provider, commercial transactions between buyers and sellers, data and information accumulated over a long period of time and available centrally.

Consequently, they have a global view of the movements of funds and the commercial transactions between buyers and sellers internationally, information that the banks of buyers and sellers do not have. They can easily reconstruct commercial transactions and movements funds between different countries and persons in the world.

Certain Internet payment service providers have the opportunity to access data and information on the commercial transaction underlying a financial movement of funds because they provide payment facilities to commercial websites belonging to the same financial group. Nevertheless, certain Internet payment service providers providing payment facilities to commercial websites not belonging to the same financial group can also obtain but in a more limited way information on underlying commercial transactions.

An easy data sharing of information with commercial websites reduces the risks of misuse and the risks of ML/TF.

If Internet payment service providers adequately monitor the financial transactions of their customers by detecting deviations from their customer's known profile of transactions, the non face-to-face contact at the beginning of the relationship with the commercial website and Internet payment service provider may not constitute a problem.

Nevertheless, it is worth mentioning that an Internet payment service provider will be able to build a better and much accurate customer's profile of transactions if the number of transactions performed by a customer is significant.

Exchange of information between commercial websites and Internet payment services providers possibly located in different countries is sometimes not easy because of the differences in the privacy legislation.

As already mentioned, AML/CFT reporting obligations are applicable to Internet payment service providers in the country in which they are physically located. Certain commercial websites and Internet payment service providers work closely with law enforcement. They encourage regulators and law enforcement to play an active role in the fight against the use of commercial websites and Internet payment service providers for criminal activities.

Second level controls vs third level controls

Internet payment service providers, licensed as e-money providers or as a bank, have several obligations in the field of identification of customers, detection, monitoring and reporting of suspicious financial transactions. As explained in the section above, they have access to a wide range of information for monitoring the transactions of their customers and certain Internet payment service providers have implemented ongoing due diligence mechanisms which include: scrutiny of transactions undertaken throughout the course of the relationship to ensure the transactions conducted are consistent with their customer's known profile. In many cases, the profile of a customer can only be deducted from previous transactions with the payment service provider.

When services of Internet payment services providers are used, banks of buyers and sellers do not have a global view of the flow of funds between buyers and sellers, as this information is only known by the Internet services provider itself. A customer of a bank may order his bank to transfer funds from his bank account to his account with an Internet payment service provider. Afterwards the customer will request the Internet payment service provider to transfer funds for a purchase on a commercial website. The bank can be totally unaware of this purchase and the reasons for funding the account with the Internet payment service provider. In the United States, similar cases have been identified with payments requested by customers of banks in favour of Internet payment service providers and used thereafter by these customers on gambling websites, without the bank knowing the funds were used for this illegal activity in the United States.

Banks still have an important role to play in the monitoring and detection of suspicious transactions, even if the funds are transferred to or originate from an Internet payment service provider. For instance, a transaction with an Internet payment service provider can be abnormal or disproportionate to the bank with regards to the known profile (professional activities, professional revenues, customer bank transactions profile) of its customers.

It is also important that financial institutions, such as the banks, do not exonerate themselves from their AML/CFT responsibilities, in particular the detection of suspicious financial transactions, when the funds originate from an Internet payment service provider, and even if the transactions concern relatively small amounts. A statement or a printout of a screen of the commercial website showing an item on sale must not immediately and unconditionally considered as an invoice or justifying a financial transaction on the bank account of the customer. Conversely, the presentation of such justification document could be used as a red flag or indicator for the financial institution.

Policy implications

Analysis of the ML/TF risks associated with commercial websites and Internet payment systems and the focus has been put on the type of electronic commerce identified for various reasons (increasing popularity, easy access, available to private individuals, high volume of cross border trade transactions ...) as being the most susceptible to be used by criminals for ML/TF: mediated customer-to-customer. The analysis shows that:

- Criminals have shown adaptability and opportunism in finding new channels to launder the proceeds of their illegal activities and to finance terrorism. As the Internet becomes more and more a worldwide phenomenon, commercial websites and Internet payment systems appear to be subject to a wide range of risks and vulnerabilities that can be exploited by criminal organisations and terrorist groups.

- Various vulnerabilities of commercial websites and internet payment systems have been highlighted: the non face-to-face registration which may lead to identification problems; the speed of transactions, the limited human intervention and the high number of transactions, which may cause problems concerning audit trails, monitoring and detection of transactions; the international character, which is inherent to the Internet, which may create issues concerning jurisdictional competences; difficulties for traditional financial institutions to monitor and detect suspicious financial transactions with the consequence that their abilities in the detection of suspicious financial transactions, when an Internet payment service provider is used, could be affected.

Some of the ML/TF risks associated with trade-based money laundering and non face-to-face business and financial transactions apply also to commercial websites and Internet payment systems. The financial transactions that are initiated from a bank account or a credit card (which is the majority of online payments) already involve a customer identification process as well as transaction record keeping and reporting obligations. While low value transactions do not equate to low risk, these transactions are subject to the regulatory controls already applicable to the financial sector and may be consequently less risky.

Regarding the risks associated with the non-face-to-face registration and the possible anonymity of the users the study highlights the need for online identity verification solutions (the electronic identity card used in certain countries for instance) to help commercial websites and Internet payment service providers mitigate the risks of criminal activity. The report also indicates that if Internet payment service providers adequately monitor the financial transactions of their customers, monitoring for and acting on deviations from the customer transaction profile, the lack of face-to-face contact at the beginning of the relationship with the commercial website and Internet payment service provider may not constitute a problem. Online and offline retail merchants and payment services should have comparable AML/CFT obligations.

It is also important that efforts to fight against fraud and ML/TF by commercial websites and Internet payment service providers in different countries not be hampered by privacy legislation, potentially interfering with the amount of customer information that service providers could exchange regarding suspected ML/TF.

Although the challenges to identifying TF apply equally to Internet payment systems (the suspicions being mostly based on name matching with the names provided by the competent authorities), it is not always necessary for Internet payment service providers to identify TF in their STRs in order to help counter terrorist financing. Any suspicious activity is important to report regardless of the type of activity. Some Internet payment service providers have put in place systems to detect, monitor and analyse suspicious transactions – even for small amounts.

Concerning the risk-based approach to combat ML/TF I would refer to the June 2007 FATF Guidance which stated that : 'By adopting a risk-based approach, competent authorities and financial institutions are able to ensure that measures to prevent or mitigate money laundering and terrorist financing are commensurate to the risks identified. This will allow resources to be allocated in the most efficient ways. The principle is that resources should be directed in accordance with priorities so that the greatest risks receive the highest attention.'

Applying this principle to online transactions, the private sector should be allowed to consider low value consumer payments initiated from financial institutions or credit card account (which require customer identification and verification procedures, as well as transaction record-keeping and reporting policies), to be of lower risk than transactions initiated through services providers without AML/CFT obligations.

The risk of fraud and the sale of illegal goods are among the concerns of commercial websites and Internet payment systems. These concerns are among the motives for commercial websites and Internet payment systems to secure their communications, websites and payment systems. In some jurisdictions online commercial websites are not as such required to detect or fight against ML/TF, but have a market incentive to detect fraud.

Some commercial websites and Internet payment service providers, aware of the risk of being used for illegal activity, have set up departments to screen and monitor the transactions of their customers, using a risk-based approach. In addition to monitoring for fraud, some commercial websites and Internet payment service providers have also set up AML/CFT mechanisms. Best practices in the sector, including customer due diligence, monitoring transactions, not accepting anonymous forms of payment (cash for instance) imposing transactions limits, maintaining transactions records, and reporting large or suspicious transactions to the competent authorities, could be helpful for other parties of the private sector.

The collaboration between commercial websites and Internet payment service providers to exchange information on commercial transactions underlying financial transactions is a factor which mitigates money laundering and terrorism financing risks, as well as risk of fraud. Legal dispositions encouraging such exchange of information could be very useful.

Because of the international character of commercial websites, international cooperation is a key factor. Cooperation between, for example, FIUs, law enforcement and other parties involved is therefore important.

Internet payment service providers report in the country where they are established (got a license) and not in the country of residence of the individuals involved in the suspicious financial transactions, which for FIUs and law enforcement may lead to identification and follow-up problems (it is difficult to confirm the true identity of the parties involved in the transactions in the country of the disclosure given that the individuals do not live in the country and the transactions are difficult to explain/justify as they does not take place in the country where the Internet service provider is located and reports.

Issues for consideration

Looking ahead, because of the international scope of the internet there is an obvious need for the various jurisdictions to agree a unified approach to the problems of money laundering and terrorist funding on the internet. The FATF have completed various studies and made recommendations but it will probably be a long process to get multinational agreement.

13

Trade Based Money Laundering

Money laundering and terrorist financing through the trade system

Various experts and regulatory bodies have identified the misuse of the trade system as one of the main methods by which criminal organisations and terrorist financiers have moved money for the purpose of disguising its origins and integrating it into the formal economy.

Where effective anti-money laundering (AML) and counter-terrorist financing (CFT) standards that have been applied making some of the previously used money laundering schemes more difficult to implement, the abuse of the trade system is an attractive alternative. It is, however, doubtful whether the various regulatory bodies are as capable of identifying and combating trade-based money laundering as they are in dealing with other forms of money laundering and terrorist financing.

Research and various studies indicate that criminal organisations and terrorist groups are exploiting vulnerabilities in the international trade system to move value for illegal purposes. A number of specific money laundering cases have been identified which involved the proceeds from various types of criminal offences to including:

- drug trafficking,
- trading stolen or other goods,
- corruption and bribery,
- fraud,
- counterfeiting/piracy of products
- and smuggling.

The most basic of these 'schemes' involve fraudulent trade practices such as:

- over- and under-invoicing of goods and services,
- multiple invoicing of goods and services,
- over- and under-shipments of goods and services,
- and falsely describing goods and services.

The more complicated schemes integrate these fraudulent practices into a complex web of transactions and movements of goods.

The inherent vulnerabilities within the international trade system, especially the enormous volume of trade flows, which can obscure individual transactions, provides many opportunities for criminal organisations and terrorist groups to transfer value across borders.

The following are examples of this abuse:

- moving value through the financial system (e.g. using cheques or wire transfers),
- the use of front companies,
- the physical movement of banknotes (e.g. using cash couriers), and concealing bulk cash in cargo.
- misrepresentation of the price,
- quantity or quality of imports or exports;
- and money laundering through fictitious trade activities and/or through front companies.

There is a substantial amount of data available to help the investigator to analyse what may be going on. this information or data will include import-export forms or supporting documentation.(description of the goods being imported or exported, their quantity, value, weight, customs or tariff code number, the mode of transportation by which the goods are being imported or exported, and/or the name and address of the exporter (consignor), importer (consignee), and shipping company. In some cases, financial or banking data is also included).

All of this information should be examined by the appropriate regulatory organisation whether it be Customs & Excise or whoever the jurisdiction empowers to carry out those controls over imports and exports.

Similarly the appropriate investigative authorities who are responsible for investigating money laundering, terrorist financing and/or the underlying criminal offences (e.g. customs fraud, smuggling, drug trafficking) should be examining this data for the indications of criminal activity.

The financial institutions who provide financial instruments for the facilitation of trade should also be applying appropriate anti money laundering controls and standards with the reporting of suspicious transactions, etc.

The other participants in the international trade are anyone who facilitates the exchange of goods and related services across national borders, international boundaries or territories. This would also include a corporation or other business unit organised and operated principally for the purpose of importing or exporting goods and services (e.g. import/export companies).

The FATF has reviewed current practices of various jurisdictions and the review showed that there is need for a stronger focus on training programs for competent authorities to enhance their ability to identify the techniques used by the criminal/terrorist in the international trade system. One can only speculate to how effective the authorities are at this current time but there is no doubt that identification of this form of money laundering should be a top priority not as the current vogue in the United Kingdom and other jurisdictions where they all claim how well they are doing in detecting money laundering because anyone who is caught stealing and put the ill gotten gains into the bank (quite openly) is charged with 'money laundering'. Give me a break – who knows I'll be charged with carrying a knife in my kitchen just to make the crime figures look good.

Countries should be encouraged to provide training on international trade/terrorist financing techniques to the staff of trade authorities, investigative authorities, customs agencies, tax authorities, the financial intelligence unit, prosecutorial authorities, banking supervisors and any other authorities that the country identifies as being relevant to the fight against money laundering/organised crime and terrorism. Given the global nature of this aspect of money laundering participation of experts from other jurisdictions would aid implementation of both training and development of investigation techniques. There is no doubt that criminal investigations involving customs fraud, VAT fraud-related money laundering, black market peso exchanges, tax and excise offences could involve international trade and/or terrorist money laundering.

The FATF recommend that it is best practice in this area to tailor training programmes to meet the specific requirements and needs of different authorities. For example, financial and trade data analysis is a useful tool for identifying trade anomalies, which may lead to the investigation and prosecution and as such training programmes for analytical and investigative authorities may include a focus on the existence and relevance of financial and trade data to crime targeting, and techniques for conducting such analysis. Such investigative techniques could include:

- Comparing domestic and foreign import/export data to detect discrepancies in the Harmonized Tariff Schedule, country of origin, manufacturer, importer/exporter, ultimate consignee, broker, unit price, commodity activity by time period, and port of import/export.
- Analysing financial information collected by the FIU to identify patterns of activity involving the importation/exportation of currency, deposits of currency in financial institutions, reports of suspicious financial activities, and the identity of parties to these transactions.
- Examining cargo movements through the comparison of import/export documentation between two counties to verify that the data reported to one country's authorities matches the data reported to the other country's authorities.

- Examining domestic import data with an automated technique, such as Unit Price Analysis, to compare the average unit price for a particular commodity and identify traders who are importing commodities at a substantially higher or lower price than the world market.
- Comparing information such as the origin, description and value of the goods, particulars of the consignee and consignor, and the route of shipment with intelligence information in existing databases to detect any irregularities, targets or risk indicators.
- Using statistical analysis methods, such as linear regression models, on trade data concerning individual, non-aggregated imports and exports.
- Comparing export information with tax declarations to detect discrepancies.
- Paying particular attention to trade transactions that display known red flag indicators of trade/terrorism funding money laundering activity.
- Cross-comparing known typologies of risk (such as those identified in the FATF Typologies Report on Trade-based Money Laundering) with trade data, information on cross-border monetary transfers associated with the payment of goods, intelligence, tax and wealth information.
- Taking appropriate follow-up action when anomalies and discrepancies in trade and financial transactions are identified. Depending on the circumstances, appropriate follow-up action could involve asking the trader for further explanation and supporting documents; auditing traders who have presented discrepancies to check the volume of their business, regularity of their operations.

It is also best practice to include in any training programmes for banking supervisors a focus on the importance of evaluating the adequacy of a bank's policies, procedures and processes for handling trade finance activities. Important aspects to cover include:

- Assessing the adequacy of a bank's systems for managing the risks associated with trade finance activities, including whether the bank effectively identifies and monitors its trade finance portfolio for suspicious or unusual activities, particularly those that pose a higher risk for money laundering.
- Determining whether a bank's system for monitoring trade finance activities for suspicious activities, and for reporting suspicious activities, is adequate, given the bank's size, complexity, location, and types of customer relationships.
- Sample testing trade finance accounts with a view to verifying whether the bank is meeting its customer due diligence, record keeping, monitoring and reporting obligations.

- Providing Anti Money Laundering training to financial institutions' global trade services departments and personnel.

Currently, many financial institutions focus their Anti Money Laundering training at the customer level and not at their personnel working in their trade services departments. It is important that the financial industry formulate with the appropriate regulatory bodies a system and training plan to focus on the international trade market and potential manipulation to facilitate money laundering by criminals/terrorists.

14

The Law

Evolution of money laundering laws

Until the 1980s, only a handful of jurisdictions had criminalised money laundering, but as it became obvious that something needed to be done to protect the financial stability of the United States and other countries, the last ten years have seen an increase in the enactment of laws and regulations. As mentioned earlier, money laundering can have a detrimental effect on the social fabric of a country and its national security as the facility to launder dirty money enables the criminal to expand his activities whether it be drug trafficking, terrorism, illegal arms trading, blackmail or fraud.

The USA were the first to enact anti-money laundering laws with any transaction over $10,000 being the subject of mandatory examination. This resulted in 'smurfing' by the criminals to disguise the deposits. Even with the enactment of these laws, many financial institutions in the USA only paid lip service to them, and it was only when very large fines were imposed by the Federal Courts did they sit up and take notice.

The G-7 Nations implemented the Financial Action Task Force (FATF) in 1989 who are now the major driving force promoting action against money laundering, their 40 recommendations being the standard against which anti-money-laundering regimes are measured. Some 26 member jurisdictions are participants of the action plan.

Other multilateral regional groups such as the Organisation of American States, the Caribbean Action Task Force, the Asia/Pacific Group, and the Council of Europe have all addressed the problem of money laundering within their regions.

Since 1990, various jurisdictions have created Financial Intelligence Units (FIU) who process information received and pass the information on to the appropriate law enforcement agency. To act as a forum for the various FIUs to network with each other and solve common problems, the Egmont Group was formed, and the Egmont Secure Web enables FIUs to communicate securely over the internet. To date, 38 jurisdictions meet the Egmont definition of an FIU, and that includes the United Kingdom, Channel Islands, and Isle of Man. 22 of these FIUs are connected to the secure web.

So the various financial regulatory bodies laid down regulations for the financial businesses to abide by, these regulations being associated with existing and, in some cases, new criminal laws.

UK regulations

In the United Kingdom, the money laundering regulations were linked to various criminal statutes such as the Drug Trafficking and Prevention of Terrorism Acts. For example, Section 1(1) of the Prevention of Terrorism Act includes the power to order forfeiture of any money or property for the use of the terrorist organisation and includes the offence of providing aid in the provision of services. Therefore it is clear that the provision of financial services is contrary to the Act and handling funds belonging to a terrorist organisation would constitute an offence.

The existing laws on money laundering can be found in:

- The Criminal Justice Act 1988
- The Prevention of Terrorism (temporary provisions) Act 1989
- The Criminal Justice Act 1994
- The Drug Trafficking Act 1994
- The Criminal Law (Consolidation) (Scotland) Act 1995
- The Proceeds of Crime (Northern Ireland) Order 1996
- The Money Laundering Regulations 1993 (Regulation 2 (3) defines money laundering and Regulation 14(d) requires the reporting of all offences of suspected money laundering)
- Proceeds of Crime 2002
- The Money Laundering Regulations 2007

I recently read a draft for a 'money laundering book' written by lawyers. It was excellent in content from a legal point of view but quite honestly, unless one is acting as a lawyer to find ways of interpreting the various laws based on stated cases and other legal arguments, the whole concept of what the law really means gets lost in a legal fog.

You know what I mean – we have seen it all before. ('I say, old boy – clause six, subsection two of the 78 Act must mean, if one takes Mickey Mouse v Goofy, blah blah blah ...') The application of the legislation, laws and regulations should be based on the simple concept that **as a financial institution you do not wish to handle the proceeds of any criminal activity whatever that activity is.**

If you do, you are no better than the old fashioned fence and your business is profiting from criminal enterprise. The Courts usually take the stance that without 'receivers' there are 'no thieves' so the more difficult it is for the criminals to get their money into your organisation, the better.

In simple terms these various Acts can be summarised as follows:

- It is an offence to conceal, etc., another's proceeds of drug trafficking, terrorism or other criminal acts, knowing or having reasonable grounds to suspect that they are such proceeds.
- It is an offence to enter in an arrangement which facilitates the retention or control by or on behalf of another of their proceeds of crime, or which allows the other's proceeds of crime to be used to secure funds or be used to obtain benefit to acquire property by way of investment, knowing or suspecting that the person concerned is, or has been, involved in criminal activity or has benefited from criminal activity.
- It is an offence to acquire, possess, or use another's proceeds of criminal activity, knowing that they are such proceeds.

➔ **Conviction on indictment for the above offences is punishable by up to 14 years imprisonment, or a fine, or both.**

- It is an offence to fail to report knowledge or suspicions of criminal money laundering or the control of criminal funds to either the Police or a supervisor in accordance with an employer's established system.
- It is an offence to prejudice an investigation, or possible investigation, by tipping off another person information that is likely to be prejudicial.

➔ **Conviction on indictment of these offences is punishable by up to 5 years imprisonment, or a fine, or both.**

Obviously the enforcement of the criminal laws is the responsibility of the law enforcement agencies whether that is the Police or HM Customs & Excise. The Money Laundering Regulations are separate laws written for the financial marketplace and are a mandatory obligation for all financial institutions. As such, they require additional administrative requirements. For example, Regulation 5 provides that all financial businesses must establish and maintain specific policies and procedures to guard against their businesses and the financial system being used for money laundering.

The Regulations cover:

- internal control and communication of policies
- identification procedures
- record keeping
- recognition of suspicious transactions and reporting procedures
- education and training of relevant employees.

→ **Failure to comply with any of the requirements of the Regulations constitutes an offence punishable by a maximum of 2 years imprisonment, or fine, or both, irrespective of whether money laundering has taken place.**

Note that:

1. Whether the offence is committed by a Corporate Entity and proved to have been committed with the consent or connivance, or to be attributable to any neglect on the part of, any director, manager, secretary, or officer of the Corporate Entity or any person acting in any such capacity, they as well as the Corporate Entity they as well as the Corporate Entity shall be guilty of that offence and shall be liable to be proceeded against and punished accordingly.

   → **In simple terms, the individual who does not follow laid-down anti-money-laundering procedures will be prosecuted as will his or her employer.**

2. Where the affairs of the Corporate Entity are managed by members, any acts and defaults will be treated as if the member was a director.

3. Where the offence is committed by a partnership or an unincorporated association, the individual, whether he be a partner or person connected with the management or control of the association will be guilty of the offence and shall be liable to be proceeded against and punished accordingly.

Enforcement of the Regulations are now the responsibility of the Financial Services Agency who assess the adherence to the regulations during visits to financial institutions. The Joint Money Laundering Steering Group, an advisory body funded by the financial marketplace, also issue guidelines to financial businesses to help in the fight against money laundering.

15

Procedures for Prevention

Controls and compliance

Probably the best protection against money laundering is a commitment by the whole organisation to defend itself actively against attack. This principle must be instilled in all members of staff whatever their position and regardless of rank. Frequently, I have seen a cavalier attitude to regulations by senior executives. This attitude is dated and can prove very expensive as the various regulatory bodies are becoming extremely proactive in their stance against those that ignore the rules. Practical policies, procedures and systems need to be implemented.

The vital administrative elements of self-protection are:

- a formal statement from the Board of Directors or senior management team clearly spelling out the organisation's commitment to combat the abuse of its facilities for the purpose   of money laundering
- a system of internal control procedures to recognise and deter   money laundering by implementation of the following:

  ☑ a designated money laundering officer and deputy responsible for ensuring compliance with internal controls on behalf of the company and with direct access to, but independence from, the Board of Directors.

  ☑ client and counterparty approval procedures and transaction procedures which facilitate the recognition of suspicious transactions and other reportable transactions. Plus the deterrence of fraud, assessment of credit worthiness and ensuring that the client receives the full services offered appropriate to its needs.

  ☑ record compilation and retention procedures that establish a full transaction audit trail with records that can be admissible as evidence where appropriate.

  ☑ process for the prompt reporting of suspicious transactions to the designated money laundering officer and relevant authorities which complies with both confidentiality and tipping-off laws.

  ☑ an annual self assessment programme to review both the vulnerability of the company and its business lines to both fraud and money laundering and the effectiveness of its money-laundering deterrence procedures.

☑ a system to test the procedures implemented by either internal audit, compliance or a competent external source.

☑ pre-employment screening systems.

☑ appropriate employee training for both new and to refresh existing staff.

Personal obligations

As mentioned earlier, all employees have obligations under the law and regulations. The main thrust of the legislation is that staff meet their obligations as long as they comply at all times with the approved vigilance policy of their particular financial services business. Obviously one does not wish to have whistleblowers within the organisation who may go outside to report their suspicions, especially if their reports are ignored. It is essential that all employees have the facility to report any suspicious transaction and that appropriate documentation is available for them to make the report. Verbal reporting should always be confirmed by documentary follow-up. Appropriate procedures should be included in any staff handbook issued and the reporting should be to the delegated reporting officer.

Reporting of incidents procedures

It is important that one does not try to discover the source or reason for the suspicious funds that arrive at your business – that is the job of the law enforcement agencies. The golden rule is – *report it*, then leave the processing to the experts.

Key staff should report to either the Reporting Officer or Line Manager (if so required for preliminary investigation in the event of there being other facts that may negate the suspicion). An internal report form should be used and signed by the staff involved with the suspicion and formal reporting.

Acting on information received

The reporting officer, on receipt of the internal report form, needs to assess the information to establish whether it supports the suspicion. The details need to be investigated so that it can be determined whether a report be submitted to the Economic Crime Unit, NCIS, or Financial Crimes Unit.

Most regulatory bodies will expect the Reporting Officer to act honestly, reasonably and to make his or her decisions in good faith. If he or she decides that the information does substantiate a suspicion of laundering, NCIS/FCU should be advised immediately using the standard form prescribed by them. In urgent cases, NCIS/FCU should be advised initially be telephone.

If the reporting officer is uncertain that the information substantiates criminal activity, NCIS/FCU should be advised using the report form as mentioned.

If, in good faith, it is decided that the information does not substantiate the suspicion and no report is made, there is no liability for non-reporting should the judgment be subsequently found to be wrong.

Within the organisation, it is recommended that the vigilance policy include internal reporting procedures so that the appropriate management, whether it be the Compliance Manager, Inspection Department, Group Security Manager or whoever, are informed by the Reporting Officer of suspicious customers/transactions.

A register should be kept, recording:

- date of report
- the author of the report
- the person(s) to whom the report was forwarded
- a reference by which supporting evidence is identifiable.

A separate register should be kept detailing all enquiries made by the FIU or other agencies. This should show:

- the date and nature of the enquiry
- the name and agency of the inquiring officer
- the powers being exercised
- details of the financial services product(s) involved.

It is important to note that the Regulatory Bodies will also require separate reports to be made to them where:

- the financial services business' systems failed to detect a transaction and the matter was reported to the business by an outside source such as NCIS/FCU
- the transaction may present a significant risk to the reputation of the financial centre and/or the business
- it is suspected that a staff member of the financial service business is involved
- a staff member of the financial service business has been dismissed for serious control breaches.

As mentioned, the regulations require record keeping so that an audit trail is maintained so that, in the event of an investigation, the document/transaction sequence can be followed.

These records must be kept to certain prescribed Time Limits, and, depending on whether transactions or electronic transfers, certain details. A full list of these requirements can be obtained from the regulatory body (usually available on CD-

Rom or floppy disk). Usually it is required that they be kept in readily retrievable form, so do not pack them away in a dusty storeroom so that it takes five years to find them. If kept on computer, the condition of the records should be examined periodically to ensure they are in good condition. Disaster recovery procedures should also be regularly monitored.

Self-assessment programme

This should be completed annually to review any vulnerabilities to money laundering, fraud and the effectiveness of the deterrence procedures.

A report should be completed documenting the work performed, who carried it out, how it was controlled and supervised, together with findings, conclusions and recommendations.

Management should be advised whether the internal procedures and statutory obligations have been properly completed.

The following questions should be answered:

- what have been the changes to our risk profile?
- what changes have there been to money laundering methods?
- do our money laundering deterrence procedures suit our risk profile?
- to what extent and in what manner are they being adhered to?
- how do they interact with other policies, controls and statutory requirements of the business?

Independent testing

Internal Audit or Compliance should implement an annual independent test of the effectiveness of the money laundering deterrence procedures which should include:

- interview of employees handling transactions and supervisors to determine their knowledge and compliance with the procedures
- sampling types of transactions with a review of associated transactions, record retention documentation and suspicious transaction referral reports
- testing the reasonableness and validity of any exemptions granted to clients
- testing the record keeping system set up in 'Record Retention'. Any deficiencies should be reported to the appropriate manager with a request for corrective action and a deadline for implementation.

Should staffing levels prohibit such testing consideration should be given to using an external contractor.

Pre-employment screening and employee training

Recent studies show that the number of job applications that contain false information are as high as 25%. In the United Kingdom it is a criminal offence to gain employment by false references and qualifications. The subject of pre-employment screening can easily be the subject of a separate book and we have mentioned this subject in Chapter 5. Obviously, it is important that all prospective employees are vetted to ensure that the financial business does not suffer the consequences of employing the dishonest. With the law and its obligations, the last thing needed is the employment of an individual who may be vulnerable to dishonesty, especially bribery. Appropriate vetting procedures for new employees and appropriate anti-money-laundering training programmes for both new and existing employees are all essential.

We recommend that a pre-employment screening programme be implemented if not in place. Existing programmes should be evaluated and where appropriate improved to prevent the rotten apple slipping through the door.

Conclusion

I hope that you have enjoyed this small book, but even so, no doubt the problems of money laundering will continue. It is important to remember the statement at the beginning of this book – there is no dirty money, only dirty people Without the criminal and his dishonest banker, accountant, insurance man, and/or lawyer, there are no proceeds of crime to convert to what appears to be legitimate assets. Most of the money-laundering cases in this book and other publications are the result of either internal dishonesty or lack of diligence. How often when a case hits the proverbial fan does the financial institution claim that they thought that the institution that transferred the money to them had completed proper verification?

- Can you be sure their procedures are as good as yours?
- Even though they are on the FATF approved list, are you sure about them?

There is no doubt that the problems of money laundering will continue and with the current increase in fraud throughout the world the clever fraudster will find ways to lose his ill gotten gains in a web of untraceable transactions to continue the legend of Meyer Lansky.

There has at last been some success in the investigation of the Hawalla banking system but the political climate throughout the world puts the cleaning up of that system way down the list of priorities.

Some jurisdictions will continue to make appropriate noises as to their compliance with FATF standards but politics will always take the lead to the integrity of a country's ethics and standards.

No doubt the so called experts will continue to pontificate and some massive fraud will hit the headlines yet again and all the same questions will be asked as to why? how? when?

I will end by saying good luck in your hunting for the launderers and thank you for buying this book.

Bob Blunden
2009

Recommended Reading

The Laundrymen, Jeffrey Robinson, Simon and Schuster, UK 1994

A Full Service Bank, James Ring Adams and Douglas Franz, Simon and Schuster, New York, 1992

Evil Money, Rachel Ehrenfeld, HarperCollins, New York, 1992

The Dragon Syndicates, Martin Booth, Doubleday/Bantam Books, UK, 1999

Review to Identify Non-Cooperative Countries or Territories, 22 June 2000, Financial Action Task Force on Money Laundering

Altavista live – news web site http://live.altavista.com

Jersey Financial Services Commission Guidance Notes/Regulations/Law

Guernsey Financial Services Commission Guidance Notes/Regulations/Law

Isle of Man Supervision Commission Guidance Notes/Regulations/Law

Gibraltar Financial Service Commission Guidance Notes/Regulations/Law

Guidance Notes for the Financial Sector – Joint Money Laundering Steering Group

The Merger, Jeffrey Robinson, Simon and Schuster, UK, 1999

www.offshore-net.com/newshot/offshorescam

Appendix 1
Dulles

Note: The background to Dulles and his alleged German connections dates from the 1920s when a number of wealthy Americans invested in what remained of Germany after the 1st World War. Dulles was in fact a state department delegate in Paris at the time of the Versailles Treaty and major American companies such as Du Pont were unhappy that there was an arms embargo on Germany. Dulles agreed to turn a blind eye to any such trade. Subsequently based in Berlin, Dulles left government service and joined a firm of Wall Street lawyers.

W.A. Harriman, a member of a railway Baron family, had set up an investment company to invest in Germany and made contacts and formed a relationship with the Thyssen family. Thyssen had set up their own banks in Berlin and Rotterdam enabling them to transfer funds without any regulatory control. A third bank was set up in New York, the Union Bank Company. Thyssen was now able to launder money, move assets around, conceal profits and evade tax.

In 1931 Harriman merged with Brown Brothers, a British company, and they directed investors money into German companies. Standard Oil was a prominent investor with the Rockefeller family and they formed a close relationship with chemical industrialist I G Farben. Dulles became lawyer for Thyssen's Rotterdam ban and represented , amongst other German companies, I G Farben.

IG Farben became very rich as they supplied most of the German military with fuel, chemicals, rubber etc during the war. In fact they made substantial secret donations to fund the Nazis enabling Hitler to seize power. Of course they became infamous for the development of the gas used in the concentration camps.

In 1933 German industrialists agreed to back Hitler and a deal where all German trade with the United States would be coordinated with a syndicate headed by a member of the Harriman family. The Union Bank became a Nazi money laundering machine and was used as a basis for a complex, deceptive system of holding companies. When the Second World War broke out Dulles was based in Berlin and he continued to look after American interests in Nazi Germany. Even when transferred to Switzerland he continued his relationships and looked after U.S/Nazi business links .Even as late as 1939 after Germany had invaded Austria and Czechoslovakia, Standard Oil sold $20 million worth of Avgas to I G Faben.

Appendix 2
Reichsbank Gold

On 3 February 1945, the United States Army Air Force (8th AAF) bombed Berlin dropping nearly 2,300 tons of bombs on the city causing the near demolition of the Reichsbank including the currency printing presses.

Walter Funk, the president of the bank, decided to send most of the gold reserves ($238 million) and a large quantity of monetary reserves to Wintershals AG's Kaiseroda Ppassiumk mine at Merkers, a small village 200 miles south-west of Berlin.

On 4 April Merkers fell to US troop of the US Third Army commanded by Lieutenant General George Patton. The Americans found Werner Veick, Head Cashier (Foreign Notes Department) and a Dr Paul Ortwin Rave, Curator of the German state museum and a director of the National Galleries in Berlin at the mine.

Rave claimed that he was there to look after paintings stored in the mine. Apparently 25% of the major works held by 14 of the main state Museums were stored there. Veick claimed that the gold stored was the entire reserve of the Reichsbank in Berlin.

However on examination, some of the gold, silver, diamonds, currency etc was found to be property confiscated by the SS from concentration camp victims'

Inventory

- 8,198 bars of gold
- 55 boxes of crated gold bullion
- Hundreds of bags containing gold items
- 1300+ bags of gold Reichsmarks, British gold pounds, French gold francs.
- 711 bags of US$20 gold coins
- 100's of bags of gold/silver coins in various foreign currency
- 9 bags of valuable collectable coins
- 276 billion Reichsmarks in notes
- 20 silver bars
- 40 bags containing silver bars
- 63 boxes/55 bags silver plate
- bag platinum bars
- 110 bags of assorted valuables

Estimated value: US$ 520,000,000

Apparently Patton tried to keep the discovery secret and when questioned claimed that his soldiers were of two minds: *Make the gold into medals, one for every soldier in the US Third Army,* or *Hide the gold so that when the government refused to buy new weapons dig it up and use the loot instead.*

The financial branch of US Army intelligence searched Germany for other stores of loot and only found three with Reichsbank gold valued at US$ 3 million.

Meanwhile the desperate Nazis in Berlin with the Red Army only 55 miles away decided to transfer the remaining contents of the Reichsbank to the Oberbayern in southern Bavaria where they planned to retreat, regroup and fight on.

Within days 9 tons of gold, hundreds of sacks of foreign currency, crates of unstamped coins and other valuables was transported out of Berlin. This shipment was unloaded by soldiers of an Alpine regiment and hidden by Lake Walchensee (720 gold bars, 164 sacks and crates of gold coins and US currency). The German officer in charge of the Alpine Regiment refused to give the Reichsbank official a receipt for this shipment.

Ernst Kaltenbrunner, Chief Reich Security Head Office, amassed a private fortune which he also shipped to Bavaria. The one remaining document lists the hoard as follows;

- 50 cases of gold coins and articles (each case weighing 50 kg, total weight 2.5 tonnes)
- 2 million $US, 2 million Swiss francs
- 5 cases diamonds and gemstones
- Stamp collection worth 5 million gold marks
- 50 kg gold bars

Goering transported his vast art collection and a large collection of vintage wines many of which were opened and drunk by US troops when discovered in a cave near Bertchesgarten.

Gold was also shipped by U Boat to Argentina.

After the war 16,000 troops of the US 10th Armoured 'Tiger' Division occupied part of southern Bavaria and key officers dug up hundreds of tons of Nazi gold, currencies, diamonds and other valuables. In those early summer months they estimated that they had found Reichsbank gold valued at about $US 11 million and estimated that they had recovered 98.6% of the $US 255.96 million of gold shown on the closing balances of the Precious Metals Department of the Berlin Reichsbank. This meant that some $US 3 million of gold (1945 prices) was missing.

There has been some speculation that some of the gold buried at Walchansee was dug up and the officer who refused to give a receipt for the shipment (Colonel Franz Pfeiffer) left Germany and spent the rest of his life with other Nazis in Argentina that well known rest home for old Nazis.

It is also known that SS General Josef Spacil robbed the Reichsbank at gunpoint of some $US 9 million and it was also taken south to Bavaria although some was divided between various Gestapo officers and Otto Skorzeny who fled to Spain where he lived very well and ran the 'Die Spinne' (the spider) escape route for wanted Nazis.

Since then the Guinness Book of records lists the disappearance of the Third Reich's treasures as the largest robbery in the history of the world. Treasure seekers from all over the world have searched for this missing treasure. There is no doubt that American, German and others helped themselves to some of this treasure and no doubt the gnomes of Zurich probably helped with the laundering of it. In fact many books and articles have been written about how Swiss government officials and banks conspired to keep billions in gold and other valuables from their rightful heirs.

I can recall watching yet again 'Kelly's Heroes', a film about a troop of American soldiers who decide to rob a bank of its German gold with the help, at the end , of a German tank commander. The robbery was successful and Clint Eastwood (Sgt Kelly) drove off into the sunset in his jeep with bars of Reichsbank gold ingots. As a cynic I now wonder how they disposed of the gold and realized its cash value.

Appendix 3
Proliferation financing and export of
WMD/nuclear technology

While the following cases do not provide any proven direct link of proliferation to the financial sector, they do provide some additional intelligence as to the complexity of the detection of proliferation activity in general

---

Customs authorities

A suspected procurement network operating in Canada attempted to supply targeted entities operating in Jurisdiction 1 with goods controlled under Canadian export laws.

Jurisdiction 1 was a jurisdiction of proliferation concern. A shipment of 'industrial equipment' was presented for export at a major Canadian port by an exporter that was subject to a Canadian Border Services Agency (CBSA) national security/export control lookout due to suspected proliferation activity.

Shipping documents were presented to CBSA indicating that the consignee of the equipment was an import/export trading company. Customs officials detained the shipment at the Canadian port for examination and export permit verification. The following documents were analysed:

- ***Export Declaration Form*** *detailing*
  - *the exporter,*
  - *the consignee,*
  - *the commodity,*
  - *transportation details (routing, carrier) and the value.*

  The exporter had listed the consignee as an Import/Export Trading Company located in Jurisdiction 2, a known trans-shipment hub. The goods were described as 'industrial equipment' without further elaboration.
- ***Bill of Lading*** *providing cargo shipping information.*
- ***Invoice*** *indicating the value of the 'industrial equipment' as $500,000.*
- ***Certificate of Origin*** *indicating that the goods originated from Jurisdiction 3.*

An **Export Permit** was not presented for the goods (Note: Depending on the commodity, its origin and its destination, exporters may be required to indicate a General Export Permit number on their export declaration or they may be required to obtain an Individual Export Permit from competent authorities.

The exporter was the subject of a customs authority lookout (targeted shipment) for procurement activity and had a history of export control contraventions.

The consignee was a trading company in a known trans-shipment country.

The description of the goods as 'industrial equipment' was not specific enough to ascertain what the goods actually were or what their intended use might be. The value of the goods was high, which could indicate specialized use or high technological content.

Customs officials at the Canadian port were instructed to contact the exporter and obtain technical specifications for the goods and an end-use certificate from the consignee. The technical specifications revealed that the goods were a 'five-axis milling machine', which, depending on their cutting capabilities, are controlled nuclear dual use goods and subject to Canadian export control laws.

The end-use certificate stated that the goods were to be used in Jurisdiction 2 at a wood working plant. Furthermore, a trading company was probably not the true end-user since it was likely the goods would be sold or re-exported. Searches indicated that the trading company in Jurisdiction 2 was state-owned by Jurisdiction 1. At this stage, customs authorities are concerned that the milling machine is a controlled commodity and that it will be diverted or transhipped to the nuclear industry in Jurisdiction 1.

Canadian Customs officials then asked the export permit authorities what required export permits were required. Goods originating from Jurisdiction 3 required a general export permit when destined to Jurisdiction 2. Since the exporter did not declare that the goods were being re-exported through Canada, customs authorities issued an administrative monetary penalty to the exporter for failing to properly declare this. There was not sufficient evidence to prove that the goods were destined for jurisdiction 2 and therefore the goods were not seized and were released for export despite suspicions on the part of customs officials.

Numerous indicators in this case gave the authorities concern as to the true end-use and destination of the goods. They continued to develop an intelligence file on the exporter and consignee. The intelligence file work-up included reviewing various intelligence, enforcement, and commercial *databases (including both open and classified sources). A review of the Canadian exporting company's previous exports revealed that it had already exported 8 five-axis milling machines with a combined value exceeding $4 million. As such, in addition to the current shipment, CBSA would now expand the intelligence probe to better understand the circumstances (i.e. end-users, routing, destination, etc.) surrounding all the shipments of five-axis milling machines (possible controlled nuclear dual use goods).*

Customs officials subsequently intercepted the Canadian exporter two weeks later at an airport returning from a trip to Jurisdiction 2. An examination of his luggage was conducted under the authority of the customs laws and a bill of lading was discovered in his carry-on baggage, which described the movement of a milling machine from Jurisdiction 2 to an electronics company in Jurisdiction 1. Classified intelligence indicated that the electronics company is a known front company for Jurisdiction 1's nuclear and missile industries.

In this example, CBSA was unable to seize the five axis milling machine, without proof of the true end-use and ultimate consignee in Jurisdiction 1.

Proof for trans-shipment to Jurisdiction 1 might include:

- *Letters of credit from Jurisdiction 1's nuclear industry to the Canadian exporter;*
- *Financial transactions between the Canadian exporter, the trading company in Jurisdiction 2, the front company in Jurisdiction 1, and Jurisdiction 1's nuclear industry.*
- *Financial intelligence analysing complete financial proliferation networks linking all the various entities involved.*

Source: Canada

Accelerometers

The United States Immigration and Customs Enforcement, Office of Investigations, in conjunction with the Defense Criminal Investigative Service (DCIS), conducted an investigation in which led to a federal indictment against a foreign national. The indictment was for conspiracy to commit offenses against the United States in connection to exporting Endevco 7270A-200K accelerometers, which are designated as a defense article on the United States Munitions List and cannot be exported from the United States without permission from the United States Department of State. The Endevco 7270A-200K accelerometer has many military applications including use in 'smart' bombs, missile development and the measurement of nuclear and chemical explosives.

From April 2007 through October 2007, ICE agents conducted undercover operations, in which an identified foreign national conspired with agents to export the Endevco 7270A-200K accelerometers in violation of United States Export laws. Undercover agents were advised that if the items were delivered overseas in proper working order, larger orders would follow. Undercover agents along with identified suspects negotiated price, payment, and delivery terms of the accelerometers in furtherance of the conspiracy. Undercover discussions included the delivery of the accelerometers to either a third party country or the country of final destination. Financial terms were discussed between the Undercover agents and the suspect utilising the formal financial sector through either an escrow account for payment or making payments through bank wire transfers.

The defendant was charged under Title 18, of the United States Codes, Section 371, with conspiracy to Commit offenses Against the United States and faces a maximum penalty of five (5) years in prison and a $250,000.00 fine.

Source: United States

Shipping of electronics to a number of countries

Canadian Individual A was the sole owner of Canadian Company A, whose business included the shipping of electronics to a number of countries. Canadian Individual A contacted Canadian Company B to purchase a number of computer chips (power amplifiers) designed for use in radar and satellite communication systems. These goods are dual use with potential military applications and are subject to export controls. Individual A reported the end-user as Canadian Company C and refused to allow Canadian Company B to meet with representatives of Canadian Company C. Canadian Individual A ultimately cancelled the order entirely.

Significant suspicions were raised on the part of Canadian Company B once Canadian Individual A refused to coordinate a meeting with Canadian Company C. The addresses given by Canadian Individual A on the US Traffic in Arms Regulations (ITAR) form for both the purchaser (Canadian Company A) and the purported end-user (Canadian Company C) **were the same.**

Further investigation revealed that Canadian Company C was actually based overseas, and was also run by Canadian Individual A and another person. Had the purchase of computer chips from Canadian Company B gone through, the items would have been shipped through Canada overseas.

The following year, an intermediary for the military of a foreign country requested a purchase of US-origin military-grade night-vision cameras from the same Canadian Individual A. The cameras have potential dual use WMD applications in addition to regular military use and are subject to export-controls. Canadian Company A placed an order for one camera with US Company 1. US Company 1 notified US authorities, who confirmed that the camera, after arriving in Canada, was then re-exported overseas and is currently located near an important nuclear site in a country of proliferation concern.

In addition, Canadian Individual A has been involved in other procurement deals designed to circumvent US export restrictions using Canadian Company A. For instance, Canadian Company A was believed to be in the midst of procuring F-5 fighter aircraft spare parts from US Company 2, also on behalf of Foreign Company X, purportedly for a foreign Air Force.

Canadian Company A has also attempted to re-label a US-origin airplane propeller as originating in another country in order to avoid prohibitions regarding shipment and re-export of US-origin goods. Although this particular shipment was stopped by Canadian authorities, other similar orders have been carried out. Canadian Company B has also fielded requests for other military-related goods, such as helicopter parts and jet fuel, although it is not known if these particular orders have been completed.

Source: Canada

Use of intermediaries to circumvent export restrictions

Canadian Company A dealt in medical products and laboratory equipment and was in contact with Foreign Company X regarding the sale of multiplexers and potentiograph laboratory equipment. (Foreign Company X is a procurement entity associated with a foreign nuclear programme of proliferation concern).

Inquiries revealed that Canadian Company A had ongoing business dealings providing potential dual use goods to a number of foreign enterprises, including Foreign Company Y. Foreign Company X was known to utilize Foreign Company Y as an intermediary, as part of its deceptive practices to avoid revealing the foreign nuclear programme as the end-user of purchased equipment. Goods are instead described as being for 'educational purposes'.

Further investigation revealed that the proprietor of Canadian Company A, Canadian Individual A regularly engaged in deceptive practices to conceal the end-user of dual use equipment. Some deceptive techniques used in this particular case included the following:

- *Individual A frequently provided the name of a Canadian University as the end-user for US-origin and other goods, despite having no actual connection with the university. The products would then be re-shipped to various foreign countries via commercial courier, with the description 'laboratory equipment' or 'medical instruments' given on the customs declaration, regardless of the true nature of the product being exported.*
- *Canadian Company A falsified documents in order to hide US-origin goods, re-labelling them as Canadian products manufactured in a southeast Asian country in order to permit export to embargoed countries.*
- *Canadian Company A exploited the fact that a country's export authorities generally did not inspect exported items as rigorously as imported items.*
- *Canadian Company A exploited a loophole in export reporting requirements for goods valued at less than $2,000.00 dollars, by re-invoicing products at a far lower value to avoid having to complete a paper export declaration.*
- *Canadian Company A was also involved as part-owner of Foreign Company Z, which is used as the principal point of transit for goods going from Canada to overseas.*

In addition to a number of potential nuclear/WMD dual use exported to the companies noted above, Canadian Company A also conducted business with several other entities of procurement concern. These entities have been connected to procurement activities on behalf of various nuclear/WMD programmes in different countries of proliferation concern. Canadian Company A is currently the subject of a joint investigative effort by Canadian agencies aimed at uncovering the nature and extent of its procurement activities on behalf of the nuclear/WMD programmes of several high-interest countries.

Source: Canada

Illicit Brokering

A suspected procurement network operating in Canada aimed to supply entities in a jurisdiction of proliferation concern with controlled and strategic goods.

While executing a search warrant related to an offence of the Customs Act and the Export and Import Permits Act at the business address of the Canadian exporter, Customs authorities uncover shipping documents and commercial invoices related to a shipment of titanium-stabilized stainless steel tubes with an outer diameter of 750mm and a wall thickness of 2.5mm (controlled under 6-6.C.9 of the ECL). This shipment was not related to the offence being investigated. The documents related to this shipment indicate the tubes were manufactured in a European country; purchased by the Canadian company; moved by rail to a second European country; loaded into a maritime shipping container; shipped to a Free Trade Zone and once there, re-manifested and shipped to the jurisdiction of proliferation concern.

CBSA did not have enough evidence to enable it to act upon this illicit brokering activity. Furthermore, the above example is based on the fact that CBSA authorities had obtained a search warrant on an unrelated matter. If CBSA had not been searching the business records, this infraction would have gone undetected. However, financial information could have formed the basis for an initial investigation.

Source: Canada

Kahn

The Khan-case (which consists of several different proliferation cases over a long period) concerned nuclear weapon programs in several jurisdictions of proliferation concern. The process of proliferation for each item to be constructed consisted of many steps in order to disguise the activities of the network and the true nature and end-use of the goods. Many individuals, companies and countries were – knowingly or in good faith – involved. There is not much published concerning the financing in the Khan proliferation networks, but at least the following is mentioned in 'Proliferation Networks and Financing' by Bruno Gruselle (Fondation pour la Recherche Stratégique, March 2007):

'Although some operations appear to have been settled in cash, others were settled through international transfers within the framework of duly established contracts. For example, this is the case for the contract made between the Gulf Technical Industries (GTI) company and SCOPE, for an amount of 13 million dollars.'

'In terms of the financial organisation, the few data available highlight two types of transaction:

- *Interbank:* for remuneration of agents or suppliers outside the network. In other words, transfers between suppliers, intermediaries and/or front companies. Thus, the contract between SMB and SCOPE appears to have been financed conventionally, probably through letters of credit or bills of exchange.
- *Cash transactions within the network and with customers.* The amounts thus obtained (possibly in several payments) could then have been deposited in bank accounts of emerging or offshore countries before transactions were made between banks for final beneficiaries. Even if payments were made in cash, some operations could have been made through written contracts between Khan (and/or Tahir) and the intermediary concerned.'

An illustration from the Centre for Non-proliferation Studies concerning gas centrifuge components to Libya illustrates the puzzle of proliferation of WMD – and also illustrates why detection is so difficult:

Many centrifuges are needed and a numerous components are required for each centrifuge. Several entities will be involved in the different networks used to acquire the components – including in payments and financing – but if someone sells e.g. 10 vacuum pumps to a country which is not a country of special concern one may not have WMD as the first thought.

Source: Gruselle, Bruno, (2007)

Appendix 4
Glossary of Terms

Accountants industry
American Institute of Certified Public Accountants, Canadian Institute of Chartered Accountants, European Federation of Accountants, German Institute of Auditors, Hong Kong Institute of Public Accountants, Institute of Chartered Accountants of England & Wales.

Beneficial Owner
The natural person(s) who ultimately owns or controls a customer and/or the person on whose behalf a transaction is being conducted. It also incorporates those persons who exercise ultimate effective control over a legal person or arrangement.

Casinos industry
European Casino Association (ECA), Gibraltar Regulatory Authority, Kyte Consultants (Malta), MGM Grand Hotel & Casino, Unibet, William Hill plc.

Competent authorities
Competent authorities refers to all administrative and law enforcement authorities concerned with combating money laundering and terrorist financing, including the FIU and supervisors.

Country
All references in the FATF Recommendations and in this Guidance to country or countries apply equally to territories or jurisdictions.

Credible Sources
'Credible sources' refers to information that is produced by well-known bodies that generally are regarded as reputable and that make such information publicly and widely available. In addition to the Financial Action Task Force and FATF-style regional bodies, such sources may include, but are not limited to, supra-national or international bodies such as the International Monetary Fund, the World Bank and the Egmont Group of Financial Intelligence Units, as well as relevant national government bodies and non-governmental organisations. The information provided by these credible sources does not have the effect of law or regulation and should

not be viewed as an automatic determination that something is of higher risk.

Dealers in precious metals and dealers in precious stones industries
Antwerp World Diamond Centre, International Precious Metals Institute, World Jewellery Confederation, Royal Canadian Mint, Jewellers Vigilance Committee, World Federation of Diamond Bourses, Canadian Jewellers Association.

Designated Non-Financial Businesses and Professions (DNFBP)
- Casinos (which also includes internet casinos).
- Real estate agents.
- Dealers in precious metals.
- Dealers in precious stones.
- Lawyers, notaries, other independent legal professionals and accountants – this refers to sole practitioners, partners or employed professionals within professional firms. It is not meant to refer to 'internal' professionals that are employees of other types of businesses, nor to professionals working for government agencies, who may already be subject to measures that would combat money laundering.
- Trust and Company Service Providers refers to all persons or businesses that are not covered elsewhere under these Recommendations, and which as a business, provide any of the following services to third parties:
  - Acting as a formation agent of legal persons.
  - Acting as (or arranging for another person to act as) a director or secretary of a company, a partner of a partnership, or a similar position in relation to other legal persons.
  - Providing a registered office; business address or accommodation, correspondence or administrative address for a company, a partnership or any other legal person or arrangement.
  - Acting as (or arranging for another person to act as) a trustee of an express trust.
  - Acting as (or arranging for another person to act as) a nominee shareholder for another person.

Express Trust
Express trust refers to a trust clearly created by the settlor, usually in the form of a document e.g. a written deed of trust. They are to be contrasted with trusts which come into being through the operation of the law and which do not result from the clear intent or decision of a settlor to create a trust or similar legal arrangements (e.g. constructive trust).

FATF Recommendations
Refers to the FATF Forty Recommendations and the FATF Nine Special Recommendations on Terrorist Financing.

Identification data
Reliable, independent source documents, data or information will be referred to as 'identification data'.

Lawyers and notaries
Allens Arther Robinson, American Bar Association, American College of Trust and Estate Council, Consejo General del Notariado (Spain), Council of Bars and Law Societies of Europe (CCBE), International Bar Association (IBA), Law Society of England & Wales, Law Society of Upper Canada.

Legal Persons
Legal persons refers to bodies corporate, foundations, anstalt, partnerships, or associations, or any similar bodies that can establish a permanent customer relationship with a financial institution or otherwise own property.

Politically Exposed Persons (PEPS)
Individuals who are or have been entrusted with prominent public functions in a foreign country, for example Heads of State or of government, senior politicians, senior government, judicial or military officials, senior executives of state owned corporations, important political party officials. Business relationships with family members or close associates of PEPs involve reputational risks similar to those with PEPs themselves. The definition is not intended to cover middle ranking or more junior individuals in the foregoing categories.

Real estate industry
International Consortium of Real Estate Agents, National Association of Estate Agents (UK), the Association of Swedish Real Estate Agents.

Self-regulatory organisation (SRO)
A SRO is a body that represents a profession (e.g. lawyers, notaries, other independent legal professionals or accountants), and which is made up of member professionals, has a role in regulating the persons that are qualified to enter and who practise in the profession, and also performs certain supervisory or monitoring type functions. For example, it would be normal for this body to enforce rules to ensure that high ethical and moral standards are maintained by those practising the profession.

Trust and Company Service Providers (TCSP)

This refers to all persons or businesses that are not covered elsewhere under these Recommendations, and which as a business, provide any of the following services to third parties:

- Acting as a formation agent of legal persons.
- Acting as (or arranging for another person to act as) a director or secretary of a company, a partner of a partnership, or a similar position in relation to other legal persons.
- Providing a registered office; business address or accommodation, correspondence or administrative address for a company, a partnership or any other legal person or arrangement.
- Acting as (or arranging for another person to act as) a trustee of an express trust.
- Acting as (or arranging for another person to act as) a nominee shareholder for another person.

Relevant trade associations include The Society of Trust and Estate Practitioners (STEP), and the Law Debenture Trust Corporation.

Appendix 5
Sources of Further Information

Various sources of information exist that may help governments and real estate agents in their development of a risk-based approach. Although not an exhaustive list, this section highlights a number of useful web-links that governments and real estate agents may wish to draw upon. They provide additional sources of information, and further assistance might also be obtained from other information sources such AML/CFT assessments.

Financial Action Task Force Documents

The Financial Action Task Force (FATF) is an inter-governmental body whose purpose is the development and promotion of national and international policies to combat money laundering and terrorist financing. Key resources include the 40 Recommendations on Money Laundering and 9 Special Recommendations on Terrorist Financing, the Methodology for Assessing Compliance with the FATF Recommendations, the Handbook for Countries and Assessors, methods and trends (typologies) reports and mutual evaluation reports. See **http://www.fatf-gafi.org**.

Other sources of information to help assist countries' and real estate agents' risk assessment of countries and cross-border activities

In determining the levels of risks associated with particular country or cross border activity, real estate agents and governments may draw on a range of publicly available information sources, these may include reports that detail observance of international standards and codes, specific risk ratings associated with illicit activity, corruption surveys and levels of international cooperation. Although not an exhaustive list the following are commonly utilised:

IMF and World Bank Reports on observance of international standards and codes (Financial Sector Assessment Programme):
- World Bank reports: http://www1.worldbank.org/finance/html/cntrynew2.html
- International Monetary Fund:
  http://www.imf.org/external/np/rosc/rosc.asp?sort=topic#RR
- Offshore Financial Centres (OFCs) IMF staff assessments
  www.imf.org/external/np/ofca/ofca.asp

Mutual evaluation reports issued by FATF Style Regional Bodies:

- Asia/Pacific Group on Money Laundering (APG)
  http://www.apgml.org/documents/default.aspx?DocumentCategoryID=8.
- Caribbean Financial Action Task Force (CFATF)
  http://www.cfatf.org/profiles/profiles.asp
- The Committee of Experts on the Evaluation of Anti-Money Laundering Measures and the Financing of Terrorism (MONEYVAL)
  http://www.coe.int/moneyval
- Eurasian Group (EAG)http://www.eurasiangroup.org/index-7.htm
- GAFISUDhttp://www.gafisud.org/miembros.htm
- Middle East and North Africa FATF (MENAFATF)
  http://www.menafatf.org/TopicList.asp?cType=train
- The Eastern and South African Anti Money Laundering Group (ESAAMLG)
  http://www.esaamlg.org/
- Groupe Inter-gouvernemental d'Action contre le Blanchiment d'Argent (GIABA) http://www.giabasn.org
- OECD Sub Group of Country Risk Classification (a list of country of risk classifications published after each meeting)
  http://www.oecd.org/document/49/0,2340,en_2649_34171_1901105_1_1_1_1,00.html
- International Narcotics Control Strategy Report (published annually by the US State Department)http://www.state.gov/p/inl/rls/nrcrpt/
- Egmont Group membership – Coalition of FIU's that participate in regular information exchange and the sharing of good practice, acceptance as a member of the Egmont Group is based a formal procedure that countries must go through in order to be acknowledged as meeting the Egmont definition of an FIU. http://www.egmontgroup.org/
- Signatory to the United Nations Convention against Transnational Organised Crime
  http://www.unodc.org/unodc/crime_cicp_signatures_convention.html
- The Office of Foreign Assets Control ('OFAC') of the US Department of the Treasury economic and trade, Sanctions Programmes
  http://www.ustreas.gov/offices/enforcement/ofac/programs/index.shtml
- Consolidated list of persons, groups and entities subject to EU Financial Sanctions
  http://ec.europa.eu/comm/external_relations/cfsp/sanctions/list/consol-list.htm
- UN Security Council Sanctions Committee – Country Status:
  http://www.un.org/sc/committees/

Appendix 6
Kimberley Process

A worldwide regulatory scheme that governs the movement of rough diamonds across international borders, adding a certificate of the legitimacy of the trade of the diamonds and a statement of value to all rough diamonds traded across borders. It is supplemented by dealer warranties applicable to polished diamonds and jewellery containing diamonds covering each trade down to retail sales. The Kimberley Process includes all significant dealers and countries involved in diamond mining, trading and processing, and its tracking and valuation system.

Index

347